Composing History

Music in Britain, 1600–2000

ISSN 2053-3217

Series Editors:
BYRON ADAMS, RACHEL COWGILL AND PETER HOLMAN

This series provides a forum for the best new work in the field of British music studies, placing music from the early seventeenth to the late twentieth centuries in its social, cultural, and historical contexts. Its approach is deliberately inclusive, covering immigrants and emigrants as well as native musicians, and explores Britain's musical links both within and beyond Europe. The series celebrates the vitality and diversity of music-making across Britain in whatever form it took and wherever it was found, exploring its aesthetic dimensions alongside its meaning for contemporaries, its place in the global market, and its use in the promotion of political and social agendas.

Proposals or queries should be sent in the first instance to Professors Byron Adams, Rachel Cowgill, Peter Holman or Boydell & Brewer at the addresses shown below. All submissions will receive prompt and informed consideration.

Professor Byron Adams,
Department of Music – 061, University of California, Riverside, CA 92521–0325
email: byronadams@earthlink.net

Professor Rachel Cowgill,
Creative Arts Building, University of Huddersfield,
Queensgate, Huddersfield, HD1 3DH
email: r.e.cowgill@hud.ac.uk

Professor Emeritus Peter Holman MBE,
119 Maldon Road, Colchester, Essex CO3 3AX
email: peter@parley.org.uk

Boydell & Brewer, PO Box 9, Woodbridge, Suffolk, IP12 3DF
email: editorial@boydell.co.uk

Composing History

*National Identities and the
English Masque Revival, 1860–1920*

Deborah Heckert

THE BOYDELL PRESS

First published 2018
The Boydell Press, Woodbridge

ISBN 978 1 78327 207 5

The Boydell Press is an imprint of Boydell & Brewer Ltd
PO Box 9, Woodbridge, Suffolk IP12 3DF, UK
and of Boydell & Brewer Inc.
668 Mt Hope Avenue, Rochester, NY 14620–2731, USA
website: www.boydellandbrewer.com

A CIP catalogue record for this book is available
from the British Library

This publication is printed on acid-free paper

Printed and bound in Great Britain by TJ International Ltd, Padstow, Cornwall

✿ Contents

Illustrations

The author and publishers are grateful to all the institutions and individuals listed for permission to reproduce the materials in which they hold copyright. Every effort has been made to trace the copyright holders; apologies are offered for any omission, and the publishers will be pleased to add any necessary acknowledgement in subsequent editions.

Acknowledgements

A book that has been this long in the making has obviously accrued a multitude of intellectual and personal debts. Looking back over my time writing this book and thinking about paying tribute to the people and institutions who have offered support and encouragement across the years, I am deeply beholden to all those who have not only made it possible, but who have made it happen. The generosity and enthusiasm of many friends and colleagues has been a crucial part of the process, and I owe them collectively, and often individually.

Two mentors in particular have been with me since the beginning of this project. Sarah Fuller was a font of advice and support from my initial ideas to the end, as well as an inspirational example of integrity in scholarship. Byron Adams was always enthusiastic and encouraging, occasionally a stern editor, and has been an integral influence in helping me to shape my ideas about the music of the music of 19th- and 20th-century Britain. I also owe special thanks to Roger Savage, who read through the typescript, corrected my many mistakes, set me on fruitful bibliographic trails, and whose perspectives on my manuscript have been crucial.

I owe an enormous debt of thanks to Michael Middeke, my editor at Boydell, whose kindness, patience, and occasional prodding kept nudging me towards the finish line, and Megan Milan, who kept the channels of correspondence open, despite my occasional attempts to ignore them. I thank Rachel Cowgill for her personal encouragement as one of the editors of The Boydell Press's series Music in Britain, 1600–2000.

Many colleagues over the years have listened to my ideas and responded with beneficial comments, as well as generously sharing their work with me. In particular, I would like to thank Joseph Auner, Jennifer Bain, Tim Barringer, Renée Clark, Hugh Cobbe, Dorothy de Val, Jenny Doctor, Alain Frogley, Christina Fuhrmann, Brooks Kuykendall, Nathaniel Lew, Charles McGuire, Jennifer Oates, Julian Onderdonk, Eric Saylor, Christopher Scheer, Phyllis Weliver, Kirsten Yri, and Bennett Zon.

One cannot do the kind of research necessary for a book like this without acknowledging the debt of libraries and institutions that have offered research help and support. I particularly want to pay tribute to the Carthusian Trust, the Yale Center for British Art, and the RVW Trust for funding fruitful research fellowships and grants. The staff at the British Library has always been incredibly generous with their aid in finding and copying sources, as has the staff of the reading room of the V&A Theatre and Performance Collection's archives. Gisele Schierhorst and the staff of the Stony Brook University Music Library helped again and again to obtain books and manage research needs. I also thank the *Stratford Herald*, the Scottish National Gallery, and the Hessisches Landesmuseum Darmstadt for permission to reproduce images as illustrations in this volume.

I am grateful for all my friends, who offered the kind of encouragement, care, and practical help without which I could not have persevered. Though many have provided kindness and concern while I was in the midst of writing, I particularly want to thank Margarethe Adams, Rachel Begley, Keith Johnston, Kendra Leonard, Clare Talbot, Daniel Ucko, Janet Ward, David Yoon, and Martha Zadok.

Finally, but above all, I must thank my family, of course, who day by day, week by week, month by month, and year by year have listened to me, tolerated my actual and virtual absences, and who have believed in me, even at times when I did not believe in myself.

CHAPTER 1

Vaughan Williams, Stratford's Masque and the Wellsprings of England's Music

APRIL 23, 1905 was a beautiful spring day in Stratford-upon-Avon, and over two thousand spectators assembled in front of a temporary, open-air stage in the Bancroft Gardens along the riverbanks to attend a production of Ben Jonson's Jacobean masque *Pan's Anniversary*. Thousands had made the trip that day to Stratford for the Shakespeare Birthday Celebration, the high point of the annual Shakespeare Festival, and an event that had been growing in popularity since its inception in 1880. This was the twenty-fifth year of the festival, so the events planned for the year's celebration were particularly lavish, including Morris and folk dancing exhibitions, folk singing classes, educational lectures, and many dramatic productions, including that of *Pan's Anniversary*, all of which the local newspaper had been promoting heavily during the previous weeks. The Shakespeare play featured for that evening was to be *The Merchant of Venice*, marked by the long-anticipated festival debut of the very popular Shakespearean actor Sir Henry Irving who, in the end, disappointed Stratford by cancelling due to illness. The production of *Pan's Anniversary* was on the same level of lavishness as for those during the rest of the day, with a large cast dressed in Jacobean costumes, the inclusion of folk and seventeenth-century dances, and the services of professional singers. The music for the afternoon entertainment was organized and composed by the young composer Ralph Vaughan Williams, aided by his friend Gustav Holst.

At the beginning of Ben Jonson's masque, a shepherd alludes to a coming celebration for a sacred holy day, a celebration with roots reaching back into time, always the same and therefore always appropriate.

> *1st Nymph:*   Thus, thus begin the yearly rites
> Are due to Pan on these bright nights;
> His morn now riseth and invites
> To sports, to dances and delights:
>   All envious and profane away;
>   This is the shepherds' holiday.[1]

---

[1] Ben Jonson, "Pan's Anniversary," in *The Cambridge Edition of The Works of Ben Jonson*, vol. 5, ed. Martin Butler (Cambridge: Cambridge University Press, 2012), 451.

The shepherds of Arcadia live in a harmony brought about by the proper worship of their protector Pan, yet this stability is threatened by the arrival of the Thebans and Boeotians, who would like to pervert the orderly celebrations with their own celebratory rites. So as the masque progresses, Arcadia meets its foe, and the old forms and traditions are threatened by the new. Arcadia must be tested, but it also must not be found wanting. The chain with the past cannot be broken or the golden landscape of Jonson's Arcadia will disintegrate into the undeferential and disordered world of the antimasque's antagonists. For the early twentieth-century Stratford audience at the Birthday Celebrations, Pan's followers hold at bay the more implied dangers of a new century and a bleak, modern world. The masque proves that timeless verities are sufficient, and the old order is reaffirmed as the shepherds and their nymphs continue their catalogues of quaint flower etymologies against the anglicized pastoral landscape of the type painted by Claude and Poussin.

> And come you prime Arcadians forth, that taught
> By Pan the rites of true society,
> From his loud music your entire manner wrought,
> And made your commonwealth a harmony,
> Commending so to posterity
> Your innocence from that fair fount of light,
> As still you sit without the injury
> Of any rudeness folly can, or spite.[2]

When the masque ended, the insubstantial shepherds and their songs and dances, presented as an idealized, pseudo-religious ritual of the kind that reaffirms social and historical connections, were shown to be the stuff of theater – backdrop, costume, and props. Rather than eternity, or the reification of the divine authority of the Stuart monarchy encountered by the original Jacobean audience, the audience at Stratford experienced a conflation of real and imagined historical voices.[3] The mummers from Britain's distant past, in their extravagant garb, whose music and folk traditions were just beginning to be known, were as much authors of this text as was Ben Jonson, who spun

---

[2] The exact text used for the Stratford production has not survived. For the original Jonson masque, see ibid., 451–61.

[3] An extensive bibliography exists on the ideological apparatus surrounding the Jacobean masque and its function to both represent and construct the claims of the Stuart monarchy. Two useful sources are Roy Strong, "Illusions of Absolutism: Charles I and the Stuart Court Masques," in *Art and Power: Renaissance Festivals, 1450–1650* (Woodbridge: The Boydell Press, 1984), 153–70 and Martin Butler, *The Stuart Court Masque and Political Culture* (Cambridge: Cambridge University Press, 2008).

Renaissance myths of power and allegory with his magician partner, the stage designer Inigo Jones. The glorious masques of Purcell and the Restoration theaters also added their voices, a mixture of the popular, spectacular, and profound. And in 1905 there was a new, rising chorus of historians and critics who were suggesting that the past could be re-presented in a contemporary national Renaissance, and who were seeking to meld the England of the past to the triumphant and vast center of the empire of the present, binding a set of diametric contrasts in a conglomeration of national identity.

Of course, the Stratford production was hardly meant to provide a profound theatrical experience, but rather to present topical, pleasant pageantry, a Jacobean text in a place that was quickly becoming the epicenter of the widening popular fascination with England's "golden" age.[4] But the slightness of the entertainment should not blind us to the implicit importance of the choice to produce *Pan's Anniversary or The Shepherd's Holyday* in 1905. In taking on the costume of the past, the production appears to resonate with the weight of over three hundred years of seemingly inherited tradition. Yet how much of this birthday celebration is inherited tradition and how much was this tradition newly invented – a mask, so to speak, of tradition? What did it mean to produce *Pan's Anniversary*, written for the court of James I in 1625, for an audience in 1905, the first time it had been seen since its original performance?

I would argue that the issues surrounding the production of this masque in Stratford were integrally connected to the musical and ideological stances of contemporary English composers during the period in which the idea of the English Musical Renaissance was first initiated and subsequently popularized. The questions raised by a 1905 masque revival are central to this study: attempts to answer them in turn generate further queries, revealing a complex web of multivalent issues concerning genesis, composition, and reception,

---

[4] The history of the Stratford Festival during the first decades of the twentieth century makes a fascinating story of the period's urge to manufacture, and then commercialize, history. For a comprehensive history of the festival, see T.C. Kemp and J.C. Trewin's *The Stratford Festival* (Birmingham: Cornish Brothers, 1953). Ian Moulton offers a more critical discussion of the ideology of the festival and the related Stratford movement in "Stratford and Bayreuth: Anti-commercialism, Nationalism, and the Religion of Art," *Litteraria Pragensia*, 6 (1996), 39–50. Finally, Roger Savage has recently published on aspects of the Stratford Festival and movement in "The Edens of Reginald Buckley: Temples and Tetralogies at Bayreuth, Stratford and Glastonbury" and "Alice Shortcake, Jenny Pluckpears and the Stratford-upon-Avon Connections of *Sir John in Love*," both contained in *Masques, Mayings and Music-Dramas: Vaughan Williams and the Early Twentieth-Century Stage* (Woodbridge: The Boydell Press, 2014). I examine the influence of the Stratford Festival on the folk, historical and amateur character of masques written in the years just before World War I in my fourth chapter.

all demonstrating the implicit, and increasingly understood linkage between nationalism, history, and music during the late Victorian, Edwardian, and early Georgian periods.[5]

This book will explore the ways in which the masque was understood through its "revival" during these periods. It was in fact more of an invented tradition than a historical one, and a generic redefinition was necessary for its increased popularity during the period leading up to the First World War. With the term "invented tradition" – a term central to scholarship on British culture and beyond – I am of course following Eric Hobsbawm, who defines an invented tradition, distinct from custom and convention, as being a newly constituted or redefined set of ritualistic or symbolic rules or actions which work through increasing repetition, to promulgate certain ideological values and norms of behavior.[6] Hobsbawm argues persuasively that while tradition is always in a state of invention and re-invention, the latter half of the nineteenth century and the first years of the twentieth saw an explosion of newly invented traditions. This was due to the extremely rapid and extensive changes to life in the modern era, since transformations in traditional behavior occur most frequently as a response to rapid changes in, and challenges to, everyday life. As Britain's empire continued to grow and encompass an ever more varied set of territories and subjects during the second half of the nineteenth century, a crisis over the identity at the heart of that empire grew as well, and the definitions of "Britishness" and "Englishness" became a particularly fraught topic. While the location of that identity varied considerably through almost competing forms of identity – I will later argue for a tri-part division based on notions of public, private, and pastoral – traditions and their real or imagined connections to the past proved crucial for English identity. Old traditions often failed to prove capable of meeting the new demands of contemporary life, and so new forms quickly rose to take their place and just as quickly assume the ritualistic aura of tradition. But, as Hobsbawm points out, not all invented traditions were created anew. Often old models were adapted for new

---

[5] The term English Musical Renaissance is applied not to the music of England during the Renaissance period, which is much more likely to be called Tudor or Elizabethan music, but instead to the period in question here, the beginning of which saw a sudden dramatic increase in native composition and positive conditions for the reception of a new school of English music on the part of critics and public alike. The application of the term "renaissance" to this new, nationalistic movement was a contemporary one, and so entered the narrative of the rebirth of English music very early on.

[6] Eric Hobsbawm, "Inventing Traditions," in *The Invention of Tradition*, ed. E.J. Hobsbawm and Terence Ranger, 2nd edn (Cambridge: Cambridge University Press, 1983), 1–14.

purposes. Old forms were emptied of their past associations and then refilled with symbolic content which might bear little or no relation to that of the past, all the while keeping the illusion of historic continuity.

The masque is an excellent example of one of these old forms or models. Even before the turn of the twentieth century, the genre had a long, persistent and varied history in England. The masque had its earliest English roots in the folk traditions and communal participation of the mummer's play and the progresses and pageants of the Tudor monarchs, but by the first half of the seventeenth century, the Stuart kings James I and Charles I had adopted the masque as the foremost artistic expression of their political power.[7] The crucial linking point of pre-Stuart to Stuart masquing is the Entry of disguised "strangers" who turn out to be benign dancing partners for the audience members. The basic format of the Stuart court masque traced the pattern of an introductory piece of "loud music" followed by the antimasque, which contained some dialogue, a song, and then a dance. This then instigated a spectacular transformation scene initiating the main masque. The masque proper was characterized by two to three "Entries," an Entry being a set of dialogue, song, and formal dance.[8] The masque ended with an extended period called "the Revels," in which the masquers and the audience danced together, which was usually concluded by a brief epilogue, bidding the participants to "come away." The roles within the masque were strictly categorized by class. Professional musicians danced the antimasques, sang, and provided instrumental accompaniment. The masquers themselves, varying from six to sixteen, were aristocratic amateurs from the inner circle of the king's favorites. They and their dances, both the formal dances of the masque proper and

[7] The mummer's play is a venerable folk tradition, with its roots in Celtic times. Usually performed at Christmas, a band of community participants dresses up in costumes as characters like Hobbyhorse and Robin Hood and visits one or more houses along the way, requesting food, drink, and other tokens. In return a play is performed, usually a variant of a battle between St George and the Turkish Knight, during which he is killed and resurrected by the Doctor, symbolically enacting the return of Spring after Winter's darkness. Two seminal works on the topic are Meg Twycross and Sarah Carpenter, *Masks and Masking in Medieval and Early Tudor England* (Farnham, Surrey: Ashgate Publishers, 2002) and Ronald Hutton, *The Stations of the Sun: A History of the Ritual Year in Britain* (Oxford: Oxford University Press, 2007).

[8] Everything else can be seen as ante- or post-cedent to this concept of the Entry. As far as these other characteristics go, they aren't necessarily traditionally English, though they could be: antimasques that contain disruptions by "Green Men," for example. They also might include elaborate neo-platonic mythological elements or elaborate visual spectacles derived from the Italian *intermedi* or French *ballets de cour*. These elements spawned later debates as to whether court masques were English or continental adaptations.

those of the Revels, were in essence at the center of the Stuart court masques, justifying the genre's other features. This mix of amateur and professional foreshadows the amateur component of masques prevalent after the turn of the twentieth century.

With its overt ideologies of absolute monarchy, and its strict conventions of Entries, antimasques, and Revels, the Stuart court masque in its "classic" form did not for the most part survive the Commonwealth. However, the power and the mystique of the masque was such that, with the precedent of a group of "masques-within-plays" from the Jacobean period, notably in Act IV of Shakespeare's *The Tempest*, the genre was absorbed into the public theater of the late seventeenth century, albeit in a much different shape. Built around song, dance, spectacle, mythology and allegory, and no longer on the erstwhile crucial Entry, this developmental trajectory reached an apex in the theatrical masques incorporated into the so-called "semi-operas" with scores by Matthew Locke, Henry Purcell and others. Throughout the first half of the eighteenth century, composers regularly wrote within the genre for both private and public theatrical performances, as the masque was one of the English musical-dramatic forms that offered an alternative to the encroachment of all-sung opera in London during this period. But perhaps because of its early association with the court and the dramatization of power, eighteenth-century masques continued to represent topics of history and nationalism through the exploitation of allegorical and pastoral modes.[9]

By the end of the eighteenth century, new forms of opera and musical theater had come to the fore, and masque compositions were presented far less frequently and in limited circumstances where nostalgic ties to older, more courtly forms or intense patriotism were appropriate. This situation continued throughout the first decades of the nineteenth century, as the genre almost ceased to exist in either performance or historical knowledge. Yet aspects of the masque, particularly tableaux vivants, certainly carried over into the continually popular theatrical pantomime, and later, into amateur productions like the pageant and the village fete.

The revival of the masque genre in the manner of what was thought of as its earlier and better state began in the middle of the nineteenth century, capturing the attention of composers searching for topics for new choral works generated by the rise of the amateur choral movement, or for historical subjects for popular musical theater. Scholarly interest in the Elizabethan and Stuart masques increased dramatically as part of the new historicist

---

[9] Michael Burden's "The Independent Masque 1700–1800: A Catalogue," *Royal Musical Association Research Chronicle*, 28 (1995), 59–159, offers the most complete overview of the masque during the eighteenth century.

attitude that sought to rediscover the glories of English drama and music at a time when connections to the past seemed to ameliorate anxiety about the present. Primary sources were rediscovered, scholarly articles appeared, and the first attempts at historical revivals were performed in London and in the Oxford and Cambridge colleges. This, then, created the cultural context for a heightened interest in the genre on the part of young English composers, who were attracted either by the contemporary understanding of the genre as a unique, English musical-dramatic form, with roots in country folk traditions and strong associations with the glories of the Elizabethan and Jacobean periods, or felt that a grand imperial statement could be made in an appropriate way in the masque tradition.

The contemporary understanding of the masque around the time of the Edwardian production of *Pan's Anniversary* certainly was not clearly defined in a strict or unified way as a set of formalized generic characteristics. Masques were being produced and performed which held little resemblance to the 1905 pageant-like revival of Jonson's masque in Stratford. Cantatas or other choral works, including those both semi-staged and unstaged, could be entitled masques, especially if they set a text that resonated with the folk festivals of springtime or Elizabethan al fresco entertainments. More elaborately staged masque scenes occurred in operettas and other musical theater pieces, again especially when connected to Elizabethan or country village settings and when the plot required a convenient crowd scene. Shakespeare's masques occasionally received settings, while settings of lyrics from masque texts by other sixteenth- and seventeenth-century dramatists, such as Ben Jonson, also were increasing in number. The last decade of the nineteenth and the first decade of the twentieth century also saw a revival of Purcell's inset masques, including those from *Dioclesian* and *King Arthur*. The newly written masque was also a favorite genre for presentation at patriotic occasions, where it often presented a blatant form of imperialist propaganda. During the period, the masque was appropriated for political and social messages, and the consciousness-raising endeavors associated with unions, socialism, and civic awareness. And with the expansion of what I will discuss as "pageant culture," by which I mean local manifestations of civic pride running the full gamut from nation to village, the masque furthermore became the property of ladies' societies and Sunday schools in one extreme, and of impresarios like Frank Lascelles, Oswald Stoll and Louis Napoleon Parker on the other.

With such a variety of generic amalgamations and possible performance venues, it is very difficult to talk of any set of consistent characteristics that define the masque over the four centuries of its existence. Indeed, for the purpose of this study it is the act of naming a work or part of a work as a "masque" that is the significant point, rather than some underlying formal consistency amongst the multiplicity of masques spanning the turn of the twentieth century. Rather than evoking a specific and consistent genre, to call something a masque was to link it to the tradition – the historical narrative – outlined above. It drew the mantle of history, and its sometime attendant accessory of historical nostalgia, over the work in a way that took on a special significance during this period. The difficulty of defining the masque through a single type is further complicated by the extreme variability of surviving source materials, since so many of these masques were occasional, and therefore ephemeral, works. The occasional and ceremonial components associated with the masque are a clue to the peculiar status of the genre. With their dependence on the visual, staged, and spectacular elements of their production – everything from cast choices, costumes, and context within an evening's program – they are not "fixed" works. They cannot be represented through a score and libretto only, something intuitively understood by librettist, composer, producers, and audiences alike.

However, if we look for consistent elements, most masques contained some kind of a patriotic component, on whatever terms such a patriotism was being defined within the context of the masque's performance: a love of the English countryside and the life of the country villages and provincial towns, a respect for Great Britain's glorious history over the ages, or a zealous support for the nation's current status as the ruling center of the world's largest empire, sometimes mixed with a subtly reforming idealism. Masques also usually exploited some component of spectacle, a relic of the ingenious and awe-inspiring scenes of transformation wrought by stage machines that were crucial aspects of the Stuart and Restoration masques. They were what might be called today "multi-media" presentations, incorporating solo and choral vocal music, spoken dialogue, scenic splendors, and often dance and/ or pantomime. Finally, the masque at the turn of the twentieth century, in keeping with its origins, often had a strong didactic component – implicit or explicit. Many were designed to serve as uplifting entertainment for the masses, a site of much concern both politically and socially in these years of the expansion of the vote and increased economic power of the lower classes.

The relationship between music and attitudes towards class in England was a particularly complicated and contested arena during this period. Opinions inherited from earlier writers on the topic assert the radical nature of the relationship between popular music, politics, culture, and the working classes, but these are now largely outdated in favor of an approach which sees popular culture in Britain at the turn of the century as essentially conservative in nature, mediated, of course, by specific issues and topics. It is important to note, however, that Victorian and Edwardian masques were not necessarily "popular" works in the sense that they expressed some aspect of popular culture or the culture of the lower classes. Rather, they served as pseudo-popular entertainments, an "official" attempt to mold the tastes and opinions of the people.[10]

Concentrating on the history of masque composition and theatrical production during the Victorian and Edwardian periods, it can be seen how easily the masque's historically nationalistic and patriotic generic character made it continually attractive to dramatists and composers seeking to represent a national identity during a period when such representations were increasingly multi-faceted due to tensions over definitions and sources for English and British identity. By focusing this investigation on several individual masques as case studies and relating them to larger trends in English opera, oratorio, and musical theater during this period, I will explore how competing versions of "Englishness" were asserted in these works, and how history and a historical consciousness were appropriated by these competing versions.[11] Masques that will be examined include works by the Victorian composers Edward Loder, George Macfarren and Arthur Sullivan, Edward Elgar, and composers who have been identified with the English Musical Renaissance such as Ralph Vaughan Williams and Gustav Holst. Central to my study is how the genre – its definition and characteristics – were consistently redefined within the shifting parameters of current historical knowledge, or, more often, despite historical knowledge, and moreover how that knowledge was manipulated to suit the musical and ideological needs of the cultural milieu of the composers and librettists of the time.

The masque, of course, was not one of the dominant genres of the music scene of Great Britain during the nineteenth and twentieth centuries in the way that, for example, the oratorio or the art song were. Compositions in the masque genre remained generally oddities, having the air of a self-conscious historical pastiche about them. But it is these very characteristics, the sense consistent throughout this period of the masque as something connected to

[10] An exhaustive treatment of this subject, and one which offers a well-balanced approach to the larger issues, is Dave Russell's *Popular Music in England, 1840–1914*, 2nd edn (Manchester: Manchester University Press, 1997).

[11] The bibliography on the issue of national identity and "Englishness" is immense. Approaches that I have found particularly useful include David Gervais, *Literary Englands: Versions of 'Englishness' in Modern Writing* (Cambridge: Cambridge University Press, 1993); J.H. Grainger, *Patriotisms: Britain 1900–1939* (London: Routledge & Kegan Paul, 1986), and Martin J. Wiener, *English Culture and the Decline of the Industrial Spirit, 1850–1980* (Cambridge: Cambridge University Press, 1981). See also Krishan Kumar's *The Idea of Englishness: English Culture, National Identity and Social Thought* (London: Routledge, 2015). A particularly valuable volume of source readings on this issue is Judy Giles and Tim Middleton, eds., *Writing Englishness 1900–1950* (London: Routledge, 1995).

history and the nation's past, that make it an excellent entry point for an investigation into how the conflict between historical and modern aspects of fin-de-siècle "Englishness" were constituted by, and represented in, musico-dramatic works of the period. Often it is these very types of genres, relics of the past thrust into the present and therefore containing a mix of tradition and re-invention of both the self-conscious and the subconscious kinds, that particularly reveal the underlying assumptions, the tensions, and the paradoxes that figure in a national identity, musical and more broadly socio-cultural.

Several fundamental characteristics of the masque make it a convenient locus to investigate the role of history and nostalgia for the past in conceptions of the English nation. First, the masque had come to be regarded as a particularly native product, in the way that most other contemporary genres were not. At the same time, as a result of its eclectic history and its changing and diverse characteristics, both formal and ideological, the ways in which this English quality became defined and delineated in the masque were certainly never fixed. Instead, the kinds of national identities projected in the masque were multifarious, drawing on the full range of nationalistic ideologies current during the period from pastoralism to imperialism, and mimicking on a local level the development and ultimate domination of a few of these ideological strands over the breadth of British music. The very openness of the genre was what made it useful for such functions; masques from this period were often as much exercises in defining and projecting national identity, as they were works for edification and entertainment.

The masque's status as a historical genre – initially considered a relic from England's "Golden Age" of the sixteenth and seventeenth centuries and then later as an amalgam of folk customs – connected it to the most privileged sources of English national identity. This connection to privileged sources contributes substantially to the usefulness of the genre and ones like it, pageants especially, in considerations of how history factored into the way in which late nineteenth and early twentieth century Great Britain defined itself as a nation. National history, whether political, cultural, or artistic, has always been one of the primary means by which national identity has been constituted, particularly in the case of England, despite Renan's oft-quoted remark that nationalism is all about getting a nation's history wrong.[12] The Victorian and Edwardian English were always proud of the history of their political and social systems, of the history of their colonial expansion, and of the glories of their literary history. Throughout the years spanning the turn of the twentieth century, this kind of English historical self-satisfaction reached

---

[12] As quoted in Eric Hobsbawm, "Inventing Traditions," in *The Invention of Tradition*, 12.

its chauvinistic peak, as if the fierce competition Britain waged for political and economic power on a global level with other imperial super-powers should be asserted in the cultural realm as well. This initiated an explosion of scholarly research delving into this past in exhaustive detail, every new study another brick in the monument to nation. It would be hard, therefore, for history not to figure prominently in representations of national identity. Genres such as the masque, which were firmly established as having a historical component, became popular for making links between the present and the past.

Finally, from its earliest manifestations, the court masque had served both an ideological and a didactic function. Praising the ruler, asserting dynastic claims, and projecting the image of the healthy kingdom with its happy subjects were consistent rationales for the production of sixteenth- and seventeenth-century masques. And while other subject matter became attached to the masque during the late seventeenth and eighteenth centuries, the genre never lost its identification with the ideological representation of the nation and/or the social constructs that led to a successful communal existence. Toward the end of the nineteenth century, when questions of national character and mission peaked again in the face of imperial growth, increasing conflict with France and Germany, and a disillusionment with the industrial age, genres which had served in the past to "teach" the nation took on a new importance. Thus, masques and pageants became increasingly popular around the turn of the twentieth century, and within them contemporary didactic goals for teaching versions of Englishness featured prominently.

What also makes the masque particularly interesting for a study of these issues is that the way in which the masque developed and changed corresponds closely to chronological developments and changes across a broader spectrum. Textually, at least, the few examples of masques from the first half of the nineteenth century show an ideological reliance on generic models from the eighteenth century, despite experiments with fitting contemporary musical style within the context of an old-fashioned "John Bull" sort of patriotism. As the mid-century point approaches, the masques begin to take on more transitional features, exhibiting after 1850 both the rising forms of nationalism and the change in attitudes towards industrialism and class that seem a feature of the larger nationalistic tendencies of the period. Of course, the nineteenth through the early twentieth century was the period that saw the rise and triumph of the concept of nationalism and the nation-state, and the period which saw these concepts sweep through both Europe and the Americas, forming the basis for contemporary ways of configuring nations and peoples.[13] As Walter Bagehot

---

[13] A good overview of the period and its imperialist agenda remains E.J. Hobsbawm's *The Age of Empire, 1875–1914* (New York: Pantheon, 1987).

put it, the business of the nineteenth century was nation-building,[14] and new nations and claims for national identity were on the rise throughout Europe, culminating most obviously in the unifications of Italy and Germany. In an opposite tendency, larger multi-ethnic states, such as the Austro-Hungarian Empire, increasingly saw movements within their boundaries seeking to gain self-determination for linguistic or ethnic groups within smaller areas.

The national question for Great Britain during the period 1850–1940 in some ways mirrors the general issues and concerns within the rise of European nationalism as a whole. However, given Britain's status as an "historical" nation, to use Eric Hobsbawm's term, and the unification and relative homogeneity it had achieved in preceding periods, the rise of nationalism and patriotism differs in many ways from the more general trends laid out by theorists of nationalism. Previous forms of English and British patriotism tended to be popular in their roots and appeal rather than driven by intellectual or "official" considerations. But the intellectual and official sources of nationalist ideas and programs became increasingly important as the nineteenth century progressed, along with, and often in conflict with, more popular manifestations of both nationalism and patriotism. Government attempts to mold popular nationalism to a more "official" track were begun relatively late in Britain, well after the colonial expansion was well underway, and were always viewed with a certain lackadaisical attitude towards their implementation.

Nationalism and patriotism, however, whether official or popular, operated to create social cohesion: what Benedict Anderson has termed an "imagined community."[15] And community was sought by finding things – or creating things – in common to heighten social bonds and a feeling of connectedness. These might include national symbols, traditions and rituals, or national memories, stories and histories. All of these were intermingled to form a common ground for an emerging national identity, in all forms of public discourse but particularly in arenas that are frequently implicated in cultural production: literature and the arts.

As these nationalistic tendencies intensified at the turn of the twentieth century, the masque further reflected both the nationalistic propaganda and the overt, imperialist jingoism of the Edwardian and pre-war Georgian period. Finally, after World War I, the masque reveals a much more complex and problematic relationship with nationalistic expression and the rise of twentieth-century modernism.

---

[14] As quoted in Eric Hobsbawm, *Nations and Nationalism since 1780: Program, Myth, Reality*, 2nd edn (Cambridge: Cambridge University Press, 1990), 23.

[15] Benedict Anderson, *Imagined Communities: Reflections on the Origin and Spread of Nationalism*, rev. edn (London: Verso, 1991).

As I will show in detail, the changes in the masque during the period 1860–1920 offer a microcosm of cultural, political, and social change in England as a whole. Seemingly innocent dramatic and musical representations of the past, masques and the related forms of the pageants of the period forcefully communicated messages about England's modern, industrial, and imperialistic present. They reveal an overwhelming involvement with national definition, relying on a variety of sources for identity that include three central categories – the chronicle of the nation, the landscape, and personal subjectivity – all of which demonstrate various mediations between the past and the present. It was a matter of debate and contestation, however, exactly how that homeland should be delineated. To a large extent citizens were free to pick and choose which among many versions of England they upheld, so long as they clearly identified that version as having a metonymic relationship with a larger England, however elusive, and responded appropriately. This explosion of national definition contained a bewildering number of possible Englands and modes of Englishness. Some of these definitions were set forth in governmental policies and party speech-making, but even more noticeably in the cultural products of the period, in literature and the arts.[16] Whether taking up an overtly public voice, expressing a more private vision, or simply reflecting more broadly popular topics, poets, artists, and composers served as conduits of conflicting versions of Englishness in ways not available to the government itself.

The reasons for the popularity of masques and pageants with the late-Victorian and Edwardian public appear in these new attempts to locate a distinct English national identity, a purpose for which, historically, the too-often patriotic nature of the masque was particularly suited. At the turn of the twentieth century, constructions of English nationalism underwent a period of redefinition in the face of several particular challenges: the economic and colonial expansion of other European countries, particularly Germany; the public's new understanding of the realities of modern warfare and the costs of imperialism in the wake of the second Boer War; and finally worker unrest and the success of the Labour Party in the 1905 elections. Throughout most of the nineteenth century, the English had slipped into global power and imperialist possessions almost by accident. This imperialist status appeared so gradually, as the result of commerce, that the nation was, by the mid-nineteenth century, innocent of any attendant political, moral, or social philosophy or ideology to frame and justify itself. Grainger characterizes the period as one of territorial and commercial expansion based not on governmental dictums

[16] See J.H. Grainger, *Patriotisms: Britain 1900–1939*, also David Gervais, *Literary Englands: Versions of 'Englishness'*.

but instead on the natural outgrowth of certain characteristics of the British people evident since the eighteenth century. Though unconscious, this growth of imperial ambition was enormously successful.[17] It was not until that success was challenged on a number of levels through increased conflict and competition with other nations, and resistance in the colonies themselves, that the imperatives of British nationalism and patriotism became a common concern in many facets of British society.

It is hardly surprising, therefore, that music, along with other arts and literature, would experience a corresponding turn to nationalism in this period. Many facets of musical life in Britain echoed these concerns of self-definition and nationhood. Furthermore, these echoes changed as society's involvement with the issues changed. As explored later, composers labeled as early contributors to the English Musical Renaissance were nationalistic only in their goals to establish a national school and gain recognition for national composers; their nationalism did not extend to a national style of composition. By the turn of the century, a generational gap quickly developed between the older and younger composers of the group over how radically different from continental models the new English music should be, and rising nationalism certainly played a large role. As nationalistic and imperialistic competition with France and Germany escalated in the political and social realms, a version of this competitive spirit manifested itself in English musical ideology. This competitiveness reached its height just after the start of World War I, when anti-German sentiment intensified in all sectors of British society; but the challenge to German musical ascendancy on the English music scene was steadily on the rise from 1890 on.[18]

How, then, did the masque become an historical genre that offered a site for the representation of conflicting versions of national identity? An important issue I examine in this investigation concerns the interplay between history and identity that became increasingly pervasive during the second half of the nineteenth century, and that strongly influenced the attitudes and aims of composers during the early years of the twentieth century.

---

[17] Martin J. Wiener, *English Culture and the Decline of the Industrial Spirit, 1850–1980*, chapter 1.

[18] A discussion of these issues can be found in Meirion Hughes and Robert Stradling, "Being Beastly to the Hun," *The English Musical Renaissance 1840–1940: Construction and Deconstruction*, 2nd edn (Manchester: Manchester University Press, 2001), and in my remaining chapters.

❧ Revivalism and the English Musical Renaissance Movement

The socio-cultural conditions that led to the re-invention of the masque in late Victorian and Edwardian periods can be linked to an even more pervasive awakening of a spirit of revivalism. The notion of revival, associated as it is with a re-invention of tradition, is an integral concept for the masque and for its relationship to British and English nationalism, musical and socio-cultural both. The word was indiscriminately attached to many issues and movements: the Gothic Revival, the Elizabethan Revival, the cathedral music revival, the early music revival, and the folk revival, to name just a few.[19] The prevalence of a spirit of revivalism in Britain during this period is indicative of the centrality of history to formulations of British modernity, and it was in essence directed by larger cultural forces, offering a anti-modern version of English national character that was non-industrial, non-progressive, and non-materialist. I will argue later that this version of "Englishness," generated out of new areas of social and anthropological sciences, cultural and material philosophy, and literature and the arts, originally functioned as an alternative version to official progressive and imperial ideologies, but quickly became appropriated itself as an "official," standardizing view in English music and society at large.

This is especially true of music and musical institutions, and it determined the popularity of historical musical genres like the masque, which were revived and re-invented to forge links between past and present. The creation of a contemporary musical school of British composition that would bear the responsibility for defining and propagating an English musical style was one area in which this possibility of exchanging a debased modern Englishness with a historical Englishness was particularly prominent.

The historical narrative of English music during the late nineteenth and the first half of the twentieth centuries has been permeated by the overarching concept of the English Musical Renaissance. In its most general sense, the appellation "the English Musical Renaissance" has come to designate the whole range of art music written by British composers from approximately 1880 to 1940, beginning with Charles Villiers Stanford, Arthur Sullivan and Hubert

---

[19] See, for example, Kenneth Clark, *The Gothic Revival: An Essay in the History of Taste* (New York: Harper & Row, 1974); Peter Hardwick, "The Revival of Interest in Old English Music in Victorian England, and the Impact of this Revival on Music composed into the Twentieth Century" (dissertation, University of Washington, 1973); Suzanne Cole, *Thomas Tallis and His Music in Victorian England* (Woodbridge: The Boydell Press, 2008) and Georgina Boyes, *The Imagined Village: Culture, Ideology and the English Folk Revival* (Manchester: Manchester University Press, 1993).

Parry, solidified by Edward Elgar and Ralph Vaughan Williams, and concluding with Benjamin Britten and Michael Tippett, among many others.[20] A response to domination by Italian opera, German symphonic methods, the popularity of Wagner, and the cosmopolitanism of the rising early twentieth-century avant garde, the narrative of the history of the English Musical Renaissance has tended to stress the music's intrinsically English character, supported by a reliance on critical language descriptive of the English countryside and rural life, a connection to English history and literature, a utilization of English folk idioms, and a concentration on vocal genres and music for the church. During the period surrounding the turn of the twentieth century, when the narrative of the English Musical Renaissance and its attendant ideologies were in the process of being formulated, these procedures contrasted with alternative views that the idea that English music needed to succeed on the same terms as continental music, by emulating the celebrated and honored genres of the Teutonic tradition: the symphony, the sonata, and the string quartet. However, by World War I, these contrasting views towards the right path for English music were being minimized as the historical–pastoral version became more pervasive.

As early as 1890, in a book otherwise devoted to the music of the Renaissance period, Morton Latham applied the term "renaissance" to describe the awakenings of a contemporary British national musical school, tapping in to several current cultural obsessions.[21] Certainly, the fascination with the Italian Renaissance, popularized first by Burckhardt and Pater, then imitated and expanded by a host of art, literary, and music historians, played a major role in the quick absorption of the "renaissance" label. More important, however, was the heightened regard and perceived cultural bond that the late Victorians held with the English Renaissance of the sixteenth and early seventeenth centuries: the "Age of Shakespeare," the "Age of Exploration," and the "Age of Elizabeth." This was an especially powerful pull for music, since for the Victorians the English Renaissance period was the last period in English history to have produced anything close to a school of composers, and so it became a natural extension to describe the perceived rebirth or revival of British music happening during the last decades of the nineteenth century

[20] Central to my definition are several essays by Alain Frogley, including "Constructing Englishness in Music: National Character and the Reception of Ralph Vaughan Williams," in *Vaughan Williams Studies*, ed. Alain Frogley (Cambridge: Cambridge University Press, 1996), 1–22 and "'Getting its history wrong': English Nationalism and the Reception of Ralph Vaughan Williams," in *Music and Nationalism in Twentieth-Century Great Britain and Finland*, ed. Tomi Makela (Hamburg: von Bockel Verlag, 1997).

[21] M. Latham, *The Renaissance of Music* (London: Schott, 1890).

and the first decade of the twentieth in terms which rhetorically linked the present to the past.[22] By the first decade of the twentieth century, as the native art music scene continued to expand in size, popularity, and ambition, due in good part to the overwhelming popular success of the music of Edward Elgar, the term became a frequent and perhaps a somewhat clichéd feature in the proliferating discussion of national music among composers and critics alike.

There is a distinctive change of emphasis, however, when the concept of a "Renaissance" shifted from being an active process integrally related to a nationalist agenda – British music undergoing a renaissance, for example – to a signifier descriptive instead of a period and of an "official" school of composers and style of a national music. An idea of the English Musical Renaissance as a period with an ultimately homogeneous national musical style and attendant singleness of purpose was one created in hindsight, after a process of selection and authentication had taken place. Looking back today, from a position in which we are in some ways still dealing with stereotypes promulgated by such a recreation, conceptualizing a monolithic period and/or school entitled the English Musical Renaissance validated a narrative of modern English music that prioritized the pastoral, the historical, and the folk styles of the period at the expense of other types of urban, progressive, and modernist trends that are also clearly visible.[23] Canonized, the term devolved into the type of problematic usage concretized in the later surveys – Frank Howes's *The English Musical Renaissance*, Peter Pirie's *The English Musical Renaissance* and Michael Trend's *The Music Makers: The English Musical Renaissance from Elgar to Britten*.[24] It

---

[22] It is probably impossible to pinpoint exactly who first applied the concept of a Renaissance to the new resurgence in English national music at the end of the nineteenth century. Hughes and Stradling claim it was first coined by Morton Latham in 1888 in a series of Cambridge lectures and inscribed in Latham's *The Renaissance of Music*, 34. This is possible, though if, as Hughes and Stradling assert, Latham was part of the group at the Royal College of Music and *Grove's Dictionary*, it is probable that the term probably had coinage within the groups before this point: *The English Musical Renaissance 1840–1940*, 45.

[23] A quick sample of new work on Vaughan Williams alone: Daniel Grimley, "Landscape and Distance: Vaughan Williams, Modernism and the Symphonic Pastoral," and J.P.E Harper, "Vaughan Williams's Antic Symphony," in *British Music and Modernism, 1895–1960*, ed. Matthew Riley (Farnham, Surrey: Ashgate, 2010), 147–74; Anthony Barone, "Modernist Rifts in a Pastoral Landscape: Observations on the Manuscripts of Vaughan Williams's Fourth Symphony," *Musical Quarterly*, 91 (2008), 60–88; and the essays contained in the *Cambridge Companion to Vaughan Williams*, ed. Alain Frogley and Aidan Thomson (Cambridge: Cambridge University Press, 2013).

[24] Frank Howes, *The English Musical Renaissance* (London: Secker and Warburg, 1966); Peter Pirie, *The English Musical Renaissance* (New York: St. Martin's Press, 1979); Michael Trend, *The Music Makers: Heirs and Rebels of the English Musical*

quickly became firmly fixed in the narrative of British music history and as it expanded it increasingly covered a great deal of compositional territory, both stylistic and aesthetic.

Used in this way as a designator of a period, the term operates more like a series of assumptions that can be labeled, for convenience, the English Musical Renaissance, rather than as a cohesive category. The result of such a periodizing approach is that the chronicle of British music composed during the period 1880–1940 constructs a homogeneity that erases the individuality of British composers active during this period and the multiplicity of ideologies and approaches to music that was really the only consistent characteristic of the period. Many accounts that treat the English Musical Renaissance as a period obfuscate the real ideologies that worked to form the now commonly believed narrative of British music during this long and diverse span of time. Thus, an overly inclusive view of the English Musical Renaissance, to which all significant British composers of the period are co-opted on such a convenient roster regardless of attitudes and compositional style, disguises diversity and real differences between the many opposing camps in British music during the late nineteenth and early twentieth centuries. More importantly, it results in distancing the "Englishry" movement from the social and political agendas to which it was connected, both in the early years of the movement, and in its ongoing quest for self-definition and ascendancy within the whole of English musical society during the first fifty years of the twentieth century.[25]

An antidote to the period approach is to consider the English Musical Renaissance as a movement with a clear set of attached ideologies. Instead of homogeneity, such an approach acknowledges that the English Musical Renaissance was only one of several different schools within English music between 1880 and 1940. Other possible schools or groups include those composers associated with the Royal Academy of Music who were heavily influenced by Wagner during the last two decades of the nineteenth century, the set of composers associated with Birmingham around the turn of the century, and composers after the turn of the century such as Warlock, Lambert and Van Dieren, who found inspiration in the continental avant garde.

Renaissance, Edward Elgar to Benjamin Britten (London: Weidenfeld & Nicholson, 1985).

[25] An early critical discussion attacking the concept of the English Musical Renaissance as a period rather than as a movement with its own ideological basis can be found in Hughes and Stradling, *The English Musical Renaissance 1840–1940*. For balanced and insightful critiques of the factual errors and ideological problems of the book, see Alain Frogley, "Re-writing the Renaissance: History, Imperialism, and British music since 1840," *Music & Letters*, 84 (May 2003), 241–57, and Julian Onderdonk's review of the book in *Notes*, 52 (Sep. 1995), 63–6.

The renaissance began as an effort to establish a creditable school of English composers who would be part of and equal to, rather than separate from, the Austro-German "universal" tradition; in this way not much different from composers of other countries and ethnicities working to establish their own national musical style, like the Czechs, Russians, and Americans. Their focus was to gain for English composers a larger presence within the English, particularly the London, musical scene. From the beginning it was connected with the ideology supposedly shared by the faculty and governing board of the new Royal College of Music, established in 1883. The college is integral to the concept of the English Musical Renaissance, since many who can be identified as part of the English Musical Renaissance 'group' received their education there, including composers such as Ralph Vaughan Williams, Gustav Holst, George Butterworth, Armstrong Gibbs, and Herbert Howells, as well as countless performers and educators. The teaching of composition at the Royal College of Music had a large role in forming a common aesthetic and worked to create oppositions with English composers who were trained elsewhere. Examples were composers like Arnold Bax, who was trained at the Royal Academy of Music, as well as figures like Holbrooke, Smyth, and Delius, who went to Germany for their advanced training and who tended to absorb a different set of continental attitudes towards music and composition. And, given its foundation by composers, administrators, and critics living and working for the most part in London, the movement retained its London–Oxbridge base, a characteristic that served to push to the periphery composers working outside London and outside the sphere of the Royal College of Music. Even as established a composer as Elgar continually battled the stigma of being a "provincial" composer, or perhaps more truthfully, he always felt that he had to wage this battle, given Elgar's predilection for self-doubt and paranoia. But Elgar only served as a visible spokesperson for many composers such as Orr, Holbrooke and others, who felt disenfranchised as outsiders to the Royal College of Music and London–Oxbridge cliques. Much of the momentum to establish a music school in Birmingham was a response to this attitude.[26]

The advantage of treating the English Musical Renaissance as a movement rather than as a period is that it highlights how a certain version of an English national music won out over other competing ideas of what a truly national-istic musical style might sound like, particularly in its reliance on concepts of the English countryside, English history, and the English language. It allows for the deconstruction of the "official narrative" of England's musical rebirth

---

[26] For more, see my chapter 5, as well as Byron Adams, "The 'Dark Saying' of the Enigma: Homoeroticism and the Elgarian Paradox," *19th-Century Music*, 23 (2000), 218–35 and Hughes and Stradling, *The English Musical Renaissance 1840–1940*, 47–60.

by investigating how it was connected to other contemporary negotiations between popular and "official" manifestations of nationalism on a broader socio-cultural level. In this sense it is a valuable approach, because it renders visible ideological underpinnings that have tended to be effaced in traditional narratives of the English Musical Renaissance.

On the negative side, approaches that over-emphasize the idea of the English Musical Renaissance as a movement risk ascribing to it a cohesiveness and sense of purpose that certainly never existed, at least during its first decades. While such approaches assert the many competing faces of English music during this early period, and the ultimate centrality of the school of ideas that became associated with the English Musical Renaissance, they also operate through the lens of hindsight, projecting back onto its members a unity that was attained only in its later histories. The truth of the matter was that the English Musical Renaissance was never an organized movement. Composers and critics associated with this group certainly reflected ideas of their time, buying into broad ideologies of cultural nationalism, pastoralism, and the folk, but, as Byron Adams has put it, there were "no weekly meetings at the RCM [Royal College of Music] devoted to the creation of an English Musical Renaissance."[27] Stanford and Parry were ideologically poles apart, and their students were often at odds with one another. This is reflected clearly in something as simple as their political stances: Stanford was a political conservative, Parry a liberal; Holst was a socialist, Vaughan Williams halfway between. Elgar was a Tory and imperialist, Rutland Boughton eventually a communist, and so on. None of this makes for an easy sense of collegiality, and certainly does not make for any type of a cohesive movement.

The common strand in all of this variability, however, is that all of the composers and music critics who can truly be said to be associated with the aesthetics and ideologies now identified with the English Musical Renaissance were cultural nationalists, in that they believed in the equality, if not superiority, of a particular English musical character and they fostered a spirit of competition between contemporary English musical composition and that of Germany, Italy, and France. This, then, should form the basis of any attempt at defining them as a group, and eliminate native composers who, while successful and active members of the British musical scene during this period, ultimately were not terribly concerned with expressing an Englishness in their music, nor developing an intrinsically English musical language. It is important to remember, however, that while the nationalistic purpose may have formed an underlying connective seam, the means and methods for arriving at a musical Englishness varied widely. Certainly Elgar considered

---

[27] Private note, June 2002, by permission.

himself a "nationalistic composer," though he wrote in a compositional style heavily derived from modern German music and had little tolerance for the historical, "folksy" posturings, as he saw them, of younger composers of the English Musical Renaissance.[28] On the other hand, composers who are now identified with the pastoral school, such as Vaughan Williams and Holst, often wrote music firmly influenced by continental modernist trends.

✎ Elgar's "The Crown of India" and Imperial Versions of Englishness

From its earliest conception in the works and teachings of Stanford and Parry, the supposed rebirth of English music was seen as integrally connected to the revival of English music of the past, before Handel's brand of *opera seria* initiated the 150-year domination of foreign music and musicians in Britain. The demand of some for a national musical style based on national musical sources, a demand to which the new types of masques were intrinsically connected, was in its own way a patriotic challenge to the dominance, by the mid-nineteenth century, of the Austro-German canon. The English Musical Renaissance movement was, of course, influenced by, and implicated in, the nationalistic ideologies of the time, but this projected version of a new national musical style also served to disguise the contemporaneity of these ideologies with a patina of the inevitability of its history and historical sources.

It is important to counter this simplistic characterization, which has come to inform so many present-day musicological conceptions of English music from 1880 to 1940, by placing it within a framework of argument and counter-argument, since in fact the nature of English music was contested among many groups and factions. Many composers and critics did not endorse the idea that the sole path to a thriving, national musical scene would require turning away from the mainstream of continental music. Instead, many felt that English music should and could compete on equal terms with the best of particularly Teutonic music. Many English composers and musicians still sought their advanced musical training in centers like Leipzig and Frankfurt, eschewing

---

[28] Elgar's attitude towards the claims of modernity versus history will be explored in more depth in chapter 5. In this context it is enough to say that, while Elgar had a deep love for the English countryside, and often embodied an English pastoralist sensibility, he did not at all believe that an English national music would be found in a deliberate archaism or an unmediated reliance on the folk. "I don't think about it [folk music] at all. I am folk music," he is quoted as declaring to his friend Troyte Griffith. Often replicated, the quote originates in a manuscript by Griffith held by the Elgar Birthplace museum.

the perceived provincialisms of the Royal College of Music and other British music schools.[29]

The status of history, historical sources, and the character of intrinsically English genres like the masque lie at the heart of this debate. Both sides of the controversy over the creation of an English national music drew on aspects of national history, and both mobilized the attractions of the past, particularly the "Jacobethan" period, a fictional construct of a golden age, located in the Merrie England of 1550–1640.[30]

But as the various types of turn-of-the-century masques reveal, there is a serious division in their use of the topics and materials of history. While a masque like *Pan's Anniversary*, like many other works of the turn-of-the-century generation of the English Musical Renaissance, linked the sonic qualities of historical music to a nostalgic vision of England's past, other masques did not replace modern music, and by extension the modern world, with the materials of the past, though they may have represented the topics of revivalism just as noticeably.

A telling example of such a masque is Edward Elgar's *Crown of India*, produced in 1912 at the London Coliseum to celebrate the coronation of King George V as Emperor of India. This overtly imperialistic and racially triumphalist work, which I will explore in greater detail in chapter 5, projected a modern and progressive version of Englishness greatly at odds with Stratford's *Pan's Anniversary*, though no less implicated in the topics of English history. Written to celebrate King George V's Delhi Durbar, the historical topic of *The Crown of India* was at the time utterly contemporary: a celebration of subjugation and possession, of the strength and power of Britain's mercantilism backed up by military might. And instead of Vaughan Williams's reliance on musical materials associated with England's golden age – Purcell, hymn tunes, Renaissance keyboard dances, and folk music – Elgar represented imperial England through two musical topics conceived much more recently: the exotic, orientalist fantasy and the military march. Not for Elgar and his audience at the London Coliseum were the nostalgic dreams of an England

[29] Very important recent scholarly work has been done on exploding the characterization of British music from the period as essentially conservative and as ignoring modernist trends emanating from the continent. I hope this study contributes to these new views, which assert fascinating and complicated interactions between different definitions of modernist aesthetics in ways that are particularly British. A good place to start exploring this topic is the volume *British Music and Modernism, 1895–1960*.

[30] A comprehensive overview of the sacred and secular traditions and holidays of Medieval and Early Modern England can be found in Ronald Hutton, *The Rise and Fall of Merry England* (Oxford: Oxford University Press, 2005).

past and gone, but the realities of a modern superpower seizing its place in the world, fulfilling an imperial destiny.

For all of the initial contemporary relevance of its topic and musical sources, the music of Elgar's masque now seems particularly "of its time," tied by its attempt at capturing an important moment to the progressive, industrial, mercantile and urban world of the late Victorians and Edwardians. Elgar's glorification of the modern, in fact, is a world now long passed. Avant-garde styles that were just emerging in the years around the turn of the century would become the modernist styles of the years between the world wars, supplanting styles of modern composition prior to World War I. And for many, a taste for modernism was soon to be moderated and complicated by the pastoral, the folk, and the dream of the organic village, represented by the solidly English national music of history and folk.[31] The best account of this shift away from progressive and modern values towards the conservative and historical is Martin J. Wiener's *English Culture and the Decline of the Industrial Spirit, 1850–1980*. Wiener argues that the crucial period for the emergence of this return to conservative attitudes began in the decade of the 1850s. He locates the high-water mark of industrial values around the time of the Great Exhibition of 1851, but also finds in the inclusion of Pugin's Medieval Court in the Crystal Palace an indication that this was an end, not a beginning. Wiener further frames the second half of the nineteenth century in England as a period of conflict, where the idealization of material growth and technical innovation that had been the defining characteristic of the first period of the industrial revolution earlier in the century began first to be questioned and then to be supplanted by a version of Englishness which stressed a contrasting and conservative set of values.

> The English genius, it declared, was (despite appearances) not economic or technical, but social and spiritual; it did not lie in inventing, producing, or selling, but in preserving, harmonizing, and moralizing. The English character was not naturally progressive, but conservative; its greatest task – and achievement – lay in taming and 'civilizing' the dangerous engines of progress it had unwittingly unleashed.
>
> Over the years, this outlook contended with an industrial reality that sometimes was proclaimed as a source of pride. The resulting conflicts of social values – progress versus nostalgia, material growth versus moral stability – were expressed in the two widespread and contrasting cultural symbols of Workshop

---

[31] Though of course Elgar also could compose in this vein with the best of the them: witness the episode in Shallow's orchard in Part III of his symphonic study *Falstaff*, to mention just one of many instances.

and Garden (or Shire). Was England to be the workshop of the world or a Green and Pleasant Land?[32]

However, alternate twentieth-century versions of English musical modernism continued to offer a challenge to both the historic and nostalgic throughout the period, and the terms of an English nationalism, musical and beyond, continued to be a contested arena.

Until the turn of the twenty-first century, most scholarship on late nineteenth- and early twentieth-century English music promulgated an accepted dogma that the large-scale renewal of English composition during this period was a result of an uncomplicated expropriation of folk music and the exploitation of a supposed "pastoral" idiom. Such descriptions had not sought to critique the ideological underpinnings of such cultural expropriations, nor the validity of applying such a general model to the English music movement as a whole. Following in the footsteps of cultural historians who began in the 1980s to demonstrate just how ideologically charged the folk and the pastoral drive was during this period, more recent work on British music continues to extend its hypotheses to key composers such as Edward Elgar, Hubert Parry, Ralph Vaughan Williams, and many others.[33] These approaches have opened up a whole new way of thinking about the music of Victorian and Edwardian Britain, revealing its full immersion in the complex ideological and social controversies of the period.

This study seeks to link the issues raised by these reappraisals of the English Musical Renaissance with an investigation into how these issues might have affected the appropriation of a particular genre, in this case the masque. The masques of the period 1860–1920 have been virtually unexplored, yet the genre offers a valuable window into how historical genres were adapted and redefined, or more properly re-invented, to project a thoroughly modern English aesthetic, albeit one in the costume of the past. This is because of the masque's traditional associations with nationalism and patriotism, and its perceived identity as a uniquely English genre with its developmental roots in the English "golden age" of the sixteenth and seventeenth centuries.

---

[32] Martin J. Wiener, *English Culture and the Decline of the Industrial Spirit, 1850–1980*, 5.

[33] Particularly noteworthy are Eric Saylor's recent *English Pastoral Music: From Arcadia to Utopia, 1900–1955* (Champaign, IL: University of Illinois Press, 2017); Georgina Boyes, *The Imagined Village: Culture, Ideology, and the English Folk Revival*; Alun Howkins, "The Discovery of Rural England," in *Englishness: Culture and Politics 1880–1920*, ed. Robert Colls and Philip Dodd (Beckenham, Kent: Croom Helm, 1986), 62–88; Richard Sykes, "The Evolution of Englishness in the English Folksong Revival, 1890–1914," *Folk Music Journal*, 6 (1993), 446–90.

The book takes the form of a historiographic study of how a group of composers redefined a historical genre formally and ideologically to promote and disseminate various differing ideas of national identity; ideas, though, that were linked by their explicit historical consciousness and overt nostalgia. Partly a cultural study, partly a genre study, and partly an initial investigation into a little-known corner of the English music scene during the period 1860–1920, I offer it as another contribution to the now-thriving field of contemporary scholarship on the music of Great Britain.

CHAPTER 2

"With revel dance and song": The Musical Image of History in the Victorian Masque

> This shall be merrie England,
> Of which our fathers oft have told,
> 'Tis holiday, let's all be gay
> Arouse thee merrie England,
> With revel dance and song.

O N March 10, 1863, a large and enthusiastic audience gathered at the Royal English Opera House, Covent Garden, for the première performance of *Freya's Gift, an allegorical Masque in honour of the marriage of His Royal Highness the Prince of Wales*, written by John Oxenford and with music by George Macfarren[1] (see Illustration 2.1). The masque opened with a four-part chorus singing in unison, representing the voice of England lamenting the dark, the cold, and the lethargy that had settled upon the land. By the end of their lengthy complaint, the text alluded to a light beginning to shine, and its appearance stimulated the assembled voices in four-part block chords to "shake away sorrow, cloud and the dusty veil." The Norse goddess Freya then appeared on stage, and her ensuing aria described how she came from her Northern home of Valhalla to bring the people of England a gift that would keep the darkness and the cold at bay. This, of course, was the Nordic princess bride, who will "change this early season into May."

All of this deliberate textual play on the aspects of warmth, light, and joy coming from the frozen North was quite appropriate and an apt allegory

---

[1] *Freya's Gift, an allegorical Masque*, vocal score (London, 1863). The masque was presented during the last week of the inaugural season of the Royal English Opera. The schedule for the week presents an interesting window into the range of genres considered appropriate for such a company, as the official playbill of the week announced. On Monday and Friday, Donizetti's *La Sonnambula* was presented, on Monday with an afterpiece of *Harlequin Beauty and the Beast* and a Grand Transformation Scene *Moonbeam and Sunlight*, on Friday followed by *Freya's Gift*. *Freya's Gift* also served as the afterpiece on Tuesday–Thursday and on Saturday for Michael Balfe's new opera, *The Armourer of Nantes*. On Friday *Freya's Gift* and *Sonnambula* were preceded by Sullivan's *Procession March*.

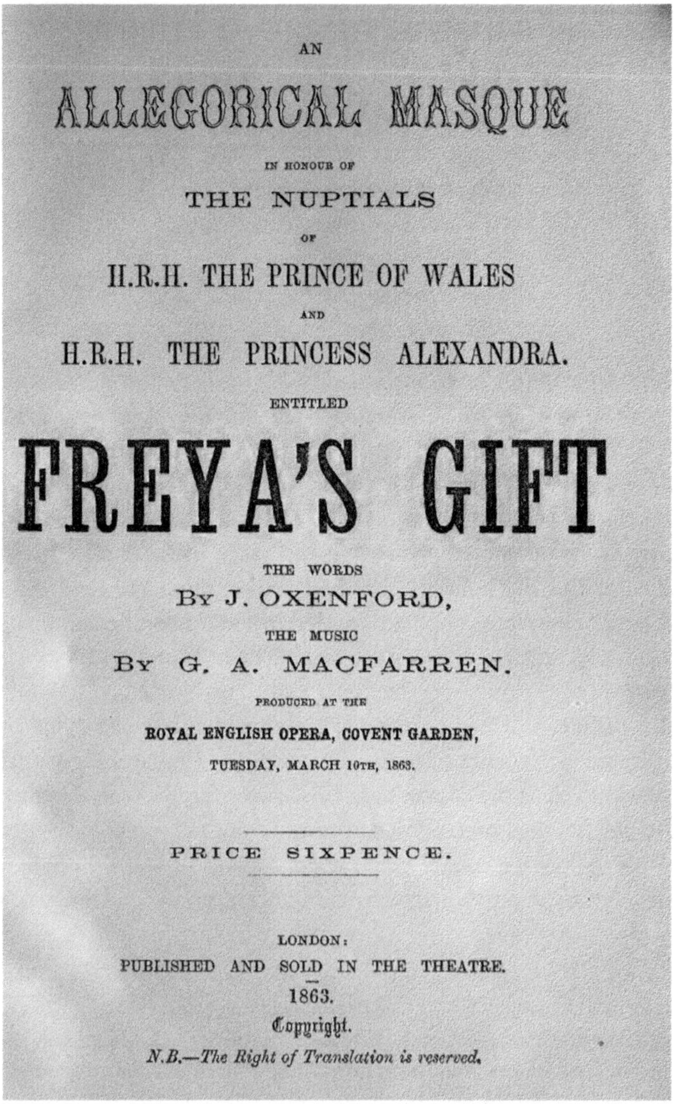

AN

ALLEGORICAL MASQUE

IN HONOUR OF

THE NUPTIALS

OF

H.R.H. THE PRINCE OF WALES

AND

H.R.H. THE PRINCESS ALEXANDRA.

ENTITLED

FREYA'S GIFT

THE WORDS

BY J. OXENFORD,

THE MUSIC

BY G. A. MACFARREN.

PRODUCED AT THE

ROYAL ENGLISH OPERA, COVENT GARDEN,

TUESDAY, MARCH 10TH, 1863.

PRICE SIXPENCE.

LONDON:

PUBLISHED AND SOLD IN THE THEATRE.

1863.

Copyright.

N.B.—The Right of Translation is reserved.

Illustration 2.1 G.A. Macfarren, *Freya's Gift*, 1863 libretto cover

that matched the occasion of the nuptials of Edward, the Prince of Wales, to Alexandra of Denmark. But Freya's aria ends with a peculiar exhortation:

> Warm, everglowing, Next to his Royal Mother,
> Knowing the two cannot be lov'd apart,
> Accept the gift, let England sigh no more,
> But be a merry England as of yore.

Apart from the rather awkwardly introduced complementary gesture towards Queen Victoria, what is intriguing in this concluding verse is its call to resurrect England's past, and the already palpable yearning for a supposedly happier time in England's history. This introduced a new nuance into the nineteenth-century masque and in many ways into English drama as a whole. The call to "be a merry England as of yore" was to be increasingly pervasive during the next fifty years.

The theme of Merry England returns as the prime textual motive in the penultimate number, appropriately enough entitled "The Revels," a term used for the concluding dances of all sorts of masques and folk festivals, usually with participation from the audience or, in the case of a theatrical production, the entire company. The text of "The Revels" clearly identifies why – beyond the death of the Prince Consort fourteen months earlier – England is merry no more. The problem is England's mercenary single-mindedness, and the text suggests the solution to be a return to traditional values:

> Our England was a merry spot
> They say in times of old.
> And have we all our mirth forgot
> In seeking after gold.
> No we have not, as we'll show,
> By revel dance and song,
> 'Twere a heavy shame
> Should Britons wear a clouded brow.
> Nor seek to recover the ancient name.
> This shall be merrie England,
> Of which our fathers oft have told,
> 'Tis holiday, let's all be gay
> Arouse thee merrie England,
> With revel dance and song.

"The Revels" continues the simple, predominantly homophonic and unison choral writing which characterized the opening number, its simplicity essentially predetermined by obvious hopes that the work would have an afterlife in the repertoire of the burgeoning choral society movement. Apart from the ubiquitous

6/8 time signature – a broad signifier during this period of the pastoral and of traditional sorts of merry-making – the music itself seems relatively free of any characteristics or historical references that would mimic the nostalgic call-to-arms of the text. It contains no contrapuntal development, other than a tendency to have imitative entries with paired voices, especially on the repeated line "with revel dance and song," no renaissance or early baroque dance rhythms and phrasing, no modal passages. However, socio-political exigencies do subtly enter "The Revels," notably in passages associated not with the references to merry England, but in those invoking the nation's imperative or the Queen herself. Lines such as "nor seek to recover the ancient name," which elicits a slight harmonic coloring by moving from D major to B minor, or the elongated rhythms of the unison writing on "Our sovereign bids us rejoice," which is followed by obvious, albeit short, echo-effects on "and the echo shall shout with a loyal voice," all point to Macfarren's awareness that the demands of the royal associations of the occasion needed to be prioritized over musical authenticity or a pastiche of a Renaissance masque's Revels (Illustrations 2.2 and 2.3).

The Oxenford/Macfarren work, formally a cantata though never designated as such, is subtitled an "allegorical Masque," and so clearly attempts to place itself within the long historical tradition of the masque genre, one strand of which has always been particularly connected to English history, royal celebrations, and spectacular sorts of pageantry from the Tudor period on. By 1863, however, the masque had been rediscovered or "re-invented" following on the heels of the almost complete extinction of the genre during the first four decades of the nineteenth century. From this point on, the genre of the revised masque grew in popularity, incorporated and merged with a wide range of other genre options, including the 1905 revival of Ben Jonson's *Pan's Anniversary* in Stratford.[2] But what strand connects *Freya's Gift*, a work written in 1863 in the newly popular cantata genre, and as such attached to the burgeoning choral movement of the 1860s, with a revival of both historical and folk customs and music such as that of *Pan's Anniversary*? While both scores are designated masques, what links these disparate works written almost forty years apart are not any formal generic characteristics, but instead a set of topics and associations surrounding the Jacobethan myth and the mood of nostalgia for the simplicities of the earlier periods of the nation's past.[3] As

[2] A list of nineteenth-century masques is contained in Appendix 1.

[3] Throughout this monograph I use the term "Jacobethan," often used to refer to faux architectural styles that draw on English Renaissance idioms, to designate the period roughly from 1550 to 1650. Technically this century includes periods properly known as the Tudor, Elizabethan, Jacobean, and Caroline. I prefer to use Jacobethan because it highlights the fictionalized and constructed aspects of this mythologized era in the ideologies during the period 1860–1920.

Illustration 2.2   G.A. Macfarren, *Freya's Gift*, "The Revels"

Illustration 2.3   G.A. Macfarren, *Freya's Gift*, "The Revels"

we see already in *Freya's Gift*, the image of Merrie England carries significant ideological baggage, such that it serves as the basis for an exhortation to transform the nation at the moment when dynastic concerns are at the fore. And, as chapter 4 will discuss in detail, the production of *Pan's Anniversary* was integrally connected to a movement which sought a similar transformation of national character through the agencies of a revived historic and folk music, drama, and dance. Throughout the intervening forty or so years, two topics – nostalgia for England's past and national reformation – mark the central features of the masque in a much clearer way than any attempts to find a defining set of formal generic characteristics for either the Victorian or the Edwardian masque.

However, there are important distinctions between a masque like *Freya's Gift* and masques after the turn of the century. For Vaughan Williams, the compositional problem presented by the Jacobean text of *Pan's Anniversary* was that of arriving at a set of musical sources that would project both historical authenticity and idealism. While the representation of a rosy-tinted past grew in importance for the Victorian masque, this idea of authenticity allied to the representation of history in musical terms was a relatively new development in 1905. And beyond the masque proper, it is a central precondition for much of the ideological bedrock of the English Musical Renaissance.

The goal, therefore, of this and the succeeding chapter is to trace in broad terms how these two central concerns – nostalgia and authenticity – merged in the Victorian masque. At the heart of this merger was the change from what is often termed an antiquarian approach of the gentleman-scholar, where the objects of history are treated either merely as curiosities to be explored or as stages in a developmental, organic model, to the more professionalized and integrative revivalist approach which characterized later investigations into the past. This change is particularly noticeable in Victorian musicology as opposed to other fields of antiquarian interest, since it clung to a progressive attitude towards the objects of the past in ways which denigrated preceding stages in a much stronger way than did the allied fields of art, architecture, and literary studies. By 1860 there was already a small but active group of musician–scholars investigating the music of the medieval and renaissance periods; the broader, more popular assumption, however, was that the musical arts had progressed so far beyond the crudities and ineptitude of earlier periods as to render early music unable to be understood, appreciated, or enjoyed by the wider public in performance or useless as a source of inspiration for the composer. Of course, there are exceptions to this generalization. Two that spring to mind are the madrigal and Gregorian chant. The madrigal continued to be a popular genre throughout much of the nineteenth century within select circles and areas, with societies devoted both to the performance of the renaissance madrigal, both English and Italian, and to supporting new composition within the genre. Gregorian chant, on the other hand, had a brief period of popularity as a key platform component in the Tractarian movement.[4] But on the whole, there was no audience for most historical music, and what it remained an interest for the antiquarian.

By the time of *Pan's Anniversary*, the situation was much different, as early music was increasingly performed in concert, studied in the schools and universities, taught to the wider public through lectures and accessible literature, and integrated into compositions in such genres as the masque. The musicological reasons for this change will be discussed in chapter 3. In this chapter I explore how the particular characteristics of the Victorian masque contributed to a deepening consciousness of the value of early music, and how topics rehearsed in the masque and similar genres played a role in constituting in an important way the national character of the English people.

ꙮ *Past Traditions*

By 1850, the Victorian public would have understood the masque to be a patriotic genre, connected to national and royal topics. Usually part of a full evening of dramatic entertainment, the masque was often an entr'acte or afterpiece in English involving a mixture of dance, solo and choral song, pantomime, and dialogue, to which was added a heavy and crucial component of spectacle through costume, scenery, and special effects. Masques prior to 1860 were performed by the leading singers of the company, augmented by the company's chorus, rather than by a separate group of performers. Production values were very high. In some ways the masque was allied to other popular theatrical genres of the period – the burlesque, the pantomime, and the extravaganza, for example – particularly in its inclusion of spectacular scenes of transformation where, as if by magic, character or scenes appeared to alter in an instant, a crucial aspect of all of these mid-century genres. Unlike these other types of popular musical entertainments, however, the masque dealt with historical or allegorical subject matter that avoided the humorous, punning quality

---

[4] For information on both, consult Peter Hardwick, "The Revival of Interest in Old English Music in Victorian England, and the Impact of this Revival on Music composed into the Twentieth Century" (dissertation, University of Washington, 1973) and appropriate sections in Nicholas Temperley, ed., *The Romantic Age 1800–1914*, vol. 5, *The Athlone History of Music in Britain* (London: Athlone Press, 1981). For more on music and the Tractarian movement, see Bennett Zon, "Plainchant in Nineteenth-Century England: a Review of some Major Publications of the Period," *Plainsong and Medieval Music*, 6 (1997), 53–75.

of the burlesque and pantomime, and the fairy topics of the extravaganza. Also, the masque at mid-century generally contained a large amount of new music especially composed for the occasion, rather than relying on pastiches of familiar tunes, as did pantomimes and burlesques.[5] This conception of the masque as a genre of allegorical and patriotic topics projected through discrete tableaux containing music, dance and spoken dialogue was to change very quickly. Within fifteen to twenty years, the masque was to become a topic for a musical work rather than a musical theater genre in itself. From the 1860s on, a masque was much more likely to be in the form of a cantata or other choral work, or to be the plot motivation for a historical scene inset into a larger theatrical work, musical or otherwise. With this generic shift also came an increase in the number of works entitled "masque".

But what kind of tradition of the masque, either remembered or experienced, did the theatrical public of the mid-nineteenth century inherit from the past?

In 1850, the theatrical public would have in some sense been aware of two broad categories of masques, the occasional and the theatrical masque. These two categories had a long history prior to the nineteenth century and continued to be a valid way of highlighting important differences in the reasons for any masque's commission and production throughout the nineteenth century as well. The occasional masque is the older of the two categories and is integrally connected to the court masque of the Tudor, Elizabethan, and Stuart periods. Outside the royal court, occasional masques were produced in aristocratic households (Milton and Lawes's *Comus* perhaps being the most famous), and for civic occasions, such as the masques written and produced in London's Inns of Court. Staged to mark particular occasions, anniversaries, holidays, and such, this category of masque included entertainments for royal visits, as in the famous masque to welcome Queen Elizabeth I at Kenilworth, and royal birthdays. Twelfth Night always served as the occasion for elaborate festivities, and throughout the reigns of James I and Charles I extensive and spectacular masques were produced to mark the end of the Christmas season, with the partnership of Ben Jonson and Inigo Jones acting as the crucial factor in the development of the Jacobean court masque, both in determining its characteristic form and content, and also in creating the mystique and power behind this ultimate expression of Stuart absolute monarchy.[6]

[5] Andrew Lamb's "Music of the Popular Theatre," in *The Romantic Age 1800–1914*, 92–108, offers a good overview of the genres and music of the popular musical theater of the nineteenth and early twentieth centuries.

[6] There is a substantial bibliography on the non-musical aspects of the masque of the period. Important older scholarship includes Stephen Orgel, *The Jonsonian Masque* (London: Oxford University Press, 1965) and Roy Strong, "Illusions of Absolutism:

After the Restoration of Charles II to the throne, the ability of the royal family to pay the huge price of producing masques on the scale of those from before the Commonwealth vanished under the financial restrictions mandated by a newly powerful Parliament. The ill-fated production of *Callisto* was perhaps the last attempt to reproduce a masque in the style of those by Inigo Jones, but masques on a smaller scale were produced among courtly circles, chamber opera-like masques such as John Blow's *Venus and Adonis*, and, as some scholarship has suggested as a possibility, Purcell's *Dido and Aeneas*.[7] Occasional masques also continued to be commissioned by all sorts of individuals and groups to mark noteworthy events or to greet eminent persons. Gibbons and Locke's *Cupid and Death*, for instance, was performed as part of the entertainments for an important Portuguese emissary, and, a century later, Arne's *Alfred* was part of a birthday offering to Frederick, Prince of Wales, from a group of supporters who were advancing his claim to be declared regent.[8] These and other masques like them speak to the political and proto-nationalistic connotations of the masque. And while mid-nineteenth-century audiences would have known few of these works in any concrete way, some audience members would have read the text of Milton's *Comus* and fictionalized accounts of masque productions in novels such as Sir Walter Scott's *Kenilworth*. They may have sung or heard sung musical selections from *Acis and Galatea*, *Dido and Aeneas*, and *Alfred*, and while this is in no ways an encounter with a real masque, it would have kept the term in modern currency. This is just to name a few avenues for possible encounters with occasional masques from the past.

Charles I and the Stuart Court Masques," in *Art and Power: Renaissance Festivals, 1450–1650* (Woodbridge: The Boydell Press, 1984), 153–70. Martin Butler's *The Stuart Court Masque and Political Culture* (Cambridge: Cambridge University Press, 2008) is a more recent treatment. For a look at the music of the Stuart masque, see Peter Walls's *Music in the English Courtly Masque, 1604–1640* (Oxford: Clarendon Press, 1996).

[7] The controversy regarding *Dido and Aeneas* comes from new research into Blow's *Venus and Adonis*, which shows that prior to the masque's performance at Josiah Priestley's school, *Venus and Adonis* was performed at court in front of Charles II. This suggests that *Dido and Aeneas* may well have had an earlier court performance, which would solve some of the dating difficulties debated by Purcell scholars. The seminal article on the side of the earlier performance is Bruce Wood and Andrew Pinnock, "'Unscarr'd by turning times'? The Dating of Purcell's *Dido and Aeneas*," *Early Music*, 20 (1992), 372–90. For two reactions to this article, see Curtis Price, "*Dido and Aeneas*: Questions of Style and Evidence," *Early Music*, 22 (1994), 115–25 and Andrew Walkling, "'The Dating of Purcell's *Dido and Aeneas*'?: A Reply to Bruce Wood and Andrew Pinnock," *Early Music*, 22 (1994), 469–81.

[8] Michael Burden, *Garrick, Arne and the Masque of Alfred* (Lewiston: Edwin Mellen Press, 1994).

The second category of seventeenth- and eighteenth-century masque contains those masques written especially for performance in the public theater. Productions of this sort were one way that Victorian audiences would have regularly encountered masque works. This category includes both masques that were self-contained works, mostly afterpieces or entr'acte entertainments, and masques that formed parts of other, longer dramatic works.[9] Originally, theatrical masques were modeled on the popularity and prestige of the occasional masque or were to serve as references for their aristocratic ambience, though quickly the theatrical masque began to acquire its own set of distinguishing characteristics. Early precedents occur in some of Shakespeare's plays – the Casket Scene in *The Merchant of Venice*, the masques in *As You Like It* and *Timon and Athens*, and Prospero's Masque in *The Tempest*, in particular, but Shakespeare was not alone among the dramatists of the period to include elements borrowed from the masque within his plays.[10] The most important dramatists of the succeeding generation, Beaumont and Fletcher, were among those who incorporated masque scenes into their plays, and the continuing popularity of these plays after the Restoration led to increasingly elaborate productions. These, in turn, were imitated by Restoration dramatists such as John Dryden, Nahum Tate and Elkanah Settle, whose texts were set to masque music from composers like Henry Purcell, Louis Grabu, and John Eccles.[11]

The heyday of the theatrical masque occurred during the last quarter of the seventeenth century, the period during which Thomas Betterton controlled the Dorset Garden Theatre. Betterton mounted a series of spectacular musical-dramatic productions now often identified as "semi-operas." This hybrid form contained spoken dialogue, isolated vocal numbers, and inserted ceremonial, military, magical or masque-like scenes which consisted, within their confines, of a combination of speaking, singing, and dancing motivated by scenarios which often invoked the supernatural or scenes of transformation, and which often were loosely connected to the plot of the framing dramatic story. This type of masque is best exemplified by those contained in Purcell's semi-operas, such as *King Arthur*. Each of the five acts of Dryden's text for *King Arthur*, for instance, incorporates one or two scenes which use a mixture

---

[9] Inga-Stina Ewbank's essay in *A Book of Masques for Allardyce Nicoll*, ed. T.J.B. Spencer and Stanley Wells (Cambridge: Cambridge University Press, 1967) offers a detailed discussion of masques inset into plays prior to the Restoration.

[10] As Shakespeare grew in canonical status and productions of his plays increased during the eighteenth century, music continued to be written to support these new, often "updated" versions of his plays. See Stanley Wells, ed., *Shakespeare in the Eighteenth Century* (Cambridge: Cambridge University Press, 1998).

[11] An important recent source on the masques of the Restoration period is Andrew Walkling's *Masque and Opera in England, 1656–1688* (London: Routledge, 2017).

of song, dance and declamation in a masque-like combination; "The Frost Scene" at the end of Act III is perhaps the most famous. The final scene of the play, when Merlin calls forth an entertainment for the victorious Arthur and his bride Emmeline, is a masque proper, with all of the previously mentioned elements within several contrasting, allegorical tableaux.[12]

The scope and expense of these semi-operas could not be sustained by the public theater of the time, and this, added to the increasing competition from Italian opera in the 1720s, led to virtual death of the English semi-opera and the emergence of a number of other musical-dramatic genres, most notably the ballad opera. But masques continued to be produced in the theaters, again either inserted into larger pieces, or serving as shorter entertainments like afterpieces. Noteworthy in this respect are the masques by Pepusch, Galliard, Boyce, and, of course, Arne.[13]

A few of these Elizabethan, Jacobean, or Restoration masques would have been known to the more well-read members of the theater audiences of the early Victorian period. Theatrical masques of the late sixteenth and seventeenth centuries were often embedded in longer dramas that by the middle of the nineteenth century were achieving a canonical status within English literary history, and therefore were issued in editions that could be read by the public. Along with printed editions and theatrical productions of Shakespeare plays, the collected dramatic works of Jonson, Fletcher and Beaumont, and Dryden were increasingly available for those interested. The extent of knowledge of works in the masque genre, however, should not be exaggerated. Most of the Victorian public would have had a real exposure to only a limited number of masques, in particular in Shakespeare's plays such as *The Tempest*, Milton's *Comus* and the ever-popular *King Arthur*, and a handful of musical pieces from the masques *Alfred* and *Acis and Galatea*.

They would have been less familiar with the theatrical masques of the eighteenth century, however, since these works were less important from the perspective of a developing literary canon than their seventeenth-century forebears. One change that contributed to the decreasing prestige of the masque by the middle of the eighteenth century was that the London theatrical world was witnessing an incredible proliferation of musical-dramatic forms, types, and genres. Some were imitations of, or developments from, Italian opera: first

---

[12] A good overview of Purcell's dramatic music is found in Curtis Price, *Henry Purcell and the London Stage* (Cambridge: Cambridge University Press, 1984).

[13] Michael Burden has produced the most complete catalogue of masques during the period 1700–1800, in "The Independent Masque 1700–1800: A Catalogue," *The Royal Musical Association Research Chronicle*, 28 (1995), 59–159. See also Burden's "Britannia versus Virtue in the Harmony of the Spheres: Directions of Masque Writing in the Eighteenth Century," *Miscellanea Musicologia*, 17 (1990), 78–86.

opera seria, then *opera buffa*. Others grew out of English popular theatrical traditions: the ballad opera, the burlesque, the pantomime.[14] This period also saw the beginnings of the two dominant, serious English musical genres of the nineteenth century, the oratorio and the choral cantata. As Roger Fiske reveals in his magisterial survey of the century's dramatic music, there was nothing concrete or fixed about most of these new genres during this period. They were particularly fluid and overlapping, and the masque was just one of many traditional and new genres which participated in this intermingling of forms and functions.[15]

Yet while the Victorian public probably did not know examples of the eighteenth-century theatrical masque in a real way, there must have been a sense of historical continuity between masques from the seventeenth century and the sporadic production of new masques in the nineteenth century that kept the vestiges of the eighteenth century alive, at least in a generalized way. By the last years of the eighteenth century, a selective process had occurred which prioritized certain generic characteristics of the masque; it was this reduced and historicized concept of the masque that was carried into the nineteenth century. Most significant were the patriotic and historical associations often surrounding the masque, a topic certainly explored in the Jacobean and Caroline court masques, famously displayed in Dryden and Purcell's *King Arthur* (1691), and ultimately concretized by Thomas Arne's masque *Alfred* with its hit tune "Rule Britannia" (1740). The survival of both of these masques provided a link between the Baroque theatrical masques and the newly emerging theatrical genres of the mid-nineteenth century. Pastoralism, whether classical or peculiarly English, was another strong component of the concept of the masque genre during this transitional period. Classical and mythological subject matter of the type exploited during the first half of the century within the Italianate masques of composers like Pepusch and Boyce were understood by the succeeding generation as appropriate for the masque, while the inclusion of historical subjects also came from the Dryden–Purcell masques and *Alfred*. Certainly, the allegorical features of the occasional

[14] For a discussion of the ballad opera and pantomime during the eighteenth century, Roger Fiske's *English Theatre Music in the Eighteenth Century* (London: Oxford University Press, 1973) offers an excellent starting point. For later developments during the nineteenth century, see G. Rowell, *The Victorian Theatre, 1792–1914* (Cambridge: Cambridge University Press, 1978) and Michael R. Booth, *Victorian Spectacular Theatre, 1850–1910* (London: Routledge & Kegan Paul, 1981). Finally, several essays contained in *The Cambridge Companion to British Theatre, 1730–1830*, ed. Jane Moody and Daniel O'Quinn (Cambridge: Cambridge University Press, 2007) offer additional views into the theater of the period.

[15] Fiske, *English Theatre Music in the Eighteenth Century*, esp. 397–486.

masque remained strong. Despite a loose definition of the masque generated by antiquarians and those interested in "ancient" literature and music, however, it seems clear that by the end of the eighteenth century the genre in contemporary performance had lost a clear sense of formal character. Nor did it possess a set of conventions that might operate as a horizon of expectations for a modern theatrical audience.

This lack of generic identity, along with the competition brought on by newer and more fashionable musical-dramatic genres, explains the decline in new masque compositions during the late eighteenth and early nineteenth centuries. However, masques did continue to be written and produced, albeit sporadically, and this, along with revivals of the more culturally significant older masques (namely those with music by Henry Purcell, albeit in limited and often truncated form, and Thomas Arne) and new settings for the masques in Shakespeare's plays, kept the genre alive.

William Earle and Gesualdo Lanza's "musical masque" from 1825, *The Spirits of Dew, of Evening, Night & Morning*, offers a good example of the difficulties encountered by those attempting to create a work within the masque genre in the first part of the nineteenth century, given the virtual obliteration of a consensus of what the genre entailed.[16] Earle's masque offers a variety of scenes set in the countryside, showing characters typical of the pastoral setting, working the land and caring for animals.[17] In dramatic works before the nineteenth century, this setting and group of characters would either have exploited the artificial, high-art ethos of the classical or Italian pastoral or would have featured in works that burlesqued this tradition, as in Gay's *The Shepherd's Week*. Instead, the classical landscape was replaced by the English countryside, as if the painted vistas of Claude Lorrain were being supplanted by those of John Constable. The masque designation in this case is applicable because of the conventional elements of supernatural characters and scenic transformation consistent within the masque from its earliest manifestations.

---

[16] Gesualdo Lanza, *The Spirits of Dew, of Evening, Night & Morning*, a musical Masque in three parts ... with an introductory symphony to each part, a Pianoforte & Harp accompaniment ... The Words by Mr. W. Earle (London: [1825?]). I have not found any evidence to support the idea that this masque was ever professionally performed.

[17] These, of course, were common late eighteenth and nineteenth century topics. One important precursor was Haydn's oratorio *The Seasons*, which was extremely popular in England during the first decades of the nineteenth century. David Gramit has written on the importance of *The Seasons* for musical pastoralism and ideas of folk culture: David Gramit, "The Dilemma of the Popular: The *Volk*, the Composer, and the Culture of Art Music," in *Cultivating Music: The Aspirations, Interests, and Limits of German Musical Culture, 1770–1848* (Berkeley: University of California Press, 2002), 63–92.

Even beyond this, concepts of transformation are at the center of Earle's text, but transformation in a native and naïve, rather than classical, landscape, infusing new, Romantic, and above all English, notions of topography into the older genre.

The masque falls into three parts, "illustrative of those highly interesting periods of Day and Night." But it is the transformation of the one state into the next that interests the author. As the title page briefly describes the action, "First: the Setting Sun with the approach of Night. Second: The Wane of Night and the approach of Twilight. Third: the Dawning of Day, the rising Sun," each part having an introductory "symphony." The summary of the action of Part One will suffice to show how these various transformative states are dramatized in a mix of pastoral and supernatural:

> The masque begins with a description of the setting sun and a trio of villagers returns from their labour. The shades of Night advance and the cries that haunt the pensive hour are represented in the character of two evil spirits – Nightshade and Hemlock. The darker shades increase and the Night and her sable train appear in contrast of the former Spirits of the Twilight, yielding repose to toil and care, and ministering good. Will-o-the-Wisp, a mischievous and subtle Sprite, is introduced – also as an associate of tipsy mirth and jollity! Night bids her train to their various offices – they disperse, and the part concludes.[18]

The other scenes or parts of the masque show a similar mix of peasants and supernatural spirits contained in the natural landscape around them. Lacking from the masque text, at least as it survives, is the typical mix of dialogue, song, and dance, and instead, the masque reads as an attempt to lift aspects of pantomime and music into something more serious and artistic.[19]

Apparently, this attempt to meld conventional aspects of the masque genre, such as tableaux, transformations and the supernatural, with new ideas of narrative, setting, and theatrical resources failed to find resonance with either theatrical impresarios or the public. In the published text of the masque, Earle includes a long introduction in which he both describes his goals for the project and complains of the difficulty in getting the masque produced on stage. The introduction is interesting, as well, for its ideas of the union of the arts in the masque and in its emphasis on the visual quality of the production:

---

[18] William Earle, "Introduction" *Spirits of Dew, of Evening, Night & Morning*, 1. The language here points to Milton's *L'Allegro* and *Il Penseroso*, used as a basis for Handel's pastoral ode. Theatrical representations of the night had been a recurrent feature of the masque, pageant, and ballet since the Renaissance, and had featured in works, including the night masque in Purcell's *The Fairy Queen*.

[19] See Michael R. Booth, *Victorian Spectacular Theatre, 1850–1910* for more on the very popular genre of the pantomime during the nineteenth century.

The effect intended to be produced in this scene, as it was proposed to proceed from the united efforts of Music, Poetry, and Painting may be easily imagined, although with difficulty described. One scene undergoing all the various changes of light and shade, from the setting sun to the moon's rise, is not beyond the art of the Mechanist and Painter, and the Author was of the opinion that such a scene would be received with more interest by an audience than those expensive pageants which fill the stage, fatigue the eye, and never interest the heart. The figurative characters are a necessary illustration – the music is tempered to the changes, and if judiciously managed by the Ballet Master, the Author cannot refrain still offering it as his opinion, the effect would be considerable. This effect was not to depend on any of the three branches of Art, but by their combination, and the harmony of their arrangement; – to judge, then, of the interest they might excite in union, by any one of the arts taken abstractedly, would be to determine of an Artist by an examination of his canvass, his paint, and his brushes, before they had been used in giving form and feature to his inventive genius.[20]

It is clear from the introduction that most of the action of the scenario was meant to be communicated through dance – another reason, perhaps, why the piece was designated a masque. As a pantomime the piece may have more easily seen a theatrical production, but the author's generic aspirations and his seriousness of purpose, two aspects that are definitely intertwined, influenced the work in ways that made it unproduceable because it was unclassifiable.

It seems obvious that the average Victorian concert- or theater-goer would have had little or no sense of the history of the masque as outlined above, nor would the audience of the period have appreciated an exact revival of any of the older masques even had they some understanding of the historical context of such an artifact. But in some aspects the masque did retain a sense of tradition for the early Victorian public, albeit in limited ways, and this was carried forward into the second half of the nineteenth century. Throughout the late eighteenth and all of the nineteenth centuries, Purcell, Handel, and Arne were not only important figures in the developing musical canon, but also national and patriotic figures. Though the public experienced only a very limited group of works by these composers, it believed that they in some way represented Englishness in their music.[21] Furthermore, the idea that the masque was an

---

[20] William Earle, "Introduction," *The Spirits of Dew, of Evening, Night & Morning*, 2.

[21] Several popular works by these composers that continued to be performed were connected to the masque genre, including Purcell's *King Arthur*, Handel's *Acis and Galatea*, and Arne's *Alfred*. More information is offered in Ellen Harris, "*King Arthur*'s Journey into the Eighteenth Century," in *Purcell Studies*, ed. Curtis Price (Cambridge: Cambridge University Press, 1995), 257–89. Roberta Marvin has

intrinsically English genre, part of a group of other English theatrical genres like the ballad opera that represented a native alternative to the ever-popular continental operas, heightened the connection during the first half of the nineteenth century between the masque and patriotic and nationalistic topics. For the masque genre to avoid becoming obsolete, however, it was necessary for the genre to be transformed and recreated in ways that allowed it to retain a sense of historical continuity, whether on the stage or in the newly popular historical novel such as Scott's *Kenilworth*, and at the same time meet expectations that the Victorian public brought to the theater.

≈ Two Masques for the Queen's Marriage

The process of re-invention began during the 1840s, a decade which saw the initiation of at least two crucial factors which were to affect the masque tradition. First, extensive changes in the English theater, starting with the abolition of the patent system of theaters and its attendant restrictions on the kinds of theatrical productions that could be produced and in what theaters, encouraged a greater number of theaters to attempt more extensive musical productions. For instance, in the 1840s at Drury Lane, Macready staged productions of "masque-relevant" pieces *Acis and Galatea*, *King Arthur*, and *As Your Like It*, all with extensive musical scenes included.[22] Second, occasions integral to the nation during the early years of Queen Victoria's reign, such as her coronation and wedding, demanded ritualistic, ceremonial entertainments, of which the masque had an impressive pedigree as a genre connected to court and ceremony under the Tudors and Stuarts. These two developments, coupled with accelerating social and technological changes discussed in the first chapter, led to changes in the masque. These moved the masque away from the confusing morass of competing formal characteristics, an identity almost empty by the time of Earle and Lanza's *The Spirit of Dew*, towards a genre essentially defined not by formal characteristics but by a set of topics and associations that could be inserted into the framework of other genres.

The beginnings of this initial period of re-invention and its attempts to recapture the masque as a nostalgic, nationalistic genre can be traced to 1840, the year of the young Queen Victoria's marriage to Prince Albert of Saxe-Coburg. The nuptials were publicly celebrated on a lavish scale, including the production of at least two competing masques: George Macfarren and his

chronicled the adaptations of *Acis and Galatea* in "Handel's *Acis and Galatea*: A Victorian View," in *Europe, Empire, and Spectacle in Nineteenth-Century British Music*, ed. Rachel Cowgill and Julian Rushton (Aldershot: Ashgate, 2007), 249–64.

[22] Alan Downer, *The Eminent Tragedian William Charles Macready* (Cambridge, MA: Harvard University Press, 1966).

son G. Alexander Macfarren's *An Emblematical Tribute on the Marriage of Queen Victoria*, and J.R. Planché and Henry Bishop's *The Fortunate Isles, an allegorical, national masque*. Unlike Earle and Lanza's "musical masque," both of these works were more easily contained by conceptions of generic propriety as occasional masques – the occasional masque being typically connected with royal festive events – and their reliance on well-known models such as Dryden and Purcell's *King Arthur*. Both attempted to locate a source for an English national character, as a people and a nation, mediated by the figure of the then-romantic Queen Victoria, and both used music to project and represent this conception of national identity.

The more elaborate of the two masques presented was *The Fortunate Isles*. The work is interesting because, while in many ways quite forward-looking in its utilization of the genre as an informative and didactic platform, it also blends modernity with a conscious attempt to incorporate antiquarian interests.[23] The masque's text was provided by one of the quintessential Victorian purveyors of theatrical works, J.R. Planché, a prolific and popular English playwright and director during the first half of the century.[24] Of course

[23] The British Library holds both a printed libretto for the masque and a manuscript score of several of the numbers (Add. 27729). The playbill for the production held in the Theatre and Performance Archives of the Victoria and Albert Museum is quite extensive. The masque was produced at the Theatre Royal, Covent Garden, under the management of Madame Vestris. It was preceded by Leigh Hunt's play *The Legend of Florence*. It was described as "A Grand Allegorical and National Masque, in honour of Her Majesty's Nuptials, entitled *The Fortunate Isles! Or The Triumphs of Britannia*. The music composed and selected by Mr. H.R. Bishop, Mus. Bac., The Action entirely arranged by Mr. Oscar Byrne. The Decorations and Appointments by Mr. W. Bradwell, the Dresses by Mr. Head and Mrs. Stroud, Machinery by Mr. H. Sloman." Notice the prominence (perhaps unusually for a masque) of the composer's name, and the lack of mention of even the name of Planché (this is perhaps because Planché was well-known and the stable playwright and producer for the company). The playbill also contains an extensive list of performers: Jupiter – Mr. W. Harrison; Saturn, or Time – Mr. Borrani; Mars – Mr. Bingle; Neptune – Mr. S. Jones; Mercury – Mr. A. Giubilei; Bacchus – Mr. Granby; Apollo – Mr. Kerridge; Hercules – Mr. S. Smith; Cupid – Miss James; Hymen – Miss R. Isaacs; Juno – Mrs. Osborne; Amphitrite – Mrs. E. Knight; Minerva – Mrs. Cummins; Venus – Miss Charlton; Diana – Miss Lane.

[24] While most known for his burlesques, and his classical and fairy "extravaganzas," Planché also wrote many straight dramatic plays, plays with music, English adaptations of French and Italian opera and plays, and several operatic libretti, the most notable being Weber's London commission *Oberon*, whose lack of cohesion and somewhat improbable plot has unjustly tainted Planché's current reputation. Alan Fischler has attempted a renovation of the libretto's poor reputation in his "*Oberon* and Odium: the Career and Crucifixion of J.R. Planché," *Opera Quarterly* 12, 1 (1995), 5–26. For a good discussion of Planché's contributions to

there are no concrete details extant about the commission or genesis of this work. It is likely, however, given Planché's important position within Vestris's theatrical organization, that he would have had considerable input into the choice of the masque genre for this production, in consultation with Madame Vestris. An aspect of Planché's theatrical career that may have strongly influenced his choice of the masque genre as the vehicle for his nuptial offering were his well-documented antiquarian interests, since so much of the masque revolves around historical tableaux. Planché was famous for his knowledge of historical costume and passion for old furniture and other relics of England's past, and he brought this knowledge to bear on his historical stage productions for Madame Vestris's theaters.[25] He was one of the first stage producers and designers to champion historically accurate stage productions in a wide range of dramatic fare, from Shakespeare to his own "extravaganzas." This interest in history may have suggested the choice of the masque and the panoramic, pageant-like view of English history it dramatizes, offering ample opportunities for authentic details in costume and stage properties.

Planché subtitled his work "an allegorical national masque." The allegorical component is understandable, since allegory had a long pedigree as a conventional trope for royal, courtly occasional works. The masque is "national" because it displays a series of historical scenes and national myths that dramatize early periods or events in England's history.[26] The first scene dramatizes the classical

nineteenth-century English drama, see Donald Roy's introduction in *Plays by James Robinson Planché*, ed. Donald Roy (Cambridge: Cambridge University Press, 1986).

[25] Planché was not only a dramatist but was also essentially stage producer for Madame Vestris's theater during this period. He is also the author of the influential volume, *The History of British Costume* (London: C. Knight, 1834).

[26] The playbill offers this information. "The Following New Scenery by Mr. Grieve, Mr. T. Grieve, and Mr. W. Grieve.
Part I.
  The Ocean – 'When Britain first at Heaven's Command, Arose from out the azure main'
  Forest of Oak and Druidical Cromlech
  Tableau vivant – Runnymede. King John Signing Magna Carta (cast)
  The Palace of Chivalry. Dedicated to the Military Triumphs of Britain (cast)
Part II.
  The Weald of Kent – 'In the Golden Days of good Queen Bess'
  Panorama – Tilbury Fort, with Queen Elizabeth on horseback reviewing the Troops – Advance of Spanish Armada – Its Defeat and Dispersion
  Commemoration of the Naval Triumphs of Britain
  Tableau vivant – King Charles the Second Landing at Dover. (From the Picture By West)
  Rising of the start of Brunswick!
  The Triumph of Peace and Love!"

topic of the birth of Albion, then continues in succeeding scenes through time in vignettes portraying the Druids, the Romans, the Saxons, Danes and Normans. Concrete moments in history are shown in tableaux vivants: King John signing the Magna Carta, Queen Elizabeth sounding the alarm against the Spanish Armada.[27] The masque concludes, appropriately enough, with a tribute to Queen Victoria and the values of English liberty.[28]

The implication of this historical narrative is that all of England's history reaches its culmination not just in the figure of Victoria itself, but in the current state of Victoria's nation, the England of 1840. The attributes of the nation rather than the ruler are glorified. But at the same time, the masque has a didactic purpose: the audience as the nation is also being instructed as to what constitutes its own Englishness, here focusing on the love of liberty. This connection is made explicit in the first scene of the masque, as the sea creatures hail Albion as the "heir of Neptune," with words set to the now-iconic melody of Arne's "Rule Britannia" from the masque *Alfred*. Upon the rendition of this symbol of patriotic Englishness, Liberty enters and decides to make Britain her new home, a move reminiscent of Venus's similar choice at the conclusion of Dryden and Purcell's *King Arthur*. The means of representing the central characteristic of British identity, that they are born free and live in freedom, is through direct reference to items from famous masques of the past – the title of Planché and Bishop's masque is an obvious gloss on Venus's air "Fairest Isle" from the final masque of *King Arthur*, and Planché's theatrical antiquarian interests most probably also exposed him to Jonson's 1624 masque, *The Fortunate Isles and Their Union*. Through this presentation the audience as a nation is shown to embody the characteristics of liberty and patriotism – not just in the past, but the nation is encouraged to define itself in this way now. This is an early example of the common tendency later in the period for the connection to be made between the masque as a relic of history and the masque as a medium for retelling history. As history became "popularized" through the exploitation of historical subject matter in literature, theater, music, and the fine arts, nationalism too became popularized through the dramatic presentation of iconic historical scenes.

[27] Planché was taking a bit of a risk by including a tableau representing Elizabeth reviewing her troops during the threat of the Armada – Sheridan's well-known play *The Critic* (1775) offers a satirical and very funny version of such a scene, which Planché certainly would have known.

[28] For a fascinating look at the issue of patriotism in eighteenth century and early nineteenth century Britain, see Linda Colley, *Britons: Forging the Nation 1707–1837* (New Haven: Yale University Press, 1992). For an alternative view, see Krishan Kumar's *The Making of English National Identity* (Cambridge: Cambridge University Press, 2003).

These aspects of *The Fortunate Isles* are authentic precursors of the later "re-invented" masque. However, *The Fortunate Isles* also looks back thematically and formally. The conventional aspects that link patriotism and allegory have their roots in the masques of Arne as well as those of Dryden and Purcell. *King Arthur* seems a possible candidate as a model for Planché and Bishop, since there are several striking similarities between the two works. In particular, Planché seems to have consciously referenced the final masque of Act V of the Dryden and Purcell semi-opera, which occurs after the conflict between Arthur, Oswald and their cohorts, human and spiritual, has been resolved, and Merlin provides Arthur and Emmeline with a vision of the glorious future of Britain and its descendants, an expanded version of which could be said to form the topic of Planché's scenario for *The Fortunate Isles*. Specific elements from *King Arthur* reappear in the Planché's masque; Dryden and Purcell's masque also begins with a mythologized oceanic scene focused on Britannia, during which Venus's descent to the "Fairest Isle" occurs. Dryden and Purcell's scene of the peasant harvest song corresponds in spirit to Planché's Elizabethan scene, and the final paean to the Order of the Garter with its Evocation of St George corresponds to the similar final scene of Queen Victoria in *The Fortunate Isles*.

It seems logical to assume that, given the resemblance of aspects of *The Fortunate Isles* to scenes in *King Arthur*, Planché knew the Dryden work. Dryden's status as a canonical English literary figure solidified during the eighteenth century, and editions of his plays and essays were repeatedly printed through the early years of the nineteenth century. *King Arthur*, albeit in modified versions, was produced on the London stage in 1819 and 1827. Specific knowledge of *King Arthur*, however, may have come through the composer of the music of the masque, Sir Henry Bishop. Bishop was an extremely prominent composer of English dramatic music during the first half of the nineteenth century, supplying song settings and incidental music for some seventy productions, as well as holding several important conducting and academic positions. He was a highly conservative composer, reaching back to late eighteenth and early nineteenth-century traditions of English musical drama rather than remaining abreast of continental developments, especially in opera.

This conservative bent was complemented by his musicological and antiquarian interests, revealed by his editorial work and his leadership of the Concerts of Antient Music from 1840 to 1848.[29] A manuscript currently

[29] George Biddlecombe, *English Opera from 1834 to 1864 with Particular Reference to the Works of Michael Balfe* (New York: Garland Publishing, 1994); Christina Fuhrmann, "'Adapted and Arranged for the English Stage': Continental Operas Transformed for the London Theater, 1814–1833" (dissertation, University of

housed in the British Library supports the idea that Bishop had a more extensive knowledge of the history of the masque than was usual during this period. It contains arrangements of several pieces from Matthew Locke's masque *Cupid and Death*, originally written in 1653. The manuscript contains a handwritten copy of the music of the masque with some explanatory notes and then several added pages at the end of the manuscript in a different hand, presumably Bishop's. Locke's introduction was copied out, as was the title page, and the following copy of the Locke work is clean and seems quite faithful to the original.[30]

On folio 29, there is a heading, "Selection from the masque Cupid and Death, (solos, soprano and basso and chorus) A.D. 1653, the words by Ja. Shirley." There follows Bishop's arrangement of the first scene of the Locke work, scored for horns, flute, oboe, bassoon, violin, viola, and bass. Bishop begins with the Introduction, expanding it by developing its opening ritornello. Arrangements then follow of the bass solo "Though little be the God above" with choral interjections, the soprano solo "One smile of Venus," and the duet "Thus Love can." The fact that Bishop actually began to arrange the masque and provide it with a somewhat contemporary orchestration speaks to a projected performance of the work, possibly for the series Antient Concerts.

This, however, is only one example of Bishop's antiquarian work, and one that points to a concrete knowledge of the masque genre. Further evidence of his interest is his editing of Handel's cantatas and other works, including the serenata *Acis and Galatea*, frequently performed in choral festivals throughout the late eighteenth and nineteenth centuries. In addition, he was involved in the Musical Antiquarian Society, which issued editions of both of *King Arthur* and *Dido and Aeneas* in 1840.

Planché and Bishop's masque is noteworthy in two important ways that were to exercise a profound influence over the masque revival: first is the ideological ploy used by the authors to represent English history as a source of English identity and to represent that historical identity on stage in a didactic manner; second is through the antiquarian interests revealed by choice of the genre

---

Washington, 2001) and "Between Opera and Musical: Theatre Music in Early Nineteenth-Century London," in *The Oxford Handbook of the British Musical*, ed. Robert Gordon and Olaf Jubin (Oxford: Oxford University Press, 2016).

[30] British Library Additional Manuscript 17800. The manuscript copy is most certainly from the early 1800s. Probably a performance was projected and someone other than Bishop copied out the pieces from the Locke masque, and then handed it over to Bishop, who began to edit and add to that copy to bring the work into some kind of arrangement for performance. A potentially interesting topic, but very little work has been done on Bishop's antiquarianism and interests in early music.

and the music developed for the masque. Both of these aspects strengthen the association of the masque with history and its topics. They also reinforce the understanding that the masque can be used to communicate historical topics within a popular sphere. For Planché and Bishop, British history is progressive, each step a successive improvement on that which went before. Yet the sense projected by this masque that the past contains valuable lessons for the present does not seem all that far removed a desire to recapture those values and integrate them into the modern world. In other words, for all their antiquarianism, Planché and Bishop eschew a dramatic idealization of the past and instead represent the present reality looking toward the political future.

A different sort of didacticism and a new source for emerging nostalgic topics, gendered rather than patriotic, can be found in the second of the masques performed in London celebrating the marriage of Victoria and Albert, George and G. Alexander Macfarren's *An Emblematical Tribute on the Marriage of Queen Victoria*.[31] This masque, produced at the Drury Lane theater, was written very quickly in order to compete with Planché and Bishop's production at Covent Garden, the management realizing a bit late that the theater should not pass up the lucrative opportunity presented by such an occasion. Macfarren later recounted how his father was annoyed that Covent Garden was getting the jump on the nuptial bandwagon (the government would pay the theaters to provide some kind of suitable production to celebrate the wedding), and two days before the event decided to pull something together quickly, roping his young son into providing a musical score within twenty-four hours. To protestations from the theater owners that the Covent Garden masque had been in the works for several months, Macfarren senior replied "the slow motion of the planets controlled not the velocity of a comet!" And apparently, at least according to Macfarren, *An Emblematical Tribute* was as well received as the *The Fortunate Isles*, despite the rush.

The surviving pieces from the masque suggest that the production worked as a fairly simple series of musical numbers offering praise and wishes for happiness and prosperity to the newly married royal couple, interspersed with ballets and spectacular scenic effects.[32] There is an opening choral number,

---

[31] This masque was never published, and a very few sections exist in manuscripts contained in the Fitzwilliam Library, Cambridge. My descriptions of this piece are dependent on these manuscripts and G.A. Macfarren's personal account reproduced in H.C. Banister, *George Alexander Macfarren* (London: G. Bell and Sons, 1891).

[32] Once again, the Theatre and Performance Archives of the Victoria and Albert Museum holds a playbill advertising the production which contains valuable information. The company was presenting three major offerings that week: Shakespeare's *Macbeth*, Barnett's popular *The Mountain Sylph*, and one of the first

"Albion's Queen and her thrice happy Lord," followed by a five-voice part-song written for Drury Lane's featured performers, invoking each of the four seasons to do its part to welcome the happy pair.[33] A concluding choral finale expresses the wish that:

> Nought shall sever
> Albert from his bride
> Victoria, Old England's pride.
> May they live forever.

Avoiding the representation of history and the allusions, musical and national, to England's past, the Macfarrens instead concentrate on the double character of Victoria as both monarch and woman. These sentiments are made most clear in a cavatina for Venus, perhaps another slight gesture towards her famous aria "Fairest Isle" from *King Arthur*, though the allusion does not follow through to either music or topic:

> Hail to Albion's lovely isle,
> Triumphant and serene.

London adaptations of Weber's *Der Freyschutz* (sic). The masque was advertised as "to Conclude with an Emblematical Tribute in honor of Her Majesty's Nuptials. With selected and original music by Mr. G. Alexander Macfarren. The New Scenery designed by Mr. Marshal, and executed by himself, Messrs. W. Marshall Parker, Meadows Wilson, and George Macfarren. The extensive machinery by Mr. Brickell. The Dresses by Mr. Palmer and Mrs. Harris. The Pyrotechnic trophies by Mr. Southby. The Banners, Emblems, and Embellishments by Mr. Blamick. The Pageant arranged and the whole produced under the Direction of Mr. Gilbert." The playbill goes on to offer the key performers and their roles, ones remarkably similar to some of those advertised on the *Fortunate Isles* playbill (dramatic piracy was rampant during this period!): Venus – Miss Cooper; Hebe – Mrs. Alban Croft; Cupid – Miss Marshall; Hymen – Master Marshall; Flora – Miss Ballin; Zephyr – Mr. Gilbert. Loves, Zephyrs, and Celestials. Britannia – Miss Daly. Europe, Asia, Africa, America, with their Emblematical Attendants. Chief Bard – Mr. Leffler. Bards, Druids, Vestals (cast).

The playbill seems to try to appeal to all tastes. "Celestial Bower of Venus! Panoramic View of London! Song of Hebe … 'Hail to Albion' … Mrs. Alban Croft. Windsor Castle from the Meadows. Mid-Day … Moonlight. Pageant of the Four Quarters of the Globe! With Tributary Offerings to Britannia. National Dances and Nuptial Ballet (cast). Assembly of Druids, Bardic Ode (composed for the occasion by Mr. G. Alexander Macfarren.) Chorus … 'Strike the Harp,' Pastorale 'O Joyful Spring' (sung by 9 soloists), Air … 'Come ye Manly, Come ye fair.' Mr. Leffler. Grand Chorus … 'Hail, all hail,' Hymeneal Tableau!"

[33] The names of these performers are written out next to the staves on the first page of the manuscript, and included Mrs. Croft, Miss Betty, Miss Colley, Mad. Alati, Mr. F—, Mr. Allen, Mr. D—, Mr. Roberts, Mr. Leff, and Mr. Morley.

And hail to him who won the smile
Of Albion's lovely queen.
Happy she who born to fill
A throne that worlds obey,
Shall make that throne more glorious still
By woman's milder sway.
Thrice happy he to make her blest
Thro' smiling years to come,
The pride of every manly heart,
The star of freedom's home.
Hail …

Unlike Planché and Bishop's masque, where Victoria serves as the dynastic capstone for a nation's glorious past, Victoria comes across throughout *An Emblematical Tribute* as the personification of Victorian wedded bliss, a happy wife whose royal powers and dynastic connections are quite beside the point. Victoria's status as a powerful ruler in her own right is minimized and instead her position as the head of a nation serves to focus her role as leader to nineteenth-century ideals of appropriate gender behavior. Her power, and by extension, that of all English women, is to be the star of the home and inspire the manly heart, as the national and domestic are conflated.[34] To this purpose, in this aria both history and the ideologies of political power are avoided, though the gendered sentiments are just as modern a construct. This is arguably early for the representation of Victorian attitudes towards gender, family, and domesticity, which became more established and prevalent a decade or two later. Their appearance here probably has to do national sentiment surrounding the wedding of the young queen. But it also suggests that new ideologies of women and gender were beginning to emerge, though not expressed as overtly as would be the case after the 1850s. Victoria's public persona, molded jointly by the young queen herself and those who represented her to the public, crucially balanced anxieties over female royal power through an insistence on the private and domestic life of Victoria and Albert. At the same time, this aria opens up a new arena for the incursion of sentiments located in a domestic, personal space and private subjectivity rather than the political and public space of nationalistic allegory.

This contrasting site of nostalgia, validating the virtues of the English home as a source for national identity, seems to be a constant for Macfarren, as the same domestic ideology resurfaces twenty years later in *Freya's Gift*. In that

---

[34] Margaret Homan's "Queen Victoria's Sovereign Obedience" in her *Royal Representations: Queen Victoria and British Culture, 1837–1876* (Chicago: University of Chicago Press, 1998) offers a more general treatment of this topic.

work, Freya's appearance is followed by the necessary, conventional ballad-type aria, conventional since it is on a vague and universal topic that allowed for its necessary marketing for home music making. There are strong echoes of Bishop's enormously popular ballad "Home, Sweet Home," also endorsing domestic joys.

> In search of bliss without alloy
> To fancied realms you need not roam.
> Those who would look for tranquil joy,
> May find it in an English home.

And so it continued, negating the satisfactions of "fame, wealth, and honour" for the priceless possession of an English home. While the preceding scena is fairly virtuosic, a showpiece for soprano Louisa Pyne, the ballad was very simple, making it accessible for the amateur performer. Obviously, the gender relationships that created the joys of English domesticity were one important component in the awakening of England to new happiness and productivity.[35]

This domestic and gendered program became an important option for the kinds of national identity projected in the masque and other similar works with a didactic mission and popular appeal. As represented in *An Emblematical Tribute*, however, English domestic and feminized virtues were often teamed with masculine virtues that symbolized the nation's growing imperial power over its expanding colonies. In this masque, such a contrast happens through a scene which allegorically represents Britain's imperial conquests, as Asia, Africa, America, and Europe offer gifts to Britannia signifying their subjugation to her imperial destiny, each characterized through appropriate "exotic" musical conventions such as ostinato rhythms and repeated short melodic phrases.

These two masques, presented in tandem during the same week in 1840, demonstrate several divergent options for the masque at the mid-century point. Some of the past traditions are still active: the reliance on topics of allegory and history, the connection to royal and patriotic occasions, the gestures towards textually and musically canonic masques of the past, at least in the case of *The Fortunate Isles*. In contrast, several key characteristics found in these masques are quite different;[36] the gendered evocation of domesticity

---

[35] See, for instance, Elizabeth Langland, "Nation and nationality: Queen Victoria in the developing narrative of Englishness," in *Remaking Queen Victoria*, ed. Margaret Homans and Adrienne Munich (Cambridge: Cambridge University Press, 1997), 13–32.

[36] Of course, the growing popularity of historical novels such as those by Sir Walter Scott offered an increasingly influential precedent, such as the fictionalized masques in chapters 12 and 14 of *Kenilworth*. It would be fascinating also to explore the connection between historical tableaux in musico-dramatic works during the early Victorian period and the rise in popularity of panoramas, dioramas and other popular tourist sites housing types of historical representations.

through English genres of vocal music such as the contemporary ballad; and the exoticized representations of colonial possessions in *An Emblematic Tribute*. Both masques were inherently monarchist and, given Victorian tastes, didactic. The tension in them between tradition and modernity was not to be easily resolved. A slightly later example from 1852, George Sloan and Edward Loder's *The Island of Calypso, an operatic masque*[37] also contains a mix of traditional and modern elements, though its libretto is quite conventional and perhaps antiquarian in its similarities to Purcell's *Dido and Aeneas* and assorted eighteenth-century operas and secular cantatas,[38] while the music reflects a mixture of Handelian pastiche and contemporary English operatic styles.[39] That the masque was perhaps a problematic genre for the uncomplicated realization of a nostalgic view of history is perhaps exemplified by one masque that was never written; according to his son, Tennyson originally thought to write his treatment of the Arthurian legends as a masque, and went as far as producing a sketched scenario, only to change his mind and use the material as the basis for *Idylls of the King* instead.[40]

---

[37] The masque, originally written for the Grand National Concerts at Her Majesty's Theatre, but never produced, actually premiered on the second New Philharmonic Society Concert under the baton of none other than Hector Berlioz, last on a program that also contained Beethoven's Symphony in C minor and the Overture to *The Magic Flute*, along with other shorter works. The performance was obviously under-rehearsed (understandable given the length and breadth of the program – *The Island of Calypso* alone ran over an hour) since a review of the opening night in the weekly musical journal *The Musical World* describes the work as "one of the ablest and most beautiful works that has ever proceeded from the pen of an English musician" but goes on to lament the disservice done by the Philharmonic's performance. Interestingly enough, the following week's issue included a letter from Berlioz diplomatically praising Loder's work and laying the blame for the poor performance at the feet of Mr. and Mrs. Sims Reeves, who apparently refused to attend rehearsals!

[38] The review in *The Musical World* seems to imply that this historicist position was understood. "A few words will describe the general intention of Mr. Loder's new work, which he entitles a 'Masque' (after *Comus* and *King Arthur*). The subject is an episode in Fenelon's *Telemaque*."

[39] English "opera" of the period was quite different from both the Italian and French traditions of the first half of the nineteenth century, and it continued to reflect the historically consistent dislike of English audiences for sung dialogue in their own language. A good description of the permutations of English opera is contained in George Biddlecombe's *English Opera from 1834 to 1864*. For more on Loder, see *Musicians of Bath and Beyond: Edward Loder (1809–1865) and His Family*, ed. Nicholas Temperley (Woodbridge: The Boydell Press, 2016).

[40] Hallam Tennyson, *Alfred, Lord Tennyson: A memoir by his son* (London: Macmillan, 1897), vol. 2, 24.

❧ *Topics of the Past*

Given the importance of masque traditions, textual and musical, within the masques by Bishop, Macfarren, and Loder – and their involvement with emerging issues of nostalgia and authenticity – Oxenford and Macfarren's *Freya's Gift* is remarkably free from references to the masque of the seventeenth or eighteenth century, either formally or musically. Instead, the historical associations of the masque are moved from the realm of imitation and pastiche to one of reference, and a nostalgic reference at that. While a work like *The Fortunate Isles* is constructed to reference a concrete set of formal and musical characteristics that belong to masques of the recent past, *Freya's Gift* abandons connections of this type and adopts instead the form and musical conventions of a contemporary genre, which suggest that these kinds of connections to the past are no longer important. At the same time, Oxenford and Macfarren are still self-consciously exploiting similar ideological and topical associations of the masque genre as did Planché, but at a distance created by the adoption of these new musical conventions. A shift has occurred: as masques attempt to connect to history, the history has ceased to be one of inclusion in a continuous, evolving line, but instead has become discontinuous. History has become "other" – something distant, removed – all of which is a condition for the idealization of an imaginary Merrie England reflected in the text. The masque participates in what Gilles de Van has described as the interaction between the exoticizing impulses of the second half of the nineteenth century and representations of historical reality, "a process of knowledge that transforms into a metaphor of desire … an impetus toward the other which becomes a mirror of the self, the search for a foreign land which changes into a reflection of one's own country, the quest for the different which sends us back to the same." De Van's definition of historical realism in opera as a form of exoticism is particularly valuable way of thinking about the historical obsessions reflected in English drama, musical and otherwise, during the Victorian period, especially in the vogue for "archaeological productions" discussed below.[41]

The fact that the nostalgic references in the text of *Freya's Gift* are not supported by references to early music is noteworthy, given that Macfarren, like Henry Bishop, was a composer who had a keen interest and involvement

---

[41] Gilles De Van, "Fin de Siècle Exoticism and the Meaning of the Far Away," *Opera Quarterly* 11, 3 (1995), 77–94, esp. 78. Quite rightly, de Van later describes how the push for knowledge moving outward from exoticism necessarily resulted in the proto-anthropological and ethnological discourses of the day – one only needs to think of James Frazer's *The Golden Bough* emerging at the height of exoticism in the 1890s, and of course, the famous opening lines to L.P. Hartley's *The Go-Between*: "The past is a foreign country; they do things differently there."

in the music of England's past. An extreme conservative both in the harmonic idiom reflected in his own compositions and in his rabid abhorrence for "progressive" modern music, Macfarren's conservatism merges into historicism in many ways. Historicism is implicated as well in the incipient nationalism that is reflected in Macfarren's clear preference for historical English settings and stories for his stage and choral works.[42] Editorial work was a major focus of Macfarren's antiquarian interest, since he prepared several editions that provided concrete knowledge of important works from the past, most notably an edition of Purcell's *Dido and Aeneas*, but also Handel's *Belshazzar, Jephtha,* and *Judas Maccabeus,* and works by the seventeenth-century composers Orlando Gibbons, John Dowland, and Thomas East. Macfarren brought to all of these endeavors an extensive knowledge of English musical styles of the past.[43]

Perhaps more crucial was Macfarren's utilization of folk songs and ballads several decades before the folk song revival. One of his earliest pieces, an overture for a theatrical play *Chevy Chace*, inspired the composer to track down the old ballad and feature the melody in the overture. However, during the late 1850s, Macfarren was involved in two projects that brought him into a deeper contact with folk and popular music of the past: providing harmonizations for Chappell's seminal edition of folk songs, *Popular Music of the Olden Times* (1855–9), and preparing an edition of *Moore's Irish Melodies* (1859–61). After 1860, there is a noticeable increase in the inclusion of early popular and folk music in his dramatic works. In the cantata *May Day*, for example, Macfarren incorporates the Staines Morris, a tune Chappell had linked to a May Day lyric. In works like *Robin Hood* and *The Soldier's Legacy*, both from the 1860s, Macfarren incorporated a selection of folk and early popular song, and also wrote new music which aped the quality of the old ballads, including many modal gestures that prefigure the "rediscovery" of modality as a musical sign for England's past in the music of English composers in the twentieth century. An apt example is one of the "crowd" scenes of *Robin Hood*, a country fair against which the conventional archery contest is conducted, so that the

---

[42] A chronology of pieces that fit into this category of English historical and pastoral topics include: *An Emblematical Tribute* (masque, 1840), *King Charles II* (opera, 1848), *May Day* (cantata, 1857), *Robin Hood* (opera, 1860), *Freya's Gift* (masque, 1863), *She Stoops to Conquer* (opera, 1864), *The Soldier's Legacy* (chamber opera, 1864), *Songs in a Cornfield* (cantata, 1868), *Lady of the Lake* (cantata, 1876) and *Kenilworth* (Italian opera, 1880).

[43] My discussion of Macfarren's historicist and nationalistic interests is heavily indebted to Nicholas Temperley's discussion in "Musical Nationalism in English Romantic Opera," in *The Lost Chord: Essays on Victorian Music*, ed. Nicholas Temperley (Bloomington: Indiana University Press, 1989), 143–57.

historical musical idiom adds to the nostalgic scene from Merrie England being presented on stage.[44]

That *Freya's Gift* does not include music reflecting such antiquarian interest, although other of Macfarren's dramatic and choral works with nationalistic themes date from precisely the same period, provides a clue to the status of the masque in 1863. The connection between the masque topic and the revival of early music made in *Pan's Anniversary* in 1905 is singularly lacking in Macfarren's masque. There are two possible reasons why Macfarren eschewed such a connection. Pragmatically, the masque needed to be popular on several levels. It needed to be easily comprehended by its public, both on the occasion of its première and for its hoped-for future as a staple for choral society performances. But it also needed to be popular in its didactic goal, like *The Fortunate Isles*, to serve as a tool for the edification and moral improvement of the working classes, for such a moralizing intent was a major component of the initial efforts of the choral movement of the 1850s and 60s. Written in the relatively new style of the nineteenth century, English choral cantata genre, works like *Freya's Gift* strongly aimed at the uplift of the public, an aim that combined with the patriotic and dynastic ideologies of the royal wedding celebrations. This combination was quite different from the one arrived at by Macfarren twenty years earlier for another royal wedding in *An Emblematical Tribute*.[45] Many would have argued that music that reflected what was still a scholarly and antiquarian interest in early or folk musics was not the most effective means for reaching

---

[44] A scene set in a country town became almost a necessary accoutrement to a historical dramatic plot, almost an iconic presence for representation of the England of the past. Vaughan Williams's 1924 ballad opera *Hugh the Drover* opens with just such a crowd scene, climaxing in the boxing match between Butcher John and Hugh the Drover.

[45] During the second half of the nineteenth century, the English cantata was a genre set apart in compositional and performative characteristics from contemporary continental cantatas, which were more often than not student or competition works. The beginnings of the English secular cantata are linked in many ways to the masque. During the first decades of the eighteenth century, the terms masque, serenata, and cantata were used somewhat interchangeably for elegant, pastoral entertainments on a relatively small, chamber performance scale, the serenata and cantata specifically from Italian models. However, by the nineteenth century, the cantata was usually defined with and against the oratorio, both generally unstaged choral genres and both forming the primary repertory of the great choral festivals. The cantata of this period was unstaged. The libretto was based on a poetic text, either newly written or adapted from well-known works by such authors as Longfellow, Tennyson, or Coleridge. Mandatory were key arias or songs for the prominent soloists lured to the regional choral festivals by lucrative fees, such as Jenny Lind Goldschmitt. These solo sections would alternate with choral movements sung by a large choir, for the most part simple homophonic settings with occasional imitative openings.

the public at large in 1870. It was not until the connection was made between the perceived moral and social needs of the working classes and the efficacies of the products of folk and historical culture that folk and early music could be seen as belonging to all of the members of English society.

More theoretically, for Macfarren, Oxenford and the many others involved in determining the topic and content of their allegorical offering for the newly wed Prince Edward and Alexandra of Denmark, the modern needed to be emphasized over the historical. Yes, history must be invoked, but in a didactic way to influence the present, and it was that "presentness," that modernity, perhaps, which still characterized the masque, at least in this production. Rather than an item for static contemplation, history needed to be shown to have an active influence on the present, and this includes the actual, heard music. The contemporaneity of the cantata genre reinforced the notion of up-to-date modernity, and thereby Macfarren refrained from the inclusion of early music that could easily have been seen as an outmoded curiosity of cultural history.

Certainly, in his other works, Macfarren's representation of topics of English history and country life through references to folk and early popular song contributed in an active way to the link between nostalgia and authenticity that manifested itself forty years later in *Pan's Anniversary*. During the second half of the nineteenth century, Macfarren was only one of a growing number of English composers, however, who found opportunities for the commission and performance of works in the growth of new, populist venues for music calculated to appeal to a wide public drawn from different social strata, especially the choral society movement and the public concert. Many composers met this demand by inflecting their music with self-conscious nationalistic signifiers that were historically oriented in topic, though generally not in musical style. For instance, the May Day cantata became almost a subgenre itself, with many versions being produced for all of the major choral festivals, most notably by William Sterndale Bennett in *The May Queen*. These works, as well as scenes in English operas and musical theater like that in *Robin Hood* mentioned above, are witness to an incredible proliferation of the almost free-standing dramatic topos of the country fair. These are set in the English countryside during an unspecified time period from the past, with characters either from farms, villages, or small towns, and they recreate one of several folk traditions of well-known historical pastimes: choosing the May Queen, celebrating the harvest, conducting the rural market.[46] This is the new pastoral, the pastoral

---

[46] The May topic also appears in *Hugh the Drover*, as the drunken village youths leave the tavern to pick may flowers for their sweethearts. And this whole topic is wickedly satirized in Eric Crozier and Benjamin Britten's opera *Albert Herring*. Conversely, Britten plays the May Day scene beautifully straight in the finale of his

historicized and nationalized, which is a prominent and pervasive feature of the poetic literature and the novels of the period. On Macfarren's *May Day*, for example, the people of a small bit of the English landscape debate among several possible choices for the May Queen, choose a suitable young woman, and then proceed to call her to the Maying. Finally, all participate in a pageant-like procession that recreates various folk traditions like the hobbyhorse and Robin and Maid Marion. As already mentioned, the work ends with masque-like Revels, to the music of an arrangement of the Staines Morris, which Macfarren had encountered in his work with Chappell's collection of folk tunes.

The picturesque representation of rural life and pseudo-folk tradition is one ideological strain found in the work of Macfarren and incorporated into the "new" masque tradition. Macfarren's historical and antiquarian interests also reflect important new topics that are reflected in the masque, topics with a chronological focus located in the "Tudor" period.

Perhaps the most important literary source for this new association between the masque and the process by which "Tudor" England was turned into a contemporary myth is Sir Walter Scott's novel *Kenilworth*, an account of the romance between Queen Elizabeth's favorite Robert Dudley, Earl of Leicester, and Amy Robsart, the third book of which is set against the backdrop of the famous masques and other festivities provided by Dudley for Queen Elizabeth's visit to his magnificent castle at Kenilworth. These were perhaps the best-known of the Elizabethan masques during the nineteenth century, due to the published account contained in Nichols's *Progresses of Queen Elizabeth*, and their subsequent popularization in the Scott novel. *Kenilworth* itself proved to be a favorite among Scott's novels for musical-dramatic treatment, serving as the basis for numerous operas from Donizetti to Macfarren.[47] Theatrical recastings of the novel were even more popular in the theater. Philip Bolton

---

Spring Symphony, written within three years of *Albert Herring*. Here, as in so much of his music, Britten demonstrates his deep understanding of the traditions and topoi of English music and musical drama of the past. It is important at this point to make a distinction between the topos of the May Day and other folk festivals circa 1860 and the folk revival of thirty years later. The reasons for this distinction will be further explored in chapters 3 and 4.

[47] Oddly enough, Macfarren's opera *Kenilworth* does not on the whole use references to English national music to a large extent, and it does not include a masque. The only scene that does refer to English historical forms comes in Act II, scene 1, which stands in for the masques offered by Leicester to Elizabeth. Here Macfarren includes a madrigal and a ballad, followed by a ballet. This lack of English content to the music is probably due to the its proposed venue, the Royal Italian Opera at Covent Garden – it actually has an Italian libretto – and Macfarren's hopes that a more cosmopolitan treatment of the subject might lead to performance on the Continent. However, the opera was never produced. For a longer description with

lists 120 productions and 240 derivative dramas, many of which are from the nineteenth century. A spate of adaptations followed the publication of the book in the 1820s, including one by Dibdin and Planché at Covent Garden. It was the basis for pantomimes and burlesques during the 1850s and 1860s, and in 1858, Halliday and Lawrence produced *Kenilworth; or Ye Queene, Ye Earle, and Ye Maydnne*, which saw several further productions during the early 1860s and which contained a scene recreating the elaborate pageants produced for Queen Elizabeth. The most popular theatrical adaptation of the Victorian period was *Amy Robsart* which premiered in 1872 and which also contained a spectacular scene entitled a "Grand Pageant Realizing the Description of Sir Walter Scott".[48]

Scott's novel directly influenced another reconfiguration of this topic, Arthur Sullivan and Henry Chorley's *Kenilworth, a masque*, written just a year later than *Freya's Gift* in 1864. Sullivan was certainly the most prolific and influential English composer of the second half of the nineteenth century. Enormously popular and successful in his time, his modern reputation is dominated by his Savoy operettas written in collaboration with W.S. Gilbert. Only recently have musicologists reinvestigated the huge amount of serious music composed by Sullivan, among which are several pieces which are entitled masques or which contain masques as sections or movements. Additionally, and importantly for the topic of historical influence in music, Sullivan also offers a good example of how later nineteenth-century composers interacted with English music from the Renaissance and translated the new musicological interest towards "Tudor Music" into actual musical works, since his forays into reference and pastiche are widely scattered and hardly systematic.

The composer was intimately involved in the music and idiom of Tudor music from the earliest days of his musical training and professional career and drew on his knowledge of this music for his compositions in many different genres. Sullivan received his musical education as a choirboy in the Chapel Royal under the Rev. Thomas Helmore. Helmore was one of the primary men responsible for defining the ideals of the role and practice of music in the new High-Church, Tractarian Movement, effecting a much-needed reform process in church and cathedral alike. Helmore's reforming enthusiasm extended to his duties as Master of the Boys of the Chapel Royal. Under Helmore, the boys received a thorough general and musical education, disciplined and caring living conditions, and the opportunity to perform a wide variety of music, both sacred and secular, in many different performance contexts. Innovatively,

some musical excerpts see Jerome Mitchell, *More Scott Operas* (Lanham, MD: University Press of America, 1996).

[48] H. Philip Bolton, *Scott Dramatized* (London: Mansell Publishing, 1992).

Helmore drew a large portion of the Chapel Royal's repertoire from the anthems and service music of the sixteenth and seventeenth centuries, and the boys also regularly sang the treble parts for meetings of the Madrigal Society. So for several years Sullivan performed older music extensively.

Many commentators have tracked down occasional references to Tudor music throughout Sullivan's well-known works. One only has to think of the madrigal from Act II of *The Mikado*, "Brightly dawns our wedding day," and "Strange adventure, maiden wedded" and "Here's a man of jollity" from *The Yeoman of the Guard*, examples from widely differing plot contexts (why a madrigal in the Japanese town of Titipu, one might ask?). Many of the so-called madrigals from the operettas are essentially Victorian part-songs with fa-la-la burdens. But this burden and the general style of the pieces were enough to act as a signifier of the Elizabethan madrigal in ways appropriate to the plot.

But a closer mediation with the music of England's past comes in other, lesser-known works by Sullivan, such as incidental music for Shakespeare's plays, and in choral and solo vocal works with topics of history based on Merrie England. Both his popularity and the content, quality, and quantity of his musical productions were important factors in providing foundations for the composers of the English Musical Renaissance and foreshadowing many of their musical and ideological concerns.[49]

An early work, written just after the young composer had enjoyed a huge success with his music for Shakespeare's *The Tempest*, the cantata–masque *Kenilworth* was commissioned by Michael Costa for the 1864 Birmingham Festival.[50] Sullivan's *The Tempest* had included a large section setting the masque conjured by Prospero to celebrate Miranda and Ferdinand's nuptials in Act IV. For the *Kenilworth* commission, Sullivan built on the success of his music for *The Tempest* and decided to employ the genre of the masque, asking Henry Chorley to provide a text.

Chorley and Sullivan settled on the topic of the Kenilworth festivities, and Chorley provided a rationale for his choice in an introduction to the published vocal score:

[49] Very pertinent to this is the late Sullivan ballet *Victoria and Merrie England*, written in 1897 for the Alhambra Theatre to celebrate the Diamond Jubilee. The ballet contains eight tableaux, including a "May Day in Queen Elizabeth's Time" and a "Christmas Revels in the Time of Charles II," which intersect significantly with the topics I have been discussing. For more, see Brooks Kuykendall's "Sullivan, *Victoria and Merrie England*, and the National Tableau," in *SullivanPerspektiven I*, ed. Albert Gier, Meinhard Saremba, and Benedict Taylor (Essen: Oldib-Verlag, 2012).

[50] For a detailed account of Sullivan's early career in London, the best source is still Arthur Jacobs, *Arthur Sullivan, a Victorian Musician*, 2nd edn (Portland, OR: Amadeus Press, 1992).

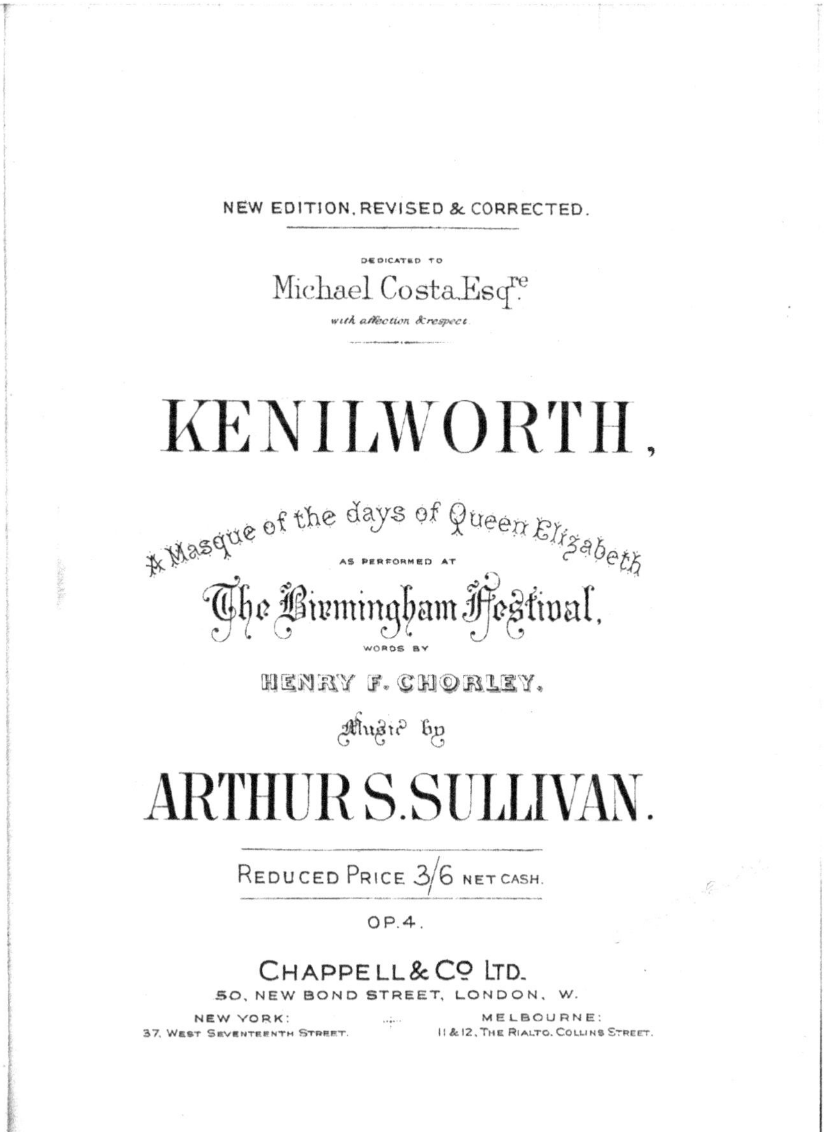

NEW EDITION, REVISED & CORRECTED.

DEDICATED TO

Michael Costa. Esqre

with affection & respect

KENILWORTH,

A Masque of the days of Queen Elizabeth

AS PERFORMED AT

The Birmingham Festival,

WORDS BY

HENRY F. CHORLEY.

Music by

ARTHUR S. SULLIVAN.

REDUCED PRICE 3/6 NET CASH.

O P. 4.

CHAPPELL & CO LTD.

50, NEW BOND STREET, LONDON, W.

NEW YORK:
37, WEST SEVENTEENTH STREET.

MELBOURNE:
11 & 12, THE RIALTO, COLLINS STREET.

Illustration 2.4   Arthur Sullivan, *Kenilworth*, title page

Once having chosen "The Princely Pleasure of Kennelworth," (sic) prepared in the summer of 1575 for Queen Elizabeth by the Earl of Leicester, as subject for an English *cantata*, nothing was required save to make rhymes fit for music; – so rich in contrast were the entertainments offered to the Queen.

"A temporary bridge, seventy feet in length," says Miss Aikin, in her careful biography, "was thrown across the valley to the great gate of the Castle. The lady of the Lake, invisible, since the disappearance of the renowned Prince Arthur, approached on a floating island along the moat to recite adulatory verses. Arion, being summoned for like purpose, appeared on a dolphin four-and-twenty feet long, which carried in its belly a whole orchestra. A Sybil, a Salvage [sic] Man, and an Echo, posted in the park, all harangued in the same strain. Music and dancing enlivened the Sunday evening, and a play was performed," etc.

My fancy was directed to this Kenilworth pageant, not merely from its local interest to those interesting themselves in our great Midland Festival, but because I have long known, almost by heart, Scott's wondrously musical, but as wondrously simple, description of the arrival of England's maiden Queen at her subject's palace on "a summer night."[51]

The libretto proceeds as Chorley describes, with sections depicting the crowd waiting for the arrival of the queen, a solo for the Lady of the Lake, a chorus for Sylvans setting up the following song for Arion, and then the inclusion of the Shakespearean duet between Lorenzo and Jessica from *The Merchant of Venice*. The cantata concludes with a "Brisk Dance" as a stand-in for the Revels, and a Finale for chorus. Even in Chorley's brief introduction, with its "musical description," "summer nights," and "maiden queens," there seems to be an underlying connection between the desire to recreate history and the nostalgic idealization of that history.

Much of the music for *Kenilworth: a Masque of the Days of Queen Elizabeth* clearly falls into the musical idioms current in the composition of cantatas during the 1860s, and some of it prefigures the music Sullivan would develop further, both in his operettas and his other serious works. Overall the *Merchant of Venice* inclusion seems to have caught the imagination of the composer, probably for the sheer beauty and concrete imagery of the text, far above the hackneyed literary efforts of Chorley. This movement calls from the composer an extended and episodic treatment at odds with the otherwise very clear cantata design of the piece. But there are also some attempts to reflect the Elizabethan setting of the masque in the music itself through historical

---

[51] Henry Chorley, "Introduction," *Kenilworth, a Masque of the days of Queen Elizabeth* (London: Chappell and Co., [1865]) 1. In actuality, the scene Chorley chose to set is more correctly what the sixteenth century would have termed Elizabeth's '*joyeuse entrée*' and not either of the "real" masques presented the following day.

KENILWORTH.

SLOW DANCE WITH CHORUS.

№ 5.

ARTHUR S. SULLIVAN.

Illustration 2.5   Arthur Sullivan, *Kenilworth*, "Slow Dance"

Illustration 2.6   Arthur Sullivan, *Kenilworth*, "Slow Dance"

KENILWORTH.

A BRISK DANCE.

№ 8.

ARTHUR. S. SULLIVAN.

12628.

Illustration 2.7 Arthur Sullivan, *Kenilworth*, "Brisk Dance"

pastiche, especially audible in the choral "dance" numbers. Most noticeably, the "Slow Dance" contains a predominantly homophonic "burden," which, despite his knowledge of Renaissance polyphony, Sullivan doesn't treat imitatively, making it less Elizabethan and more in the nature of a nineteenth century part-song, again typical of the cantata genre (Illustration 2.5). On the other hand, it also has an unusual five-bar phrase structure, with an opening that gestures towards a minuet style (Illustration 2.6). At the same time, however, the stresses on the second beat of some measures give the dance a sarabande-like feeling. The "Brisk Dance" contains aspects of a gavotte and its typical two-beat upbeat, with contrasting duple and triple meter sections, short sequences, and some play with drone-like accompaniments (Illustration 2.7).

Neither of these two dances is modeled on any one concrete historical dance form. Instead, the two are cobbled together from gestures that evoke an air of the past. The few allusions to actual dance forms are anachronistically drawn from Baroque types: obviously Sullivan would have been more familiar with these kinds of dances from such examples as Handel's keyboard suites and the *Water Music*. Sullivan's "historical" dances in this work are some of the first in what was to become a popular subgenre of English orchestral miniatures in the form of dances during the late nineteenth and early twentieth centuries. The dances from Edward German's *Henry VIII* and Roger Quilter's *Three English Dances* are just a few that immediately come to mind. Not pastiche, and in the continental vein of light ballet, they frequently include brief gestures towards modality, imitative textures, use of drones, and other signifiers of the past. Absolute authenticity is not at issue here, rather the atmosphere of nostalgia and the illusion of the past.

❧ *Pageantry, Archaeology, and Music*

Like many nineteenth-century composers of vocal and theatrical music, Sullivan was continually drawn to Shakespeare as a source and inspiration throughout his career. During the years close to the composition of *Kenilworth*, Sullivan published solo vocal settings of several Shakespeare songs. Seven years later in 1871, Sullivan returned to the source of Chorley's insertion and provided an extended piece of music for the masque at the end of Act I of Shakespeare's *Merchant of Venice*.[52] The commission came from Charles Calvert at the Prince's Theatre, Manchester and was premièred with the composer conducting on September 19, 1871. Calvert apparently rearranged the Shakespeare play, putting all of the Venice scenes together into the first,

---

[52] Arthur Jacobs, *Arthur Sullivan, a Victorian Musician*, 70.

second, and fourth acts, and the scenes at Belmont into the third and the fifth, presumably to allow for fewer but more spectacular scene designs.

The preface for Sullivan's publication contains a hint of a program for the piece:

> The masque in the Merchant of Venice occurs in the second act [sic]: the fifth to sixth scenes of which contain several references to it. It takes place in the open space outside Shylock's house; Lorenzo's two friends, Gratiano and Salarino are among the masquers, and it is under the confusion caused by the dancing that Jessica makes her escape with Lorenzo.
>
> The music being written for the stage must necessarily lose a portion of its effect when deprived of scenic adjuncts. At the commencement of the scene, when the music begins, the stage is empty and night is approaching. The distant cry of the gondoliers echoing along the canals (horns *sotto voce*), the voices of the maskers as they approach nearer and nearer, and the other accompaniments to the scene, are all depicted in music. A lover serenades his mistress, the maskers gradually throng on the ground, the revelry begins. The dances are, first, a bouree – the old-fashioned, heavy measure – next, a grotesque dance for Pierrots and Harlequins; and thirdly, a general dance in modern waltz rhythm. Night has settled down on the scene where Jessica makes her escape; after this the fun waxes furious, and amidst the glare of torches the flitter of coloured lanterns, and the shouts and songs of the revellers, the curtain descends.[53]

The idea of masque presented by this introduction and by Sullivan's program seems somewhat of an anomaly, disconnected from the strands of masque we have been examining thus far. Sullivan seems to be conflating the idea of a Shakespearean masque with that of an Italian masked ball – a masquerade – a conflation suggested, obviously enough, by the Venetian setting of the play. Sullivan may have been approached by the producer to provide the masque music and was presented with the Venetian topic of the masque, thus taking responsibility for the Venetian setting out of his hands, though details such as the kinds of dances he may indeed have chosen.

The decision to offer such a spectacular set piece, with what must have been a diverting and lavish display of costume, set design, and stage movement, was certainly conditioned by the burgeoning "archaeological" style of stage production so popular with Victorian theater audiences.[54] An "archaeological" production is a term often used to denote a nineteenth-century dramatic

---

[53] *Music to the Masque in Shakespeare's 'Merchant of Venice' by Arthur Sullivan* (London, 1871).

[54] For a good overview of this type of dramatic productions, see Michael Booth's *Spectacular Victorian Theatre*.

(or operatic) production in which money and attention was lavished on the historical accuracy of the visual aspects of the scene. This included costumes, painted backdrops, stage props – any aspect that would elevate the visual quality beyond the imagined to the absolutely real. As mentioned previously, though historically accurate dramatic production slowly crept onto the English stage from about 1780, Planché was one of the first theater producers to attempt to provide a spectacular reality of detail in all aspects of his stage productions of historical drama and period plays. This went against traditional staging methods that would play all manner of dramas in contemporary dress or translated to other times and places. By the second half of the nineteenth century, this "archaeological" style was a well-established approach, and theaters vied among themselves to outdo each other in the size and scope of these productions. This led to enormous and detailed productions that were particularly inflicted at the time on contemporary stagings of Shakespeare, as if the size and scope of a production of a Shakespeare play was required to do justice to the national status of the Bard. It is very possible that the effects present in the Sullivan masque were extensions of the archaeological pretensions of the Victorian theatrical producer.

The masque, therefore, functions as a self-contained unit inserted into a larger dramatic context but bearing little or no dramatic relationship to the whole, except to give a flavor of "Carnival of Venice" for delight of the audience, and to provide cover for the lovers to escape. The producers seized upon the setting of the play as an excuse for an extended spectacle, catering to a public conditioned to expect such displays, and, by doing so, they dropped any pretext of historical authenticity. Sullivan's score further isolates this scene as a discontinuous, self-contained entity, adding sound to a visual spectacle that divorces itself from narrative signification. Nowhere in the masque scene is there any musical reference to the historical period inherent in the Shakespearean frame of the play, though a gesture towards a vague, albeit erroneous, historicism occurs in the description of a Baroque bourrée as an implied Renaissance "old-fashioned, heavy measure." Instead, this setting provides a springboard for various Venetian musical motives – the barcarolle-like Gondolier's song, the *commedia dell'arte* figures, the "glare of the torches."[55] Odd juxtapositions occur; the "Baroque" bourrée is succeeded, incongruously, by a contemporary waltz, both presumably danced by Pierrots and Harlequins.[56] Sullivan

---

[55] Of course, Sullivan revisited the Venetian locale and musical topics in the operetta *The Gondoliers*. Venice seemed to suggest the Baroque for Sullivan, since in the famous deportment scene, the two gondolier brothers are taught to dance a gavotte.

[56] For an arrangement of the pieces from the masque scene as a suite for orchestra, see *Mascarade du Marchand de Venise, Suite de pieces pour Orchestre avec Solo pour Tenor par Arthur Sullivan* (Kalmus, [187?]).

matches the visual spectacle with its musical affiliate: a bright, flashy score clearly designed to be excerpted and performed at "popular" concerts across the country, either as a suite or as individual numbers. The numbers were also designed to be presented in a variety of arrangements, most noticeably in piano versions of the bourrée and the waltz, and the voice and piano arrangement of the solo gondolier's barcarolle.

Sullivan's score presents the genre of the masque as spectacle and as theatrical set-piece. Sullivan weaves a web of connections joining Shakespeare and Elizabethanism, offering an opportunity for scenic display within the narrative setting of the play (after all, a masque is specified), and the exotic, picturesque tableau popular in the "archaeological" strand of Victorian dramatic production. While his score was probably the nineteenth-century masque the farthest removed from traditional ideas of the genre, in many ways it is still a natural extension of characteristics central to the first decades of the "re-invented" masque – an opportunity to connect to a vague, unspecific history through a nostalgic idealization and spectacle.

As exemplified by Sullivan's works, both the popularity of Elizabethan and Tudor topics within the spectacular, "archaeological" style of Victorian drama, and the new currency of the masque as a generic topic rather than form, made the masque a popular "set piece" within stage plays and musical dramas. While the Sullivan *Merchant of Venice* masque scene is somewhat of an anomaly within this tradition, Alfred Cellier's *Doris* is more typical of how masques were interwoven into larger works both for their opportunity for dramatic spectacle and for their historical topicality.

Alfred Cellier was both a colleague and a good friend of Sullivan, serving as an associate conductor for many of the Savoy operas. His fame as a composer of musical theater came with his operetta *Dorothy*, another Elizabethan musical comedy which ran an unprecedented nine hundred performances and which managed to undermine the reign of Gilbert and Sullivan. They responded to *Dorothy*'s challenge with *The Yeoman of the Guard*, but the days of the partnership were numbered. Cellier never repeated the success of *Dorothy*. *Doris* was only mildly popular, and none of Cellier's other works captured the heart of the public.

Cellier's *Doris*, with a text by B.C. Stephenson, is subtitled a comedy-opera, with more sentiment and less satire than Gilbert and Sullivan's contemporary Savoy operas.[57] The plot circles around the attempt by the women of the Shelton household to obtain pardon for Sir Philip Carey, erroneously accused of treason, whom they have discovered in their orchard hiding from Elizabeth I

[57] See Alan Hyman, *Sullivan and his Satellites: A Study of English Operettas, 1860–1914* (London: Chappell, 1978).

on the day of her coronation. Their plan is to ask for this pardon after a presentation of a masque Master Shelton has been planning as an entertainment to Elizabeth as she rests on her long procession to London. Preparations for the masque feature as a major part of the second half of the musical comedy, and an interrupted version of the masque is presented in Act III. The masque itself follows a model derived from Elizabethan masques such as those at Kenilworth: Doris Shelton, playing Elizabeth, receives the captains of two Spanish galleons who present her with slaves and riches from the East and West. Nevertheless, in the masque what the queen craves is "of all the gifts on earth the homage of one true heart." This then offers the opportunity for Philip Carey to offer his heart to the real Queen Elizabeth, who is watching, blending the "real" with the masque.

Doris was first performed in 1889. As topics of the Jacobethan period continued to increase in popularity in musical and theatrical works throughout the last years of the century, so too did the use of a historically-inflected musical pastiche suitable for setting such topics.[58] While certainly not an invariable pattern, this pastiche style seems to be associated with two specific arenas of representation. First, it is often the musical idiom of the comic characters who personify certain stereotypes, or archetypes, of a particularly English nationality, whether purely historical or having a certain peasant or folk, hence timeless, nature. For instance, in *Doris* this type of musical representation occurs in the scene at the beginning of Act II, set in the local drinking establishment. The act's short overture introduces a sturdy melody reminiscent of a Playford country dance tune, which is harmonized through a hymn-like four-part texture, and which incorporates a short shift to the minor that gives it a slightly "antique" modal flavor. These signifiers plant us firmly within the realm of historical pastiche, albeit a chronologically vague one. This air of pastness continues into the opening number of the act, a drinking song in the style of a glee or "catch" sung by the villagers and servants of the Sheldons utilizing the tune of the overture[59] (Illustration 2.8), and then

---

[58] It seems sensible to think that this exploration of Jacobethan topics in musical theater had some effect on composers of art music, including those of the English Musical Renaissance, despite their frequent complaints about the base, popular tastes pandered to by music hall and musical theater. As testament to this, Vaughan Williams includes an excerpt from Cellier's other Elizabethan comic opera *Dorothy* in his seminal essay "National Music," a production the composer could easily have seen as a teenager in London.

[59] *The Masque Music from Doris, for the pianoforte, by Alfred Cellier* (London, 1889). The number is actually entitled a glee, anachronistically, since the glee was a type of part-song which developed around the middle of the eighteenth century, and which remained popular up until the First World War. The "catch" is an earlier term, and Cellier may have had this type of seventeenth-century part-song in mind, since it

The Alderman's Glee.

Illustration 2.8   Alfred Cellier, *Doris*, "The Alderman's Glee"

in a song by the conventionally stereotyped character of Alderman Sheldon. Pastiche style often features as the music of Jacobethan crowd scenes as well, dramatic sites which are particularly implicated in the representation of the setting of the piece, and hence, in representing history. These scenes tend also to be sites heavily imbued with a sense of historical nostalgia, connecting to settings and topics that dominated the cantata movement twenty-five years earlier: the May Day, the village market, the archery competition. An archery competition opens *Doris*, and the masque scene ends it, both ensemble scenes attempting to evoke the music of the past through broad melodic and rhythmic gestures that are reminiscent of country dances and folk tunes, and harmony and textures that allude to hymns and older choral styles.

In contrast, the music of personal expression and subjectivity in *Doris* remains dominated by the musical language and generic conventions of late Victorian England. Tuneful and accessible, the ballads and songs of operetta and musical theater were designed to have popular appeal in a way less connected to the terms of historicism and spectacle, and more to successful mass marketing for performance beyond the theater, as in Sir Philip's ballad from Act II, "Honour Bids me speed away." Within the parlor and concert hall, the demand of an emotional immediacy superseded the demand of historical reference. The authenticity of personal expression still was naturally seen to speak in the musical language of the day, not the artificial "color" of the past.

But within *Doris*, the masque functions as more than just one more instance of the division of stylistic labor within musical theater works with Jacobethan topics. More importantly, the masque becomes the nexus for a wide range of represented ideologies. Obvious enough are the imperialistic overtones: through the agency of the conquered Spanish captains, the queen received both tribute and gifts that represented her possession of both the East and the West, her subjects and captives processing in with the strains of a jaunty march (Illustration 2.9) and then the Spanish captains singing of the allures of faraway lands in an airy, pensive chorus. By the date of Cellier's *Doris*, Queen Victoria was not only queen but also Empress of India and titular head of an extensive empire. Her status is given historical validity through the implication of Elizabeth's own imperial acquisitions.

However, this Victorian author felt that material acquisitiveness, while not to be denigrated, must be presented as subservient to other, higher values.

was definitely a type of song associated with taverns and drinking. Again, though, the catch was not an Elizabethan song. The point to make is that the glee was a contemporary song form which, like the masque, carried connotations of history, with its links to the madrigal, and Cellier's audience would have associated this with some kind of authenticity, though the form by the late nineteenth century was different in significant ways from the Elizabethan prototypes.

No. 27. ENTRANCE OF THE MASQUERS & CHORUS.

Illustration 2.9   Alfred Cellier, Doris, "Entrance of the Masquers & Chorus"

In "the Masque of the Spaniard" this is represented by Elizabeth's desire for "the one true heart" – an English heart. The symbol of the "English" heart was one that necessarily embodied all sorts of nationalistic virtues. The gifts are not refused (nor would Britain's imperial "destiny" be), but they are firmly held in check by a different set of priorities which are understood in nationalistic terms. Here, in Act III, particular views of an ideology towards national identity are being represented and enacted, as they would be again and again in similar scenes of musical drama. The masque, however, is unique in its ability to serve as a vehicle for this kind of nationalistic representation. As it was understood during the last decades of the century, the masque was a historical artifact connected to the nostalgic utopia of Tudor England, and as such allowed for the presentation of a wide range of nationalistic and chauvinistic – if not xenophobic – allegory and symbolism. But, because it was historical, this created an illusion of distance and removal that partially obscured the very real, very modern ideology attached to the re-enactment of the historical ritual.

By 1880 the masque was well on its way to being understood in ways essentially similar to the assumptions upon which *Pan's Anniversary* would be predicated, as a signifier for a group of associated topics connected to the pastoral and the historical rather than as a set of formal characteristics. As such, the masque genre was important in social and cultural terms as an indicator of a contemporary predisposition to define modern Englishness through connections to the past. But as of yet the source and authenticity of the music for the genre was not important. For the most part, it perpetuated either modern and progressive styles of music, or styles specifically aimed towards popular audiences both in theaters and concert-halls. Certainly, as in Sullivan's *Kenilworth*, it was beginning to accumulate in rare instances a set of supposedly "appropriate" musical references to music of the past, to support and authenticate the topics of history. There is considerable distance, however, between the occasional musical references in these Victorian masques and the pervasive utilization of early music in *Pan's Anniversary*.

Looking back to *The Fortunate Isles* and *An Emblematical Tribute* from 1840, the tension between the modern and the historical was already present in these disparate scores. The composers and librettists drew from models of the past to lend a sense of historical continuity and to link to a previously established set of tropes and associations, and yet they reflected a particularly modern sensibility about both music and society in their goals of education and progress. The same underlying tension persists throughout the 1860s and 70s. To some extent this is a result of the fundamental problems of representing Englishness. However, the fact that this tension continues to resonate in music throughout the Victorian period testifies to the intimate connection between definitions of

Englishness and definitions of English music. As noted in the opening chapter, this dialectical tension would only increase with the onset of the ideologies of imperialism and its attendant chauvinism towards the end of the century.

Such concerns are mirrored on a larger scale within the English Musical Renaissance itself during its earliest stages. Dating the exact origin of the supposed English Musical Renaissance presents a scholarly conundrum that is virtually insoluble. Certainly, by the first years of the twentieth century it was firmly established. Part of the ideology attributed to composers categorized as belonging to the English Musical Renaissance at that point was the open expression of indebtedness to music of the past. This clear signifier was not a feature of British musical aesthetics or politics a generation earlier, when the leaders of the movement, compositional and bureaucratic, were beginning to formulate the idea of a self-conscious national music, but were still composing and supporting contemporary, continental idioms. For both the masque and the English Musical Renaissance, the connection with the sonic materials of the past had to be forged together with the historiographical element.

CHAPTER 3

The Past Speaks in English:
Historiography and the Masque Revival

B Y the last quarter of the nineteenth century the masque was well on
its way to becoming established as a genre straddling art and popular
cultures, imbedded in Shakespeare productions and musical comedies, and
casting a shadow of the historical over cantatas and other works designed
for the burgeoning choral movement. It can be argued that the Victorian
masque developed mostly apart from any in-depth knowledge or experience
of the realities of the Elizabethan and Stuart court masques, and that this
provides a reason why the new, re-invented heterogeneous genre established
itself so quickly. Without a clear sense of the concrete musical materials of
the historical masque in particular, and the Elizabethan and Stuart periods
in general, views of what "authenticity" meant were skewed by the distorting
prism of memory and nostalgia. Within the re-invented masque the topos of
history acquired an ideological significance, but as of yet there was no true
musical significance. The Victorian masques demonstrated that, apart from
the implied historicity of the topic, musical modernity prevailed, and it was in
modern terms that the masque was resurrected to serve the needs of the choral
societies and musical theaters. Musically, this meant that most masques of the
latter half of the nineteenth century avoided explicit historical pastiche or
musical references, utilizing popular genres and modern, albeit conservative,
compositional methods instead. Thematically, this meant that the creators
of these masques articulated a historical perspective that was saturated with
contemporary preoccupations of national character, empire, and the role of
the increasingly vocal lower classes in the definitions of the nation.

However, such a historical vacuum could not continue. Following closely
on the heels of proliferating productions of contemporary masques during the
second half of the nineteenth century came a heightened interest in masques
from earlier periods on the part of scholars and antiquarians, reflected in
the groundbreaking, period-style revival of the anonymous 1614 *Masque of
Flowers* at the Inns of Court in 1887. While this revival had a limited impact
on dramatic life in the 1880s, by the turn of the century antiquarian interest in
the masque was certainly part of the larger expansion of historical enquiry that
was characteristic of the period, as well as a heightened nationalistic impulse
to uncover the country's heritage. So, while English music histories as late as
John Hullah's *The History of Modern Music* of 1862, revised in 1875, have no

information at all about the masque, by the 1890s masque scholarship was well underway.[1] Beyond just the expansion of scholarly activity, what this and other studies of musical history did was to establish the importance of the music of the past, both in itself as a collection of works with the ability yet to speak to the present, and, importantly, as a means (or a source) for an authentic musical language through which modern composers could connect to their national identity and communicate this identity to others.

Even a cursory glance at the list of books and articles from the nineteenth and early twentieth centuries containing sections covering the masque, whether from the fields of social, theatrical, or musical English history, shows a steady increase in the available bibliography, which reached a peak between 1900 and 1910, the years surrounding Vaughan Williams and Holst's *Pan's Anniversary* (see Appendix 2). A revival such as that of the *Pan's Anniversary* offered at Stratford is a clear result of this new interest in the history of the masque and of a desire to recreate the experience of the past dramatically in the most concrete ways possible. However, the result of the scholarly efforts that rediscovered the historical artifacts – leading to revivals like *Pan's Anniversary* and others like it – was to place a different version, a different definition, of the masque in competition with the newly written and composed masques of the type examined in the preceding chapter. The scholars and revivers of the historical masque were much less interested in recreating the genre to make it viable for contemporary audiences than they were invested in giving their audience a new appreciation for the relics of a great and glorious national past. At the crux of the differences between the two types of masque definition was

---

[1] John P. Hullah, *The History of Modern Music*, 2nd edn (London: Longmans, Green, Reader, and Dyer, 1875). Books on music history written in Great Britain during the first half of the nineteenth century were essentially reductions and summations of the two magisterial histories from the eighteenth century by Charles Burney and John Hawkins. It was not until the establishment of periodicals like *The Monthly Musical Standard*, *The Musical World*, and *The Musical Times*, and the rise of the public lecture around the mid-century point that new ideas and information about music history were presented to the English public. John Hullah's *The History of Modern Music*, based on a lecture series, was an important step towards creating books on music for the general public. Throughout most of this scholarship, the emphasis was on the works of the great composers of the eighteenth and nineteenth centuries, particularly focused on Germans. However, as the century progressed, space was increasingly devoted to the new discoveries in medieval and renaissance music. This is certainly tied to the rise of evolutionary and organic models of history derived from Darwin and adapted to the historiographic realm by such English writers as Spencer. For a brief overview of English historiography during the long nineteenth century, see Vincent Duckles's chapter in Nicholas Temperley, ed., *The Romantic Age 1800–1914*, vol. 5, *The Athlone History of Music in Britain* (London: Athlone Press, 1981).

the tension between the claims of English authenticity and the demands of the modern. This was of course a crucial issue on a wider scale for English music as a whole during the first decades of the twentieth century.[2]

But the reality of the historiographical enterprise was such that no matter how insistent the calls for authenticity through scholarship, definitions of the masque based on historical artifacts and new research into the masques of the past model were in many ways an "invention of tradition", in Hobsbawm's formulation. The social concerns of defining and, to an extent, creating a viable national identity exerted a considerable presence, no matter how "neutral" the claims of scholarship seemed at the time. The versions of history created within this context were bound to reflect those concerns.[3] As the masque was expropriated as a populist genre with links to the nation's past in an increasing number of contemporary productions, the scholars of the masque focused on conflicting versions of the origins and early development of the genre. This in turn reflected a preoccupation with the value of high art in contrast with popular culture. Two conflicting accounts of the masque tradition were continuously debated: on the one hand, the masque was viewed as a Renaissance court entertainment, with its roots in the Italian *intermedi*; on the other hand, the masque was seen as a repository of English folk traditions. In the latter theory, the masque developed out of various kinds of disguisings and mummings, and therefore was much more intrinsically English than continentally-derived. The Italian influence upon the genre, given the evidence of descriptions and texts themselves, could not be denied, nor could the impact of the French *ballet de cour*; this is what is stressed in the earliest masque scholarship before around 1900, and which emerged again after World War I.[4] Yet almost all of the descriptions of the masque from the early years of the century contain substantial passages that claim folk traditions, as well as connections to medieval and early Tudor entertainments, as the roots for the masque so that they can argue for its peculiarly English character.

---

[2] The nature of this opposition, and how it was reflected in the masque, is the topic of chapters 4 and 5 of this monograph.

[3] For an overview of the changing concerns of British history writing during the nineteenth century in general, see A. Dwight Culler, *The Victorian Mirror of History* (New Haven: Yale University Press, 1985) and Neil McCaw's *George Eliot and Victorian Historiography: Imagining the National Past* (New York: St. Martin's Press, 2000).

[4] E.J. Dent, *Foundations of English Opera* (Cambridge: Cambridge University Press, 1928) and Enid Welsford, *The Court Masque: a Study in the Relationship between Poetry and the Revels* (Cambridge: Cambridge University Press, 1927) come to mind, both written during the late 1920s. Dent's work was begun in 1914, when he and Clive Carey were planning a production of Purcell's *Fairy Queen* at Cambridge, which would have been the first since 1693, but both projects were interrupted by the First World War. Dent subsequently rewrote *Foundations* in the early 1920s.

Obviously, more was at stake in such controversies than the question of whether Italy or the mummers provided the evolutionary momentum for the masque. Other questions are dimly visible in the margins of much of this scholarship. Some of these questions result from the urgent need for the discovery of English historical identity. Of crucial importance at the time is the utility to which English history could be employed to define various contemporary versions of Englishness in the late nineteenth and early twentieth centuries. This use of history is connected to the rising status of folk culture, and the investigation into prehistory for the sources of particularly English genres, no matter their subsequent history. Other questions involve the continuing debate over the character of English cultural productions, present and past; in particular whether they should be classified as high art or as popular and utilitarian. All of these broad social issues commingling national identity, history, and modernity were obsessively contested in the more specific arena of music, both within what we have been calling the English Musical Renaissance and among its opponents. Within the English Musical Renaissance this operated along a generational divide, as the "fathers" of the movement such as Hubert Parry clung to the principles of high art and a modern, cosmopolitan compositional language, ultimately seeking a compromise with the forces of nationalism, while composers of the succeeding generation, such as Vaughan Williams, sought to activate the movement around the rediscovery of national music of the past, including the popular and the folk. At the same time, the English Musical Renaissance movement, always a loose confederation of individuals, sought to define itself against its critics and opponents, who continued to see the progress of a national music as dependent on an aggressive modernity.

And so, a segment within turned to historiography, parsing the materials of history in order to define the musical materials of the present. As such, a historiographical project uncovering English music of the past was an exercise in authenticating various periods, genres, and figures as valid sources for adaptation within contemporary terms. For the masque, four basic historiographical premises needed to be established before the masque gained a status as a viable English historical genre. These were contested over a twenty-year period from 1890 to 1910. To examine them in detail is to discover that they mimic the authenticating activity that occurred on a larger scale within the historiographic project of the English Musical Renaissance. The first premise was the determination that the sources of the masque were idiosyncratically English, an effort that downplayed the claims for other alternative sources. The second was the identification of the masque in its heyday of the sixteenth and seventeenth centuries as a genre which combined experiment with successful works, a means for the adaptation of continental musical developments within a clearly English, national context. The third historiographic premise was the elevation of the status of Henry Purcell as the central precursor of contemporary English composers. The final aspect of this historical project was the elevation of folk music and other folk traditions through an attempt to link them to the art music of the Elizabethan and Stuart periods. Each of these hypotheses was important not merely within the context of a historical understanding of the masque and its origins and development, for the conclusions reached within each of these areas were needed to create a foundation for the broader models and theories adapted by modern English composers. Masque scholarship, alongside burgeoning inquiries into church music, the madrigal school, and the lute song, assumed an important role in determining a version of Englishness that was useful for the development of the aesthetic premises underlying the work of the composers grouped under the designation "English Musical Renaissance." Such a version of Englishness was imprinted on several succeeding generations.

❧ The Search for the Source: Early Accounts of the Masque

The "English origins" hypothesis mentioned above is present from the earliest beginnings of masque scholarship. One of the first volumes devoted to the genre was Herbert A. Evans's *English Masques*, which appeared in 1897. Evans's volume offered a number of masque texts by Ben Jonson and others, as well as an extensive description of the genre and its development. Though written early in a period that would nurture a blossoming field of masque scholarship, it already reveals several of the problems and contradictions that characterize accounts of the English masque during this period.

Evans begins his preface by alluding to the relative lack of previous interest in his subject.

> The debatable land which is occupied by the subject of the present volume has never been thoroughly explored by English writers. Our dramatic and musical historians, preoccupied as they were by questions of greater interest and weightier import, and tacitly subscribing to Bacon's dictum that "these things are but toyes to come among such serious observations," have been able to make but improvised and desultory excursions into its territories. Hence it is that the task of making a thorough exploration has been left to a German, and we are indebted to Dr. Oscar Alfred Soergel of the University of Halle for the first attempt at an adequate discussion of the Masque as a whole, in its origin, development, and decay.[5]

---

[5] Herbert Arthur Evans, *English Masques* (London: Blackie and Son, 1895), v.

Despite his mildly ambivalent inclusion of Bacon's disparaging comment, Evans criticizes his fellow English historians for not exploring the genre with any seriousness, and thereby allowing a German to co-opt what should have been a British project, that of restoring a neglected body of historically important musical-dramatic works to the fold of characteristically English masterpieces. Already, in the volume's first paragraph, the foundations of his project are evident, as is typical of the nationalistic tendencies that infiltrate most of the English masque scholarship of this period.

The nationalist project becomes clearer as Evans commences his introduction to the masque itself:

> The Masque in one form or another was long a favourite amusement at the English Court; after a somewhat chequered career of two centuries some faint foreshadowings of its literary glory are at length discernible under the last of the Tudors, but it did not reach its full development, either in this respect or in any other, till after the Stuarts came to the throne. Although the outburst of splendour which then signalized its maturity was largely due to foreign influences, and although its very name was of foreign origin, we shall see that it has every claim to pedigree indisputably English, and that as a literary product it attained a distinction to which its continental rivals could lay no claim.[6]

However clear his nationalistic intentions, Evans's opening contains what would become a source of contention: his description of the masque's origins and development. Evans feels obligated to acknowledge the "foreign influences" that provided the impetus for the genre's maturation, thus displaying the organic model of history that had grown out of Darwinian evolutionary models and that provided much of the metaphoric language found with abundance in late-nineteenth-century English historiography.[7] But it is also crucial for him to claim this genre as one of England's own, "indisputably English" in character and "pedigree." And since an English pedigree comes from a lineage traceable back to English roots, Evans wrestles throughout his discussion with the insoluble problem of securing the national sources for the masque genre.

Evans begins by tracing the derivation of the word, from the Arabic through the French to the English "maske" by the early sixteenth century, the French spelling "masque" not becoming popular until very late in the sixteenth century. He then goes on to say that "the fact that the name did not exist in England before the sixteenth century is no proof of the non-existence of the thing denoted by it." He supports this novel argument by citing several court records

---

[6] Ibid., ix.

[7] A broader overview is given in Bennett Zon, *Music and Metaphor in Nineteenth-Century British Musicology* (Aldershot: Ashgate, 2000).

and descriptions of masque-like productions, tracing his evidence as far back as a description of a night of dancing in costume at the court of Edward III in 1348. He continues to find accounts of "mummings" or "disguisings" throughout the early Tudor period, entertainments he feels are important early examples of "maskes," with their increasingly complex staging, professionalized music, and attempts at narrative continuity. To refute scholars who might reasonably assert that the masque was an imported form of Italian *mascherata* – a theory which is supported by a well-known early-sixteenth-century description of one of these court spectacles in which the writer Edward Hall specifically refers to the masque as being something newly arrived from Italy – Evans deflects possible counter-criticism by declaring that what was "new" was not the masque itself, but the innovation of asking the audience to join the maskers in a series of dances. This assertion once again banishes the specter of a non-English source for the genre. As Evans puts it, "from an early period a dance in masquerade was one of the ordinary diversions of the European Courts, the English among the rest,"[8] so that any cross-fertilization is of a rudimentary nature, unimportant to the intrinsically English qualities of this native genre.

To further emphasize the Englishness of the evolving genre, Evans offers several supporting points. He discusses how the genre developed in tandem with English drama throughout the sixteenth century, often presented in combination with an interlude or another firmly English dramatic tradition, the morality play. Implicit in this argument is that the drastic changes in the genre between the Tudor mummings and the full-blown glories of the Jacobean court masque can be accounted for by native dramatic developments rather than outside influence. Evans firmly denies the possibility of an Italian influence: nowhere in his account are the *intermedi* of the Italian courts, particularly the well-known Florentine *intermedi*, even mentioned. However, Evans is willing to entertain that there might possibly exist a slight influence on the formal plan of the Jacobean masque from the French *ballet de cour*, especially in the elaboration of the dances and the increase in spectacular effects. Evans presents a few descriptions of sixteenth-century ballets, but declines to conjecture about how much of an influence these may have had on the masque, despite the many similarities. Evans's avoidance of making these connections colors his interpretation in ways that seem directly connected to the book's requisite nationalistic agenda.

Evans then defines the essential characteristics of the Stuart court masque and its two forms of dances, the Entries and the Revels. His description is of particular interest, as it demonstrates clearly the conceptualization of the masque in the late nineteenth century:

[8] Herbert Arthur Evans, *English Masques*, xii.

The masque, then, is a combination, in variable proportions, of speech, dance, and song, but its essential and invariable feature is the presence of a group of dancers, varying in number, but commonly eight, twelve, or sixteen, called Masquers. These masquers never take any part in the speaking or in the singing: all they have to do is to make an imposing show and to dance. The dances are of two kinds (1) stately figure dances performed by the masquers alone and carefully rehearsed beforehand, and commonly distinguished as the Entry, the Main, and the Going-out; (2) the Revels, livelier dances, such as galliards, corantos, and levaltos, danced by the masquers with partners of the opposite sex chosen from the audience. The Revels were regarded as extras, and are not numbered among the regular masque dances of the programme; they took place after the Main and were doubtless often kept up for a considerable time.[9]

The rest of the introductory essay traces the partnership between Ben Jonson and Inigo Jones and describes features of their many masque productions.

There are two aspects conspicuously missing from Evans's account of the masque. The first is any substantive discussion of the music of the masque. For Evans, writing in the 1890s, the primary importance of the masque was defining it as a genre about dancing and about dramatic presentation. This would soon change, as the literary qualities of the texts, particularly those by Ben Jonson, began to dominate discussions of the genre. But nowhere does he specifically discuss what the music of the masque sounded like or what its functions were beyond the obvious one of providing for the dancing. Only once does Evans mention that songs were interspersed throughout an evening's entertainment, and that comment is within a discussion of the masque as a venue for high-quality lyric interpolations, some of which were set to music. Evans obscures the reality that these interpolations might have communicated meaning musically as well as poetically.[10]

The second important missing aspect of Evans's exegesis is that of folk traditions, an aspect that will become increasingly important in accounts of the masque over the next decade. Folk elements do not yet appear on the horizon in Evans's early account. For those authors who wrote after Evans, the sources for the masque were to be located in the medieval and popular, but for Evans the masque was born in the milieu of the court and developed as a high-art genre, specifically through royal patronage. Nowhere is any kind of populist

---

[9] Ibid., xxxii.

[10] This preference for dealing with spoken word only at the expense of music and dance characterizes much of the scholarly writings on the masque, the Florentine *intermedi*, Medieval liturgical drama, and other forms of Renaissance and Early Modern multi-media dramatic works, well into the twentieth century, despite the fact that often much of the music for these productions survives.

aspect of the masque admitted, either past or future. As a matter of fact, Evans ends his account of the genre in the middle of the seventeenth century, attributing its demise to the termination by Cromwell and the Commonwealth of the specific court culture that had supported it.

> It is the expression of the exuberant light-heartedness of an age which had not yet paused to inquire whether it was right or wise to make enjoyment an end in itself. We feel that there is inherent in the masque a freshness, an abandon, a total absence of self-consciousness, which must have been stifled in the cynical atmosphere of the court of the Restoration. The world was still young, but the great Puritan wave swept over the land, carrying away with it things evil and good, and the masque disappeared forever.[11]

As this passage shows, Evans acknowledges that masques were written and produced during the Restoration, but importantly he was unwilling to grant such later works the generic affiliation with the masque as he defined it, since they were products of a commercial rather than courtly aesthetic. It is possible that Evans's dismissal of the Restoration masque, and other similar efforts that occur within masque historiography, to a general sense of unease about the Restoration period as a whole. On the one hand, contemporary historians approved the restoration of the Stuart monarchy for the good of dynastic continuity and national identity as monarchy. On the other hand, many were uncomfortable with the frivolity and licentiousness of the Restoration court, and the specter of Roman Catholicism that hovered over Charles II and James II. Also, Evans does not discuss works like *Comus* or *Cupid and Death*, masques from the Commonwealth and immediate post-Restoration period which are largely informed and bear a close resemblance to masques that Evans does cover in his work. This supports the idea that he sees his subject as exclusively the court masque. For Evans the masque was a product of an innocent time, a time of youth and freshness, idealized into a Golden Age wantonly destroyed by Cromwell, by the execution of a doomed monarch, and by the repressive morality of the Puritans. He fails to mention Dryden, Purcell, or the masques of the eighteenth or nineteenth centuries, since as products of a different time they do not fit what he feels defines the boundaries of his topic, a topic which seems as much nostalgia as material. By closing the introductory chapter on the masque as he does, he grants the genre a status that reveals an underlying idealization of the historical period that produced it – a particular type of Merrie England revealed for all to see – and the aristocratic cultural milieu that supported it.

This is not to diminish the historical importance of Evan's partially flawed description. His crucial rhetorical move was to determine that the masque

---

[11] Herbert Arthur Evans, *English Masques*, lv–lvi.

was an essentially English invention, that it deserved a status as a national genre through both its foundations and evolution, and that it had a high level of artistic merit that would sustain contemporary interest. However, though Evans's idealization of the masque was an important step forward toward increasing interest in the genre, his exclusively literary and high-art construction of this history reflected an emerging masque ideology that was useful to those such as Vaughan Williams who advocated the use of such historic genres as a basis for a new musical language.

This assumption by younger composers of the period that such historic genres could provide the foundations of a renaissance of English music was not a self-evident step. A third historian of English music during the 1890s, Henry Davey, agreed that the masque in its time was the equivalent of early Italian opera and contained inherent promise, but went on to label the masque essentially a dead end. For Davey, the problem was that the masque was basically too aristocratic and rarified for its survival:

> The nascent Opera, which at the end of the sixteenth century appeared in Italy, had its English counterpart in the Masque; and both entertainments originally used mythological material, and were an amusement for cultivated aristocracy. The masque never advanced much beyond this limited sphere; and the stage failure of Fletcher's splendid *Faithful Shepherdess* is sufficient proof that the form was not a growth of popular life … The Italian opera, restricted in its beginnings, ever expanded, while the masque, though flourishing in the reigns of James I and Charles I, became contracted into an excrescence upon a drama.[12]

For Davey and many other music historians including Parry, the problem rested in the fundamental difficulty of the role of music in English drama, with its attendant problems of dialogue and recitative. For Davey, the weakness of the masque genre was a dramatic rather than a musical one:

> The weak side of English music has been the dramatic side. English Opera – for such the Jacobean Masque really was – made what seemed a most promising start; but its lack of vital powers has made it always a fancy of the hothouse rather than a robust natural growth. At the same time, it should be remembered that the English Drama has, during the eighteenth and nineteenth centuries, been no more elevated than the English Opera.[13]

---

[12] Henry Davey, *History of English Music* (London: J. Curwen and Sons, 1895), 193.
For an interesting analysis of Davey's ideological leanings, see Bennett Zon's "'Loathsome London': Ruskin, Morris, and Henry Davey's History of English Music (1895)", *Victorian Literature and Culture*, 37 (2009), 359–75.

[13] Henry Davey, *History of English Music*, 193–4.

Despite this half-hearted attempt to excuse English dramatic music, Davey certainly asserted that the masque genre had a limited viability. Nor did he find evidence of a continual thread that would connect the masque to the development of an English musical style. In comparison to the English music historians who followed him, particularly Hubert Parry, Davey represents a lone dissenting voice that ran counter to the emerging historical narrative that found important manifestations in the "hothouse" entertainments of the Stuart court masques.[14]

❧ Music History Accounts of the Masque

If the initial accounts of the masque were exclusively concerned with literary and dramatic aspects, music historians very quickly became increasingly interested in the Elizabethan and Stuart court masques. They had more access to the actual music of the masque, as more secular music from the late sixteenth and early seventeenth centuries was discovered in manuscript, and subsequently transcribed, edited, and published. Such research supported the hypothesis that the masque was, both dramatically and musically, an experimental genre, an arena for dramatists and composers to adapt the most modern of continental developments to an Anglicized taste, particularly in the realm of Italian monody and French dance music. As such, English musical historiography of the last decades of the nineteenth century co-opted the concept of national styles to assert a particular, and in some ways superior, English music that could be validated against that of Italy, Germany, and France. This relatively new approach was a watershed in accounts of English musical history. As late as 1875, John Hullah was generally dismissive of the importance of English music in the context of European music history, though he wrote of the church music and the madrigals of English composers of the sixteenth and early seventeenth centuries as continuing to be important to contemporary musical life in Britain in a fundamental way. A typical passage comes in Hullah's opening pages, in a discussion of "the musical nations of Europe:"

---

[14] I have found no other writer after Davey who did not validate the masque's role in the development of English music. E.J. Dent in his *Foundations of English Opera*, for example, does acknowledge the dramatic problems of the masque, especially when compared with the drama of the period – a problem that he attributes at least partially to a failure of modern audiences to understand the ideological and performative conditions that informed Jacobean audiences. However, he still devotes twenty-four pages to the Stuart court masque as an important first step in the development of English operatic traditions.

Not only does the history of modern music concern Europe only, but a very small portion of it … progress has been due chiefly to three nations; – the Belgians and Northern French … the Italians, the Germans, and more recently the French. Doubtless we (English) have had, from an early period, a school, and a great one, of our own … But it would be hard to prove that any one of these nations has contributed directly to the progress of the art; or that the art would have been other than it is, if none of them had ever practiced it. It is a little mortifying to ourselves, but no less, true, that foreigners "make a point" of ignoring our existence as a musical people … they misspell our names, credit us with works to which we have no claim, and kill us years before our time.[15]

By the 1890s, nationalistic ideologies spurred English musicologists to make revised and extensive claims for early English music. Such musicologists were aided by increasing knowledge of, and access to, early source material; this new information allowed scholars to extend further the notion that various types of English music were basic components of a national character and identity.

How English music historians maneuvered their way through their newly rediscovered history, in terms of both re-evaluating the musical products of the past and the relative claims of high versus popular culture, is apparent in the writings of Hubert Parry. As well as being one of the prominent early composers of the English national school, Parry was among the most consequential music historians active during the decades around the turn of the twentieth century.[16] His importance derives from the erudition and clarity demonstrated in his influential works of music history – *The Evolution of the Art of Music*, *The Music of the Seventeenth Century* (volume 3 of the first edition of the *Oxford History of Music*), and *Lives of the Great Composers*, among others. He was professor of music history and literature, then director, of the Royal College of Music and professor of music at Oxford University, and thereby in a position to pass his particular historical ideologies down to several generations of young musicians and composers. Parry thus had an enormous effect on the growing field of musicology as an area of study distinct from more

[15] John P. Hullah, *The History of Modern Music*, 7–8.

[16] Parry is only one in a long line of composers who were also music historians. One thinks of Sullivan's crucial role in the revival of Schubert's music. More relevant, perhaps are Ralph Vaughan Williams's writings, discussed later in this chapter. Other English composers who wrote extensively on music history include William Crotch, Henry Bishop, G.A. Macfarren, Walford Evans, Gustav Holst, Rutland Boughton, Constant Lambert, Herbert Howells, and Gerald Finzi. A broader point might actually be made that an interest in and/or an involvement with history and the music of the past is one of the defining characteristics of a certain type of English composer during the late nineteenth century and the first half of the twentieth.

general forms of antiquarianism or general music studies. His influence was well deserved; he was knowledgeable about the music of the past, especially the seventeenth century, and kept abreast of the vast amount of music of the past being edited and printed during the initial explosion of editorial music historiography during the second half of the nineteenth century. He was well educated and well read, and intimate with new trends in philosophy, history, aesthetics, and literature, all of which he brought to the task of writing music history. Parry's general method of history writing applied the evolutionary models of Darwin and Spencer to music history, thereby drawing heavily on metaphors of organicism in his account of a basic linear projection of progress through the ages.[17]

Several factors color Parry's description of English music from the sixteenth and seventeenth centuries. First is his overall pragmatism in regard to the relative importance of English music. Parry continually situates English music between some type of absolute, non-national canon of great music, which contains very little music by any English composer, and a nationalistic ideology that prompts him to rediscover and validate English music of the past. He searches for those aspects that seem especially characteristic of English music from this period, aspects that distinguish it from the better-known music of France, Italy, and Germany, resulting in a mode of historical investigation in which he evaluates the origins of various important developments and their dissemination, and then examines in detail how these originating elements are modified through their integration into (or conflict with) the existing English national style. This is exemplified in his discussion of distinctions between the Italian aria and the English air, which he theorizes at length as contrasting routes of development initiating from a single impulse but affected by different national characters.[18]

Parry's account of seventeenth-century music reflects emerging knowledge about secular music during this period, manifesting itself in his historiography through a prioritization of secular over sacred music. Indeed, this particular idiosyncrasy forms the overall thesis for the volume, given "obvious proof of the fact already insisted on, that the meaning of the musical revolution of the seventeenth century was the secularization of the art; and that even church music, in order to take new life, had to adopt methods which had been devised

---

[17] The general details of my discussion of Hubert Parry's writings on music history beyond that centered on the masque are indebted to Jeremy Dibble, "Parry as Historiographer," in *Nineteenth-Century British Music Studies*, ed. Bennett Zon (Aldershot: Ashgate, 1999), 37–51, and Bennett Zon, *Music and Metaphor in Nineteenth-Century British Musicology*.

[18] C. Hubert H. Parry, *The Music of the Seventeenth Century*, vol. 3, *Oxford History of Music* (Oxford: Oxford University Press, 1902), 196–7.

for purely secular purposes."[19] He posited that the new English school of music had to confront the dominance of the continent on secular and modern terms in order to successfully compete, and this meant weakening the traditional link between English music and the Anglican church.

Parry's secularizing impulse was extended to historiographical views of English music as well. Twenty years before, Parry's assertion concerning seventeenth-century music could not have been made with any confidence, since so little of the secular music of the seventeenth century was available in editions; knowledge of this vast repertory would have been limited to an occasional encounter with a manuscript. But the last quarter of the nineteenth century had seen an explosion in the editing and printing of sets of "musical monuments," especially in the field of English music. A small repertoire of English sacred music of the sixteenth, seventeenth, and eighteenth centuries had survived through the continuing choral tradition of the Anglican cathedral service, but knowledge of England's secular music was extremely limited. The exceptions were a handful of scores by Purcell and Handel, but only a miniscule amount of their secular works survived in print, and the continued availability of their works was due mostly to their particular high status in English music history. For Parry, as for many eager to initiate a new period in English music, church music past and present was hindered by its conservative nature. It was secular music which represented the forward thrust of musical development after the renaissance, beginning with the *nuove musiche* of Caccini and his contemporaries in Italy at the turn of the seventeenth century.

Parry treats English music of the seventeenth century in two chapters, the first describing music in England before the Commonwealth and the second discussing the music of the Restoration and late Stuart periods. His second chapter on English music comes after an intervening chapter on French music during the seventeenth century, a chapter in which he covers Lully, the ballet, and the *tragédie lyrique*. This sequence demonstrates clearly the two organizational points of Parry's historical methodology. First, chapters are organized around national styles and developments, which are then assembled to fit into an overlapping chronological schema. This methodological focus explains why he separates French and English music of the same period, 1650–1700, into different chapters, despite similarities and cross-influences between the two that could easily have been discussed together. Second, he is careful to establish a sequence of influence and derivation, again in a chronological organization. So, the treatment of French music comes between the two chapters on English music; Parry wants to prioritize the French influence on the music of Restoration England at the expense of the Italian influence,

---

[19] Ibid., 258.

implicitly supporting the points made in his first chapter on English music that outlined the differences between English and Italian styles.

The masque is treated at length in Parry's first English chapter devoted to the Jacobean and Caroline periods. After an initial discussion of the madrigal and the lute song, with longer sections devoted to the representative composers Morley and Dowland, he discusses the Jacobean masque and its music at length: almost ten pages. Unlike Evans's account, which minimizes the role and quality of the music involved, Parry asserts in a chapter entitled "Signs of Change in England" that the most advanced English secular music of the period was to be found within the masque:

> The methods of these branches of art (the lute song) admitted of transformation while still retaining copious traces of the old polyphonic style. They allowed of the continuity which is so dear to the English mind; and if art had been restricted to such branches in this country, English composers could scarcely have moved fast enough for the times. But there was a form of entertainment which just supplied the framework required to induce parallel experiments to those of the Italian promoters of the 'Nuove Musiche,' which at the same time remained characteristically English. The popularity of masques at Court and among aristocratic classes, from the early days of Tudor rule even till the outbreak of the civil war, almost compelled composers who were called upon to supply music for them to consider their art from a different point of view from that of the old church composers and composers of madrigals; and the opportunities they offered for introducing solo music and simple dance-tunes and incidental music, were among the most important inducements to experiments in the style, and ultimately became potent influences in weaning the cautious and conservative musicians of England from their exclusive attachment to the noble but limited forms of choral art.[20]

He goes on to declare that the masque, while perhaps simplistic when compared to the experiments of Monteverdi and other Italian composers, is "really of great historical interest," because it offers an English counterpart to Italian stage music, and "the first definite and undisguised departure in the direction of secular music of any dimensions in this country."[21]

In contrast to Evans, Parry downplays the dramatic significance of the masque and instead describes it as an experimental laboratory for new kinds of English secular music. As in so much of his historiography, this characterization of a past period is again underpinned by an urgent contemporary agenda. Parry presents the masque as an arena in which continental features

[20] Ibid., 195–6.
[21] Ibid., 196.

can be tested, reconfigured, and adapted to fit a national musical style, much in the same way as in his teaching of composition he advocated molding aspects of contemporary German music practice into an inimitable English style. Style, focused around a national stereotyping, becomes the locus of Parry's exploration of the past, as shown by the passage that succeeds the extended contrast of masque music with Italian music-drama as a product of differing national characters:

> The English composers of masque music had a somewhat different problem to solve [than did composers of early Italian opera]. The masque was not a dramatic product at all, but an elegant and artificial entertainment composing a good deal of fanciful poetic dialogue, with lyrical songs and and groups of dances. The interest of the subject was not emotionally human at all, though there might be moments of human interest. What interest there was for the higher faculties was rather intellectual than emotional. The subtleties of art, the conceits of lively fancy were to be preferred to the soul-stirring story of passion or the deep interest of tragedy, so that the stage performance was altogether different from the subjects of the 'dramma per musica'. It required less dialogue and recitative and more of dainty and attractive separate movements. The English composers indeed seem to have been almost incapable of producing recitative of the Italian kind. Its lack of organization seems to have been uncongenial to their orderly temperaments, and even when they set out with a suggestively indefinite beginning they soon drifted into passages of definitely declamatory style, or passages of formal or rhythmic tune.[22]

The national stereotyping in this passage is striking. The masque becomes a representative genre not only for English musical style but also for English character. Not dramatic, the masque is elegant; its qualities rest in its subtlety and "lively fancy." It is an intellectual rather than an emotional genre. This is in contrast to *dramma per musica*'s emotionalism, passion, and tragic interest. Implicitly, Parry is outlining a national English character against a foreign "other," a characterization that he extended to the contemporary English national style in music which he was actively promoting in other areas of his work.

Though not alluding to it specifically, Parry is also addressing in this passage a key question raised by the history of English dramatic vocal music: the apparent dislike by both British composers and the British public of recitative cast in English, a problem which thwarted many an attempt throughout the eighteenth and nineteenth centuries to establish a "pure," English operatic tradition. By introducing a compositional "problem" that is related to a national

[22] Ibid., 197.

attitude toward music, and resolved by adaptation, Parry implicitly offers a solution for the problems faced by his contemporaries. He solves this historical problem by tracing the beginnings of what he sees as an English alternative to Italian-style recitative, the declamatory solo, which will ultimately – and, more importantly for Parry's ideological agenda – be taken up by Henry Purcell later in the seventeenth century.

In essence, Parry positions masque music as a genre that amalgamates a host of current English stylistic tendencies found in the seventeenth century – ordered, balanced, tuneful, and rhythmic, among others. These and other such stylistic tendencies he hoped would motivate and generate new English characteristics among his contemporaries. His use of characterizations of the past to implicitly model the present was extended towards other "English" genres and other English music from the past, applying evolutionary, forward momentum in other places. This process, however, was hardly natural or even universally evident, but instead one way in which the pattern of re-invention within English music historiography in general – and the English Musical Renaissance movement in particular – manifested itself. The cultural power of the forces surrounding and supporting the composers who have been grouped under the English Musical Renaissance heading – in their particular vision of a modern English music – was such that though other dissenting opinions appear in contemporary histories, the narrative favored by the English Musical Renaissance composers and their supporters gradually obscured them.

❧ *The Purcell Revival*

The third historiographic premise at stake in the acceptance of the masque as a national genre was the elevation of Henry Purcell to the status of the "greatest English composer" of the past. For the purposes of our discussion it should be enough that Purcell wrote masques, and thus provided an easy precedent for modern composers seeking to connect with the past. For British composers of the early twentieth century, just composing masques forged an implicit bond with Purcell, given the popularity of *Dido and Aeneas* and *King Arthur*. Indeed, Ralph Vaughan Williams relied on specifically Purcellian motives and turns of phrase in the songs that he provided for *Pan's Anniversary* for solo and chorus.[23] But again, as with the other historiographic issues already mentioned,

---

[23] A detailed description of *Pan's Anniversary* will appear in chapter 4. At this point it is enough to mention that the four songs, or hymns, contained in Ben Jonson's text were set by Vaughan Williams as solo or choral movements which in many ways mimic the patterns found in many of Purcell's odes. This is not all that surprising, since at the time Vaughan Williams was composing *Pan's Anniversary* he was also editing the Welcome Songs for the Purcell Edition.

the scholarly establishment of a connection between Purcell and the masque was less than straightforward. Examination of early Purcell scholarship reveals a very real anxiety about which repertories from which periods needed to be prioritized in the search for historical connections and the establishment of a national identity resting on a particular version of the past.

Parry wrote his volume on seventeenth-century music during a decade that witnessed a steady revival of Purcell's music, initiated by the 1895 bicentennial of the composer's death. Despite the assertions of some that heralded the "resurrection" of a forgotten and neglected national genius, Purcell actually is one of the few English composers to have had a continuous series of advocates throughout the eighteenth and nineteenth centuries.[24] The beginning of this tradition came with the inclusion of the *Te Deum* and *Jubilate* on the programs for benefit oratorio concerts. Several of Purcell's works were performed at the first concert series in London aimed at the preservation of a canon of musical classics, the Concerts of Ancient Music. *Dido and Aeneas* was given concert performance at the Academy of Ancient Music in 1774 and 1778, and portions of *King Arthur* and the *Indian Queen* in 1768. Records of performances of other Purcell works in concert have vanished, though it is possible that several of his verse anthems, such as "Thou Knowest Lord" and the "Bell" Anthem, continued to be part of the repertoire of particular cathedral choirs, and various solo songs were occasionally heard.

However, already in the late eighteenth century editors and publishers turned to Purcell's works with a view of canonizing him in print. The first, aborted, attempt at a complete edition, which included volumes containing *The Tempest* (mistakenly attributed to him for all of this period, and until the mid-twentieth century), *Indian Queen*, and excerpts from *King Arthur*, was made by Benjamin Goodison between 1788 and 1790. A more successful project was Novello's five-volume set of Purcell's sacred music in 1828–32. In the 1840s, the Musical Antiquarian Society, under the general editorship of Rimbault, issued new editions of *Dido and Aeneas*, *Bonduca*, *King Arthur*, and *Ode for St. Cecilia's Day*. Noteworthy in this publication history is the repeated appearance of editions of the key works for the masque: *King Arthur*, *The Tempest*, and *Dido and Aeneas*. Within Parry's lifetime, *Dido and Aeneas* was the most well-known and accessible of Purcell's stage works, with concert performances in 1878 at the Royal Academy, in 1888 by the Bach Choir, in 1889 by the Handel Society, and a fully staged version at the Royal College of Music in 1895, conducted by Stanford, in which Vaughan Williams and Holst participated. The Purcell Society was

----

[24] A more detailed discussion of Purcell's status as one of the first canonical composers in England during the eighteenth century is given in William Weber, *The Rise of Musical Classics in Eighteenth-Century England: a Study in Canon, Ritual, and Ideology* (Oxford: Clarendon Press, 1992).

founded in 1876, and began its landmark complete edition of Purcell's works in 1889. By 1900 fourteen volumes had been published, including *The Masque in Timon of Athens, Dioclesian, The Fairy Queen,* and *The Tempest.*

As the century drew to a close, the Purcell revival picked up momentum, culminating in the performances surrounding the bicentenary celebrations of the composer's death in 1895, including Parry's own *Invocation to Music: An Ode in Honour of Henry Purcell* with words by Robert Bridges. As mentioned above, on the first day of the festival the Royal College of Music staged *Dido and Aeneas.* The following day seven Purcell anthems were sung at an elaborate service at Westminster Abbey, and that evening the Philharmonic Society revived the *Ode for St. Cecilia's Day.* During the following months, Purcell was performed in a variety of venues, offering the opportunity for many to encounter his works for the first time.

However, despite this continued activity surrounding Purcell's music throughout the century, an anonymous editor of the *Monthly Musical Record* wrote in 1895:

> So much has been written, so much more is being written, about Purcell, his life, and his works, that we have no desire to weary our readers with a fresh account of them, differing from previous accounts only in language and in arrangement of petty detail. Further, the interest aroused in Purcell by the recent Commemoration concert seemed slight, transient, easily spent. It will slumber, we greatly fear, for another century at least, unless, indeed, sixty-three years from hence, while this generation sleeps its final sleep, some few ardent souls go out to keep sacred the three-hundredth anniversary of Purcell's birth. Meantime, we have no wish to act the part of the public conscience. The English have all but forgotten Purcell, and quite forgotten the greatness of the work he did. That is their loss, and theirs only. Purcell is secure; his work stands fast. And our object in thinking of him at the present moment is not to repeat the old, old stories, nor to reproach the public with their neglect of the subject of those stories; but to point, at a time when it is acknowledged that Purcell did achieve something, to a part of the secret of his artistic success. The major part of that secret was his genius, as all know who know Purcell.[25]

The writer of this editorial was able to voice his criticism of Purcellian philistines because of the perception that Purcell had been, up until this point, relegated to the status of a few well-rehearsed obligatory paragraphs in

---

[25] Anon., "Editorial," *Monthly Music Record,* 25 (1895), 300. Reprinted in Michael Burden's *Purcell Remembered* (Portland, OR: Amadeus Press, 1995), 146–7. Burden suggests that the anonymous writer of this editorial was J.R. Shedlock, the editor of the journal in 1895, and the editor of the Purcell Society's first edition of the *Fairy Queen.*

accounts of English music history, despite the ardent advocacy and editorial efforts of a few musical antiquarians. His views mocked those many for whom Purcell did not seem to represent a viable tradition, or a tradition in which the links to the musical present could override the historic particularities of a style so at odds with the terms of contemporary musical composition. Only ten years before his volume for the *Oxford History of Music*, in his 1893 *The Art of Music*, Parry framed his account of Purcell in the following terms:

> In the late phase of the madrigal period, which was almost exclusively centred in England, composers aimed at characteristic expression of the words far oftener than the great Italian masters had done; and they often showed that tendency towards realistic expression which Purcell carried to such an excess. Purcell was indeed the greatest music genius of his age, but his lines were cast in most unfortunate places. His circumstances put him completely out of touch with the choral methods of the great period; and the standards and models for the new style, and the examples of what could and what could not be done, were so deficient that his judgment went constantly astray; and in trying to carry out his ideals according to the principles of the 'new music' he occasionally achieves a marvellous stroke of real genius and not unfrequently falls into the depths of bathos and childishness. The experiments which he made in expression, under the same impulse as Schutz in church choral music, are quite astounding in crudeness and almost impossible to sing; while in secular solo music (where he is more often highly successful) he frequently adopts realistic devices of quaintly innocent kind, for lack of resources to utter otherwise his expressive intentions.[26]

However, Parry's views on Purcell went through a radical transformation over time. In the early 1890s, neither the writer for the *Monthly Music Record* nor Parry could have envisioned the ensuing utilization of Purcell as a harbinger and model by the succeeding generation of English Musical Renaissance composers. As mentioned in chapter 1, the very last page of Latham's book on the English renaissance of the sixteenth and seventeenth centuries included a passage which characterized composers such as Parry and Stanford as inheriting the mantle of the Golden Age, and reviving English music after its two-hundred-year sleep. As this idea of the musical renaissance caught on, due in large part to propaganda by Grove, Parry, and the younger generation of composers centered at the new Royal College of Music, Purcell became the terminal point of the Golden Age, and his death administered the prick on the finger of the Sleeping Beauty that was English music of the late seventeenth, eighteenth and early nineteenth centuries, now awakened by a

---

[26] C. Hubert Parry, *The Evolution of the Art of Music*, 2nd edn (London: D. Appleton-Century Co., 1930), 184.

host of kissing princes in the guise of composers such as Parry, Stanford, and Elgar. As such, Purcell no longer represented a great (though idiosyncratic) past, but informed the present and gave hope to the future as well. The older composer had to be constantly re-presented in performance and literature to enable the "renaissance men" to connect to his particularly English virtues.

Parry was the focus for early definitions of the English Musical Renaissance and its attendant reconfiguration of Purcell. Thus, ten years after the *Art of Music*, the terms of his account of Purcell in the *Oxford History of Music* came to echo the characterization of Purcell as England's "musical Shakespeare"[27] that became prevalent at the end of the nineteenth century and that celebrated above all his sensitive English text-setting, but also his adventurous harmonic palette, the virtuosic breadth of the genres in which he composed, and his role in integrating continental musical developments into a clearly English idiom:

> Purcell's work covers more ground than that of any other composer of the century. He attempted every brand of art then known, and even developed some which can hardly be said to have been known till he mastered them; and there was no department in which he did not excel. He easily learned the secrets of the composers who preceded him, and swept the methods of all different branches into his net. Though in some respects he seems to have more natural kinship with Monteverde [sic] than with any other composer, he was equally master of the instrumental style of the French Opera, the style of the Italian sonata-writers, and the methods of dealing with chorus which had been Carissimi's peculiar glory. Probably no composer except Schubert has ever had a readier fund of melody; and it always rings true and characteristic of the country to which he belonged.[28]

By 1902, Parry is asserting that Purcell is the most astounding musical genius of English music of the seventeenth century, perhaps of any century. But he does not see beyond Purcell to other English composers of the late seventeenth or early eighteenth centuries: "Purcell's genius had anticipated all that his contemporaries were capable of. Their work after he was gone was but the afterglow of an extraordinary outburst of musical energy in the country."[29]

Even given this glowing encomium of Purcell, and his esteem for his accomplishments, Parry's developmental model of history writing overshadows the

[27] The term can be traced to Charles Burney, though it well may have had general currency before Burney's comment. See R. Luckett, "'Or Rather Our Musical Shakespeare': Charles Burney's Purcell," in *Music in Eighteenth-Century England: Essays in Memory of Charles Cudworth*, ed. C. Hogwood and R. Luckett (Cambridge: Cambridge University Press, 1983), 59–77.

[28] C. Hubert H. Parry, *The Music of the Seventeenth Century*, 306–7.

[29] Ibid., 307.

merits of the individual composer. In Parry's view, it was precisely *because* Purcell was so extraordinary, indeed unique, that the promise inherent in English music up until the last years of the seventeenth century was unfulfilled:

> The tragic fact cannot be ignored, that the essentially English attitude towards art which Purcell represented in his highest achievements for church, concert room, or theatre, led to no ulterior development. Handel possibly profited by the example of his admirable and vigorous treatment of histrionic chorus-writing; but no one followed up the possibilities of his superb conception of scenes for solo voices. The most brilliant moment in the history of seventeenth-century music thus remained outside the general evolution of European art. The style was too individual and too uncompromising to appeal to foreigners, and the advance which, mainly owing to Purcell's genius, had seemed phenomenal, came to a sudden standstill at his death. At once virile and intense, marked by not a few points of doubtful taste, the English music of the last quarter of the seventeenth century remains a supremely interesting but isolated monument of unfulfilled promise.[30]

It is odd that despite an extended treatment of Purcell's music for theater, in which Parry places Purcell above contemporary Italian operatic composers for the quality of his recitative and declamation, he never once mentions that Purcell wrote masques, nor does he discuss the relationship between the Stuart court masque and Purcell's theatrical masques. Parry's only mention of the masque is the possible influence it might have had, along with French opera of the later seventeenth century, in the amount and types of dance music included in the repertory of the period. It is hard to understand Parry's glaring omission, given his extensive and favorable treatment of the masque in the preceding chapter.[31] He surely knew of the extended interpolated masque scenes in works such as *King Arthur* and *Dioclesian*, given the sheer amount of Restoration music he discusses in the course of this chapter. Moreover, the Purcell Society had produced several of Purcell's stage works in London by this time, some, such as the "Masque of Love" from *Dioclesian*, in celebrated productions directed by Gordon Craig.[32] Parry would certainly have known of these

---

[30] Ibid.

[31] Other contemporary histories do make this connection, though it is never an overt argument. Again, Henry Davey offers a contrast to Parry. See Henry Davey, *History of English Music*, 177.

[32] Craig's ultra-modernist productions of these Purcell masques were profoundly influential upon the history of modern theater design. The contrast between the "revivalist" aspect of the production and the modernist aesthetic that represented this revival warrants its own study. For an interesting treatment of aspects of Craig's historiographic interests in his productions, see Roger Savage's "'What About an

performances, reading of them in the musical press of the day, if not experiencing them firsthand as a member of the audience. The logical explanation is that these later masques did not fit into Parry's definition of the masque as the "court masque." Like Evans, this definition is colored by an inclination to link the masque genre with the earlier period in English musico-dramatic history, a period which as a whole could serve as a more appropriate model for contemporary times, despite the singular personality of Purcell.

The reason for this inclination must rest on the evolutionary model that is at the heart of Parry's history. Having placed the masque at a particular point in a certain line of development, Parry hesitated to revive a discussion of the masque in a completely different guise, especially since he did not see the possibility of further development in the type of masque that emerged within the context of Restoration semi-opera. Much of Parry's discussion of Restoration music hinges on the theory that Restoration music was both experimental and quixotic, in large part a product of a king who "as one of the most conspicuous prototypes of modern fashionable society, insisted on being amused."[33] Parry stresses the importance of new purposes for music, and especially in his discussion of church music he details the ways in which Purcell and the others of his generation avoided the older, traditional genres of English music. To then detail the continuance of one of these genres, such as the masque, and one so different in form from the prototypical court masque, might have undermined his argument.

But Parry also succumbs to a scholarly idealization in his wish to keep the masque in an older time, the noble epoch of Shakespeare and Jonson, rather than the debased era of Dryden and Nahum Tate. England after Cromwell became a modern nation, more mercantile, expanding in wealth and power, a colonial, and soon to be imperial nation far different from the "Golden Age" of Elizabeth. A form of sentiment, conscious or otherwise, seeps into the manner in which Parry charts the evolution of English music. Parry tinged his evolutionary ideas with an urge to glance backwards affectionately at certain genres, thus saving them from the gradual dissipation that he detects in English music during the eighteenth and most of the nineteenth centuries. In this sense, Parry evinced a certain connection with Evans; both historians chose to keep the masque at a greater historical distance from the present rather than retell the actual facts of the genre's history after the Restoration. Increasingly the masque was given an idealized place in English history.

English Ballet?' Edward Gordon Craig, Music-Theatre and *Cupid and Psyche*," in *Masques, Mayings and Music-Dramas: Vaughan Williams and the Early Twentieth-Century Stage* (Woodbridge: The Boydell Press, 2014), 165–221.

[33] Parry, *The Music of the Seventeenth Century*, 307.

❧ *Masque Historiography and the Folk*

Parry offers one final theoretical distinction between English and Italian dramatic music during the first half of the seventeenth century, the kernel of which will be seized upon with a vengeance in the following decade:

> The features which mark most strongly the difference between the music of the English masques and Italian 'dramma per musica' are the lyrical songs. These are indeed complete but simple ditties, similar in style to many in the song books (of lute songs) discussed above. Their character is obviously derived from folk-songs. The English composers in this respect went through not the tortuous process to arrive at a concrete organization, such as is met with in the Italian aria. For the purposes of the masque the typical folk-song supplied organization enough; and, as it proved, infinitely greater elasticity and richer possibilities of immediate expression than the formal Italian aria. Such artistic little folk-songs seemed to have formed the most definitely attractive points in the music of the masques.[34]

Accounts of the folk music movement in England written prior to 1980 often exaggerated the importance of Cecil Sharp's initial folksong collecting in 1903 and the subsequent publication of his seminal *Folk Songs of England* in 1907, pointing to Sharp as the crusader who was responsible for the impact the folk movement would have on English musical life over the following forty or so years.[35] It is important to remember, however, that the Folk Song Society and the publication of its journal began in 1898, and that Parry was a member of its first board of directors along with Stanford, Stainer, Mackenzie and Lucy Broadwood. By this time there already existed a core of people who had been actively collecting and publishing folk songs for many years, including Frank Kidson, who in 1891 published *Traditional Tunes,* and Lucy Broadwood and J.A. Fuller Maitland, whose *English County Songs* appeared in 1893. Richard Sykes states that one of the most intensive attempts to formulate an English national musical idiom can be located in this group of folk song enthusiasts, who felt that in folk song was expressed certain of the most basic musical qualities that could be identified as typically "English."[36] Throughout the 1890s this idea

---

[34] Ibid., 200–1.

[35] This is particularly true of histories of the folk movement written by people involved in Sharp's organization, the English Folk Dance Society, and invested in perpetuating the Sharp myth. This includes Vaughan Williams, but also people like Maud Karpeles and Douglas Kennedy. More on the "political" aspects of the folk movement is offered by Georgina Boyes, *The Imagined Village: Culture, Ideology, and the English Folk Revival* (Manchester: Manchester University Press, 1993).

[36] See Richard Sykes, "The Evolution of Englishness in the English Folksong Revival, 1890–1914," *Folk Music Journal* 6 (1993), 446–90.

spread rapidly throughout the British musical community. While Parry never seriously advocated a heavy reliance on folk music, despite his work for the Folk Music Society, he and his fellow "renaissance men" quickly realized that a way of attaining the goal of creating a new, nationalistic school of composition overlapped significantly with those searching for typically English elements in the folk song. To this end, Parry was happy to provide his support.

A new-found interest in English folk songs was invigorated by Parry's interest in what he, in keeping with contemporary scholarly accounts, termed "primitive music," a term that reflects evolutionary views of history. Parry's first book, *The (Evolution of the) Art of Music* – the "evolution" part of the title added to the second edition, in a sense clarifying Parry's methodology – begins with a chapter entitled "Preliminaries," which neatly fits into one discussion the music of "primitive" cultures, folk music, and medieval music as one package of sources for the Western art music tradition. Jeremy Dibble proposes that Parry gained his interest in the links between ethnography and music from such sources as Spencer's essay "The Origin and Function of Music" (1857) and a later article on evolution and music in *Mind* (1890), as well as Edward Burnett Taylor's *Primitive Culture* (1871), which Parry had read in 1885. But these are also the years of the publication of the first volumes of James Frazer's *The Golden Bough*, and while there is no proof that Parry read any Frazer during the 1890s, the issues and interests aroused by *The Golden Bough* were certainly circulating throughout Parry's circle of friends and could very well have been found within his wide general reading.[37] Several possible prospects within Frazer's work may have influenced Parry and his successors in melding history and folk in musical historiography. First, certainly, is the endemic fascination at the turn of the century with the "primitive," partially a result of having to conceptualize the indigenous people of their expanding empire for the British of the Victorian period.[38] A related issue for Great Britain in particular is how, for Frazer, the "primitive" offered a safe haven for the projection of – and engagement with – social and psychological issues too uncomfortable to acknowledge openly in Victorian society. As so many Victorian scholars did, Frazer depended on displacement. For instance, Robert Fraser discusses *The Golden Bough*'s popularity as aided by the Victorian love

[37] The first edition of James Frazer's *The Golden Bough* appeared in two volumes in 1890, and was expanded into a three-volume edition in 1900. Frazer continued throughout the rest of his life adding detail to detail – the third edition contained twelve volumes published between 1907 and 1928. That Frazer's impulse through these editions is additive rather than revisionary is itself an important key to the comparative method.

[38] This topic is explored by Marianne Torgovnik in her *Gone Primitive: Savage Intellects, Modern Lives* (Chicago: Chicago University Press, 1990).

of indirectness, a feature in Frazer's work that allowed him to discuss the horrible and horrifying, but only obliquely.[39]

More mundane, but perhaps a more concrete influence, was Frazer's utilization and popularization of the "comparative method" of historical anthropology, a method prevalent during the late nineteenth century. The comparative method draws heavily on induction and imagination, and constitutes a creative, almost literary, approach to join elements across cultures – as well as across time – to arrive at parallels and, finally, to parse out the common source of those parallels.[40] So while readers in the twenty-first century may wince at Parry's marriage of supposed parallels in European folk music, medieval music, and the music of non-Western cultures under the broad umbrella-like term of "primitive" music, these were the years in which the search for national identity often turned to the search for sources located away from contemporary urban realities, towards the far reaches of a purer past, uncontaminated by the accretions of the modern world. The primitive, surviving as traces in present-day folk customs, joined history as a locus for a national idealization.[41]

Again, though, Parry's approach to historiography has broader implications for how he and his students such as Vaughan Williams and Holst projected their mission as self-conscious musical nationalists. It is not difficult to see the extension of this "comparative method" to embrace the forging of connections not just in the past, but also between the past and the present, as the younger

[39] Robert Fraser, "The Face beneath the Text: Sir James Frazer in his Time," in
Sir James Frazer and the Literary Imagination, ed. Robert Fraser (London:
Macmillan Press, 1990), 1–17, here 5). A passage from Anthony Powell's *A Dance
to the Music of Time: Second Movement: At Lady Molly's* (Chicago, 1995, 211),
quoted by Byron Adams in his essay on Elgar's Enigma Variations (Byron Adams,
"The 'Dark Saying' of the Enigma: Homoeroticism and the Elgarian Paradox,"
19th-Century Music, 23 (2000), 218–35) seems particularly apropos: "Lady
Warminster represented to a high degree that characteristic of her own generation
that everything may be said, though nothing indecorous discussed openly. Layer
upon layer of wrapping, box after box revealing in the Chinese manner yet another
box, must conceal all doubtful secrets; only the discipline of infinite obliquity
made it lawful to examine the seamy side of life. If these mysteries were observed
everything might be contemplated: however unsavory: however unspeakable.

[40] For more on Frazer's impact on contemporary thought, as well as a detailed
discussion of the nineteenth and early twentieth century ideas connected to it, see
John B. Vickery, *The Literary Impact of The Golden Bough* (Princeton: Princeton
University Press, 1973). And for an in-depth discussion of Frazer's connection to
Victorian anthropology, there is Gillian Beer, "Speaking for the Others: Relativism
and Authority in Victorian Anthropological Literature," in *Sir James Frazer and the
Literary Imagination*, 38–60.

[41] These ideas will receive a fuller treatment in chapter 4.

generation of Parry's students searched for identity through the models of the past. It is perhaps the imaginative and creative aspect of these comparative links which allowed for the easy and relatively unsystematic appearance of source material from art and folk musics of the past in scores from this period, such as that of *Pan's Anniversary*.

In 1903, a year after Parry's volume in the *Oxford History of Music* appeared, E.K. Chambers published his influential monograph *The Mediaeval Stage*.[42] In his preface, Chambers outlines his own evolutionary model of history, this time with regard to English drama, a model which firmly takes into account the roots of art in the folk.

> [This reflects] a very deep interest in the track across the ages of certain customs and symbols of rural gaiety which bear with them the inheritance of a remote and ancestral heathenism ... The first book shows how the organisation of the Graeco-Roman theatre broke down before the onslaught of Christianity and the indifference of barbarism, and how the actors became wandering minstrels, merging with the gleemen of their Teutonic conquerors entertaining all classes of medieval society with spectacula in which the dramatic element was of the slightest and in the end, coming to a practical compromise with the hostility of the church. In the second book I pass to spectacula of another type, which also had to struggle against church disfavour, and which also made their ultimate peace with all but the most austere forms of the dominant religion. These are the ludi of the village feasts, bearing witness not only to their origin in heathen ritual, but also, by their constant tendency to break out into primitive forms of drama, to the deep-rooted mimetic instinct of the folk. The third book is a study of the process by which the church itself, through the introduction of dramatic elements into its liturgy, came to make its own appeal to this same mimetic instinct; and of that by which form such beginnings, grew up the great popular religious drama of the miracle plays, with its offshoots in the moralities and the dramatic pageants. The fourth and final book deals summarily with the transformation of the medieval stage, on the literary side, under the influence of humanism, on the social and economic side by the emergence from amongst the ruins of minstrelsy of a new class of professional players, in whose hands the theatre was destined to recover a stable organization upon lines which had been departed from since the days of Tertullian.[43]

Likewise, Chambers's chapter discussing the masque is entitled "Masques and Misrule," a title that hints at his wider interpretation of the genre and

---

[42] E.K. Chambers, *The Mediaeval Stage* (Oxford: Oxford University Press, 1903), esp. 390–419.

[43] Ibid., v–vi.

its connection to both folk sources and history through connections to Christmas revels throughout English history. Chambers extends the masque to a time long before the Elizabethan and Stuart court masque, linking it to a wide variety of occasions involving dancing, such as the entry of anonymous costumed visitors ("mummers") with a modicum of drama. His discussion ranges from the country custom of mumming, the "disguisings" and wearing of hoods during the medieval Christmas season, to the court pageants of the Tudors. Fundamental to this extended conception of the masque are the folk customs associated with Christmas, the Lord of Misrule and the Feast of Fools. Typical is the following passage:

> The 'mumming' or 'disguising', then, as it took shape at the beginning of the sixteenth century, was form of court revel, in which, behind the accretions of literature and pageantry, can be clearly discerned a nucleus of folk-custom in the entry of the band of worshippers, with their sacrificial *exuviae*, to bring the house good luck.[44]

Though Chambers's volume contains all the paraphernalia of the historian, with extensive footnotes and quotes from primary source material, it is the less than purely "historical" identification of a Frazer-like root for tradition that motivates Chambers's interest in the masque. That this foundation of the folk is a national one is unquestionably important, though implied. Interestingly, Chambers seizes on the same passage in Edward Hall's 1513 account mentioned in Evans's history, in which the chronicler calls the masque "after the manner of Italie," that concerned Evans. He offers a different explanation than Evans, however, who ascribed the new element to the dancing between the masquers and the audience. Chambers had already proven in his chapter that such dancing can be traced back to folk customs, so he therefore offers the possible solution that the "Italian" element was the wearing of dominoes. This further removes the threat of Italian influence, at the same time further linking the Tudor pageant to a folk source.

Chambers's innovative application of Frazer's ideas regarding primitive ritualistic drama, merged with an evolutionary historiographical methodology, is symptomatic of a new set of concerns on the part of cultural historians around the turn of the century. The use of such methodologies extends far beyond the attempt to derive a theory of the development of medieval drama.[45] Concerning the masque specifically, the synthetic approach of this

---

[44] Ibid., 400.

[45] It is important here to mention in particular the work of a group of Oxbridge classicists, the "Cambridge Ritualists," who sought to apply Frazer and other similar proto-anthropological approaches to Greek culture, particularly Greek drama. The group was led by Jane Ellen Harrison, but also included Gilbert Murray, who, with

type of cultural historian mediated the tension created by the conflict between derivations and influences in attempts to define peculiarly English qualities of the masque genre and to adopt them as vehicles for the assertion of a link between an English past and present. For English music even more broadly, such an approach sidestepped the issue of the supposed lack of a continuous national musical tradition by finding continuity through a national character traceable to (and ultimately located in) the distant, and thus "purer," past. This approach contrasts with the more usual methods present in general histories of European music, where musicologists continued to create narratives which predominantly establish a continuous strand of artistic inheritance and development.

ꙮ The "New" Generation of the English Musical Renaissance: Vaughan Williams's Early Writings

The writings of Hubert Parry and the ideas and attitudes towards both music and nationalism that underpinned them represent a transitional phase. Parry's assumptions and theories articulate a position somewhere between the prerogatives of the rapidly waning Victorian period and the demands of the modern age. The tensions and contradictions regarding history, nationalism, and popular culture revealed in Parry's writings were difficult to resolve for a man molded by Victorian ideology and idealism. By the beginning of the twentieth century, Parry was at the peak of his popularity but his views were beginning to be perceived in certain circles as old-fashioned. The synthesis of nationalism, art music, and folk culture in English music and musical historiography necessarily arose from younger composers and musicologists more convinced of the need for a fresh and self-consciously "national" compositional style and less invested in retaining the divisions between art and traditional musics. This is not to say that younger composers were willing to espouse contemporary popular music in their new appreciation for traditional popular music. Nor were the modern, particularly urban, lower classes any less a problematic factor than they were during the second half of the nineteenth century. In

Francis Cornford, later commissioned Vaughan Williams to write the incidental music for his production of *The Wasps*. Roger Savage has convincingly argued for Vaughan Williams's marginal connection with this group, and for the influence of its approach on such works as *Hugh the Drover*. I would extend Savage's points to say that his kind of approach to linking literary and dramatic tropes with the folk and mythic past permeates much of the masque literature, and indeed has deeper relevance for the folk revival as a whole. Roger Savage, "Vaughan Williams, the Romany Ryes, and the Cambridge Ritualists," in *Masques, Mayings and Music-Dramas: Vaughan Williams and the Early Twentieth-Century Stage*, 304–58.

fact, the "authenticity" of traditional folk culture was seen as an antidote to the reality of contemporary class conflict.

The most influential, and perhaps the most representative, example of these kinds of new synthetic trends in English music historiography during the first years of the twentieth century can be found in the writings of Parry's pupil, Ralph Vaughan Williams.[46] Early in his career, Vaughan Williams assumed the role of an articulate and passionate advocate for folk song, which he considered one of the prerequisites for the rebirth of an English musical style. He became a primary spokesperson for the necessity of the general public to be educated to appreciate the historical and folk music of England. To do so required that he develop a newly consolidated view of the sources of English music.

As early as 1902, Vaughan Williams began writing essays on musical topics for periodicals, beginning with a set of nine articles published in *The Vocalist* on a wide range of topics including Palestrina, Beethoven, Bach, Wagner, Schumann, and Brahms.[47] Significantly, the first of these articles was entitled "A School of English Music."[48] This particular subject was to become the most important of the topics that recurred in his writings throughout his life.[49] In this concise essay, Vaughan Williams discussed the possibility of a contemporary new school of English composers, the characteristics of which he would compare in his later writings to the musical culture of the Tudor period. For the young composer, the old was already serving as a model for the new. These early articles, considered together with the set of university extension lectures on English music history given by the composer beginning in 1902, reveal that Vaughan Williams had formed strong views about the music of England's past – and what sort of music should constitute England's future – at the beginning of his career. But as of yet, none of these early articles evinces a consistent approach to English music of the past. Within just a few years, however, folk song would dominate Vaughan Williams's theories about the proper sources of English national character, musical and otherwise. At the same time, these early articles and lectures do demonstrate that by 1902 the composer certainly had begun to formulate a historical awareness of and appreciation for the

---

[46] For an overview of Vaughan Williams's writing across his lifetime and a large number of reprinted essays, see David Manning's edition of his writings, *Vaughan Williams on Music* (Oxford: Oxford University Press, 2008).

[47] Julian Onderdonk has analyzed these articles from the perspective of his views of folk music in "Vaughan Williams's Folksong Transcriptions: a Case of Idealization?," in *Vaughan Williams Studies*, ed. Alain Frogley (Cambridge: Cambridge University Press, 1996), 118–38.

[48] *The Vocalist*, 1, 8.

[49] This is true as late as 1954, in the series of lectures given at Cornell University and published as *The Making of Music* (Ithaca: Cornell University Press).

significance of past musics. Such an awareness derived from his background and education. Coming from a comfortable liberal and intellectual family (his mother's uncle was Charles Darwin)[50] where his musical studies were barely tolerated, he took a degree from Cambridge in European history and further developed his interest in music history by attending Parry's lectures. After obtaining a doctoral degree in music from Cambridge in 1899, his first job as a church choir conductor in London prodded him to explore more of the repertoire of English church music, including a large component of sixteenth- and seventeenth-century polyphonic music. Of course, this was the period of the revival of interest in Byrd and Purcell, whose music profoundly appealed to the young composer. His immersion in concepts of historiography – both musical and otherwise – challenged him to take history into account when developing theories about the correct sources of a national music, beyond one which would rest solely on the bedrock of the prehistorical folk.

By 1914, over ten years after *The Vocalist* articles and after the successes of the *Songs of Travel*, *Toward the Unknown Region*, and the *Sea Symphony*, the composer arrived at a tentative reconciliation of this tension between historical and folk music. He effected this uneasy reconciliation through a redefinition of Tudor music – its boundaries, its sources, and its description of genres. The composition of the *Fantasia on a Theme by Thomas Tallis* came in 1910, a pivotal work in Vaughan Williams's oeuvre because it furthers the compositional project initiated by the use of historical models in *Pan's Anniversary* and the incidental music for *Pilgrim's Progress*. Following this productive period, the composer supplied a four-part series on the topic of English music history for the periodical *The Music Student*.[51] Written for an audience of non-specialists, Vaughan Williams's articles do not offer a complete or even a necessarily chronological survey, but instead suggest that the reader explore the oeuvres of a handful of composers and specific important works. Within these suggestions are liberally sprinkled the author's own views on their importance for English composers and audiences today.

In his first article, in rhetoric reminiscent of his teacher Parry, Vaughan Williams's central concern is with the search for a distinctive national character. He discovers aspects of it by invoking the idea of a man "naturally

---

[50] Byron Adams has offered an insightful discussion of the impact of Vaughan Williams's family and upbringing on his future views in "Scripture, Church, and Culture: Biblical Texts in the Works of Ralph Vaughan Williams," in *Vaughan Williams Studies*, 99–117.

[51] *The Music Student*, 7 1–4 (1914): "Foundation of a National Art", 7, 1 (Sep. 1914), 5–7; "British Music in the Tudor Period", 7, 2 (Oct. 1914), 25–7; "Age of Purcell", 7, 3 (Nov. 1914), 47–8: and "British Music in the Eighteenth and Early Nineteenth Centuries", 7, 4 (Dec. 1914), 63–4.

and spontaneously expressing himself musically," but stipulates that this man must be "removed by circumstance from all extraneous and factitious influences, so that we can be sure that his self-expression is genuine and spontaneous. To achieve this he must be unlettered (this is not the same as illiterate), un-travelled; he must live among those to whom his expression would be intelligible – that is to say, he must be in a homogeneous community." In other words, Vaughan Williams's "natural man" belongs to the organic village, following the folk custom of his ancestors unsullied by the modern world. While he quickly posits the importance of folk song as a basis for national music, folk song also serves as a touchstone for the art music of the distant past. Vaughan Williams admits that not all of the good music of the past derives from folk song, so he argues that popular music is an expression of the natural man as well. This allows him to make connections between art and popular music, pointing to just such connections in the works of canonic English composers like Dunstable, Morley, and Purcell. By constructing an argument of this type, he proposes for both art music and folk music similar abilities to reveal the inherent national character.

In the second article, he discerns further connections between art music and folk music in a more specific way. Vaughan Williams strikingly suggests that the problem with much English art music is its tendency to separate art from popular music. Such an unhealthy separation causes much English art music, especially more recent music, to fail its most primary mission: to reflect the national character. Composers of art music thus abdicate their responsibility to speak to their nation, impeding the renaissance of English music in the twentieth century. Here Vaughan Williams turns to the Tudor period, holding it up as the model for the future: "Only once in its musical history has England had a school of composers. It has had great men who appeared and disappeared like meteors and left no trace behind (Dunstable, Purcell, Wesley), but a great composer may appear in a barren land as a sport of Nature: a school of composers implies a nation saturated through and through with music."[52] Vaughan Williams ascribes the development of this supposed school of Tudor composers to three factors. Two are reasonable enough: the Renaissance spirit as manifested in the secular madrigal, and the Anglican church as a national organization that required new kinds of religious music. The third factor, however, is perhaps more unusual and intriguing. Vaughan Williams believed that the composers of Tudor church music made a connection between popular music and religious music through the metrical psalm and hymn tune. He writes of the "gradual approximation of the music of the learned scholars and the music of the people" or, to put it plainly, the use by the

---

[52] *The Music Student*, "British Music in the Tudor Period" (Oct. 1914), 25–7.

Tudor school of folk and other popular songs as a source of musical gestures through which they adapted the cosmopolitan style of continental composers. He posits the hypothesis that "in Elizabethan times there was a 'folk' revival (or rather Evolution) similar to that which is taking place in England now. It is evident that Elizabethan composers and their public were well acquainted with English folk-song."[53]

By developing this hypothesis, Vaughan Williams links folk music and Tudor music in a definitive way through his idiosyncratic historical methodology, asserting that art music was in a continual process of assimilating folk and popular music during the sixteenth and seventeenth centuries. He blurs the distinctions between art, folk, and popular music by considering them approximations of one another, analogizing not just their content but ultimately the national character. While many of those opposed to Vaughan Williams's theories could mount arguments about the relevance of folk music for a modern musical style, pointing to distinctions between high and low musical culture, Vaughan Williams dismisses the very foundation of these distinctions, making both musical cultures equal as plausible sources for the English Music Renaissance of the twentieth century.

By 1914, the date of Vaughan Williams's articles for *The Music Student*, the four historiographic preconditions set out at the beginning of this chapter – the identification of the masque as a genre with purely English sources; the identification of this genre as one that competed on equal terms with new musical innovations on the continent during the seventeenth century; the forged connection with Henry Purcell as the primary forerunner of the new movement in English music; and the incorporation of the folk into a conception of viable source material – had been met. These hypotheses had become incorporated in the aesthetics and ideologies of composers identified as ascribing to the idea of an English Musical Renaissance. Though masque scholarship could be viewed as scholarly, narrow, and parochial – hardly a topic of national importance – each of these preconditions had a nationalistic component. Some scholars of the masque were certainly caught up in asserting a new status for English music past and present. Endeavors to resolve these issues strained to determine a proper relationship of English music and English composers to history, and strove to discover how sources were to be selected and prioritized, as well as how and when English music acquired its national character. Ultimately, however, this musical discourse participated in the broad debate which characterized many disciplines and discourses in fin-de-siècle Britain, all seeking to establish the terms of national identity and the connections of this identity to the past.

---

[53] Ibid., 27.

This obviously is not to deny an interest in modernism among writers, artists, and composers. Chapters 5 and 6 will both look at how modernism was offered as a means of resistance against the dominant discourses that privileged the past. But it would be hard to argue that modernism ultimately offered a serious challenge to the nostalgia seeming to permeate artistic representations of English national identity during the late nineteenth and early twentieth centuries. Thus historiography, though academic, in many ways was the central activity of cultural discourse in England during this period, and hence the terms of its construction are of crucial importance.

CHAPTER 4

Making the Commonwealth a Harmony: The Masque, the Folk Revival and Pageant Culture

Shepherd: And come you prime Arcadians forth, that taught
By Pan the rites of true society.
From his loud music all your manners wrought,
And made your commonwealth a harmony.
Commending so to all posterity
Your innocence from that fair fount of light,
As still you sit without the injury
Of any rudeness folly can, or spite;
Dance from the top of the Lycaean mountain
Down to this valley, and with nearer eye
Enjoy what long in that illumined fountain
You did far off, but yet with wonder, spy.

(*Pan's Anniversary*, lines 137–48)

THIS investigation has thus far identified two differentiated strains of "re-invention" for the masque prior to 1905: the first traces actual composition in theatrical and choral music while the second follows the development of a concept of the masque in the past as reflected in historical studies. What we might denote as the "masque as praxis," aimed to recreate a genre that would tap into an already energetic and forceful strain of nostalgia mixing spectacle and patriotism in a way that would appeal to a popular audience. Such cantata masques and theatrical masques – whether occasional or embedded into larger dramatic narratives – grew in popularity as part of a complex of representational topics that celebrated what I have called the "Jacobethan" period; a perceived golden age nebulously situated in the England of the late sixteenth and early seventeenth centuries. These celebrations – which are today echoed in village fetes all over England – were replete with May Days and Robin Hood, comical villagers, and interventions of Elizabeth Regina herself.

The second strain, "masque as historical object," fashioned the genre (particularly the masque works of the sixteenth and seventeenth centuries) into a narrative of origins and developments. By doing so, literary and music historians "re-invented" the masque of the Renaissance and Early Modern period through patterning fact and perceived fact into a representation which could be made to resonate with contemporary concerns of nationalism and national identity. Underneath scholarly preoccupations with sources and influences, masque historiography contributed to the establishment of an accepted canon of historical sources appropriate for representations of English national character. While writings from the nineteenth century excavated the early Renaissance for the origins of the masque, by the turn of the century folklore and native folk traditions were considered central to the perceived English nature of the genre. For some writers these traditions assumed an anthropological dimension, at times a mythic proportion, reflecting the considerable influence of Frazer's writings on many areas of proto-anthropology and cultural history during the first years of the twentieth century.

Though these two separate strands in the re-invention of the masque remained separate prior to 1900, using very different forms and materials and addressing very different audiences, both types of revivalist activity surrounding the masque began to be combined in the early years of the twentieth century. They began to be connected through an underlying reliance on various functions of nostalgia that drew upon emerging English attitudes towards the relationship between fraught national identity and the nation's past. Nostalgia as an attitude has always been inextricably linked to the uses of history, whether public or private. The distancing effect of nostalgia works paradoxically to assure the present moment of progress, yet also to heighten the sense that something has been irreconcilably lost in the translation of past to present.[1] This paradox cannot be easily resolved into a cohesive attitude, but rather flourishes in the slippery areas between a longing for aspects of the past and a certain satisfaction when contemplating the present. While nostalgia seems to assert a discontinuity with the past, from another perspective it asserts reassuringly that "this was once us, and so we still are," particularly valuable on the level of national identity.

The two strains of masque re-invention are further connected in that they identified concrete and transferable textual, musical, and spectacular elements associated with the masque that could be represented and reproduced repeatedly. These masque types could be inserted as iconic moments into a wide variety of frames and accompanied by an ever-expanding load of ideological baggage. These iconic moments operated as spectacle, as a conglomerate of elements that heightened a visual and aural conception of the past. At some point, through reification, they gradually assumed the force of truth. So the

---

[1] This point is made in Malcolm Chase and Christopher Shaw, "The Dimensions of Nostalgia," in *The Imagined Past: History and Nostalgia*, ed. Christopher Shaw and Malcolm Chase (Manchester: Manchester University Press, 1989), 1–17.

past became thatched roofs, not slate, half-timbered houses, not brick, and Renaissance madrigals and lute songs, not Italian opera.

Where the two types of re-invented masque differed, however, were in audience. Choral and theatrical works that utilized the transformed aspects of the masque were generally oriented towards a popular audience in ways that scholarly, historiographical accounts of the masque were not. However, within masque productions that took place during the Edwardian period, the uses of history became increasingly multifarious.[2] Audiences attending new kinds of popular entertainments witnessed historicized versions of the masque outlined by historians and musicologists. Audiences were not merely passive spectators at such performances, but increasingly became participants in the re-enactment of the past, since during this period there occurred a proliferation of masques for community participation. Thus a kind of "pageant culture" was invented. By this method, the public actually participated in the performance of history and by doing so interiorized the historical ideologies of the period in an even more effective way. A work such as *Pan's Anniversary*, for example, performed in large part by amateurs and aimed at an audience from varied class and cultural backgrounds, mixed together the historiographical and the performative strands of masque performance from the nineteenth century, re-presenting a masque from the past in association with all of the modern spectacular elements that the genre had accrued during the previous century.

To understand how the masque was shaped by these developments, it is necessary to examine the means by which Vaughan Williams, Holst, and other members of the second generation of the English Musical Renaissance adapted and modified the sources of the new English nationalism through their contact with larger cultural forces at work. Many commentators have discussed the crucial encounter with the "folk" for Vaughan Williams and many other composers of his generation. However, this chapter will look more closely at how the folk movement transformed the English Musical Renaissance by developing a new, perhaps more practical view of history for a national musical style. This new view lent itself to representations of Englishness that eschewed the overtly patriotic and subverted the imperial, preferring that of the "organic village." During the Edwardian period there was a clear move by the composers associated with the English Musical Renaissance to link folk music with a conception of English art music of the past as the appropriate source material for a national music. At the same time, many of these composers discerned that there was something lacking in history and folk culture as mere topics

---

[2] A topic that is much too large to discuss here – it is enough to note that this trend was discernable across the wider arena of cultural production during the period, in everything from literature to architecture.

for visual and textual spectacles of nostalgic indulgence. The actual musical language and structures underlying these sources had to be incorporated for the music to be both nationally and emotionally "authentic." However, underlying all of the importance given to folk music within the nationalistic ideologies of the English Musical Renaissance is the new solidarity between versions of English national identity and emerging conceptions of folk culture and the ideal of the "organic village."

✤ Living in the "Village"

The notion of the "organic village" (or the "organic community") was an integral part of the ideology of the movement that has come to be called the folk revival. Simply, a vision of an "organic village" describes an idealized agricultural English community, self-sufficient and still tied to traditional ways and means. The concept contains a historical aspect: it is only to be found in rural English communities prior to the supposed ravages of the industrial revolution, a countryside whose populace was not yet polluted by the contamination of mass culture and modern urban values. This historical construct surrounding the concept contains within it many ideological overtones, as it embraces presumptions about folk culture, popular culture, class hierarchies, and national and cultural renewal.

The term is most frequently associated with F.R. Leavis and the writings contained in the journal *Scrutiny*, beginning in the 1930s.[3] However, the emergence of the organic village as a common topic in literature, music, drama, and art began much earlier in the nineteenth century, as soon as the first effects of industrialization began to make themselves felt. Images of rural utopia appear in certain of Wordsworth's poems in the late eighteenth century, and in Blake, and multiply as the century progresses in such authors as George Eliot and Thomas Hardy. English national identity was increasingly located in an idealized version of the rural, agricultural countryside, especially in the southern counties. This was further supported by the increasing tendency for the English to deny the priorities of a modern, industrial, and imperialistic

---

[3] F.R. Leavis (1895–1978), one of the most influential literary critics of the twentieth century, was totally invested in creating and upholding a carefully constructed canon of English literature, present and past, through a combination of a new critical type of close analysis and moral imperative. He was editor and co-founder of the influential journal *Scrutiny*, 1932–53. Particularly disdainful of mass culture and modern society, he looked to the past for the roots of English society, language, and its literary strengths, located in the organic village, a term he helped to popularize. For this aspect of his theories, *Mass Civilization and Minority Culture* (1930) remains his central work.

culture which had dominated the first half of the century and had accounted for Britain's current world position, in favor of one rooted instead in the "organic village."

Ironically enough, by the beginning of the twentieth century, just when the cult of the "organic village" as the center of English national identity was on the rise, especially among artists and intellectuals, it was generally understood that the real "organic village" no longer existed. While authors like Eliot and Hardy felt they could connect with some kind of timeless rural society, albeit a threatened one, by 1900 such a vision of rural England existed only as an exercise in nostalgia. Increasingly defining the village against a monstrous modern, urban "other," the folk song enthusiasts strove to save rural or folk culture from disappearance. Yet this attempt on the part of the revivalists only added to the circular dimension of nostalgia by increasingly idealizing that culture, emphasizing its distance from the present and thereby blinding the revivalists to the reality of that culture as it still existed. The first decades of the twentieth century in Britain were dominated by a vision of England that was no longer attainable, the vestiges of which, however, needed to be fiercely and energetically collected and systematized so that the remnants could be held in trust for the nation, "returned to the people as a whole," the revivalists said. To compound the irony, the "folk" – easily seduced by the blandishments of popular culture – could no longer be trusted to embody and perpetuate rural traditions, so these traditions must be extracted from them in whatever form they remained and put into the safekeeping of the intellectual and artistic elite.[4]

From several different aspects this nostalgia for the life of the rural folk provided a contrast to the other, less benign constructions of Englishness – such as imperialism and unbridled capitalism. The "organic village" version of England was not the center of an ever-extending world empire, incorporating many peoples and their cultural identities and traditions.[5] Some in England during this period believed that England had lost its way as a nation by assuming an imperial path, with all of its attendant global concerns. "Little Englanders" believed that the focal point of national policies should be located within England herself, that "little island," and seek national renewal from within. Instead of an England bent on worldwide domination, a strictly local

[4] Georgina Boyes effectively makes this point in chapter 2 of *The Imagined Village: Culture, Ideology, and the English Folk Revival* (Manchester: Manchester University Press, 1993). And while we may be duly suspicious of the ideological motivations for the sudden intense interest in folk traditions during the first decades of the twentieth century, it must also be noted that these musical traditions would have indeed been lost without the laborious efforts of these folk song collectors.

[5] A more extended treatment can be found in Grainger's chapter 10, "Little England," in *Patriotisms* (London: Routledge & Kegan Paul, 1986).

identity was posited by exploiting a version of Englishness that was assembled from an amalgamation of myths and beliefs surrounding the historical and folk cultures of the "shires." The image of the "organic village" for them reduced Englishness to a single defining set of characteristics that exploited the countryside of the southern and central counties of England as the repository of an authentic national consciousness.

The effect of this brand of nationalist ideology was to disenfranchise a large segment of the British population, particularly those located in the North of England which contained many of England's industrial regions. Conversely, it validated certain counties easily accessible by rail or, later, by automobile for those living in London and having the means to travel outside. This is the world of Forster's *Howards End*, and Hardy's Wessex, of George Sturt and Edward Thomas: countryside and country ways lying just outside the boundaries of suburbia. In a way, though rural, this site of English national identity was near enough to the metropolis to be contained or colonized by it. This explains the apparent paradox of a rural identity supported and adopted by an essentially urban segment of the population.

Furthermore, the folk revival and other related definitions of local, rural Englishness were historical rather than modern, and defined themselves against unappealing present-day realities. This retrospective move took two forms, which were not, interestingly enough, mutually exclusive. The first moved beyond an actual historical period, pushing the location of the historical ideal further and further away from the modern in an attempt to locate a pristine village folk culture. Eventually history was virtually left behind, located in a space that had devolved into a mythic and timeless locale. The second form fixed certain periods in the nation's history for the location of this ideal. These fixed moments in the nation's past were both real and imaginary – real in that they could be investigated and reconstructed through scholarly enterprise, but imaginary in their idealization and embedded ideologies of nostalgia. These periods shifted. During the second half of the nineteenth century the ideal was located in the medieval period, as part of a late phase of the Gothic Revival and other forms of Victorian medievalism. However, by the turn of the century the historical ideal was firmly ensconced in the later "Jacobethan," a move away from the urbanized and cosmopolitan medievalism that exalted castle, cathedral, and city to a view that posited a different symbiotic relationship between the great house and the village, punctuated by the progresses of the monarchs through the countryside.[6] Thus, paradoxically, the organic village

---

[6] This point can easily be made by noting the change in popular architectural styles. The years surrounding the mid-nineteenth century saw the emergence of Pugin and the subsequent fad for Gothic Revival architecture. Yet by the end of the century, historically inflected architectural styles were much more likely

was both outside of time, annexing the ahistorical, almost magical power of timeless and mythic folk traditions, and at the same time associated with specific chronological periods, having the appearance and factual structure of "real" English history. This paradoxical desire to have both magic and reality was to have important consequences for the English Musical Renaissance, with its twin poles of national identity located in both folk and Tudor music.

Versions of Englishness embedded in the desire for the organic village hinged on the importance of history in conceptions of English national identity. They rested upon an ideology of popular culture, but on a histori-cized popular culture rather than the actual popular culture of contemporary Edwardian society. As a direct outcome of the distrust of new forms of popular culture that dominated much of the cultural discourse of the second half of the nineteenth century, this preference for the historical folk went hand in hand with the distrust felt by the aristocratic classes and, more importantly, by the articulate intelligentsia of the upper middle classes, for the modern urban working classes. The urban working classes were perceived as dangerous and undisciplined, which led to a nostalgia for the class systems of the organic village, where everyone knew his or her assigned role in an established social hierarchy and felt the necessity and naturalness of that order. If popular culture was an expression of the potentially destabilizing presence of the restless urban working classes, then folk culture was an expression of the happy inhabitants of the organic village. Condemnations of modern popular culture arose from this ideological construct.

All of these features of alternative versions of Englishness circulating around the organic village stood in direct contrast to the real England: a modern, industrial, and imperial world power. Such a nostalgic ideology was taken up by a plethora of political and cultural stances towards England's path in the twentieth century. To make such an assertion, however, is not to suggest that such a stance lacked inherent patriotism. These stances simply sought a different source for the features of national identity and an alternative path for revitalizing the national spirit. Just as the orientalism of the Victorian and Edwardian periods sought to concretize English identity through an exploration of the "otherness" of non-Western cultures, the primitivist aspects of rural nostalgia and the rediscovery of English folk culture constructed a

to be a conglomerate of Jacobethan and village cottage styles, exemplified by the designs of Lutyens. For more, see Wiener, *English Culture and the Decline of the Industrial Spirit, 1850–1980* (Cambridge: Cambridge University Press, 1981) and David Cannadine, "The Context, Performance and Meaning of Ritual: The British Monarchy and the 'Invention of Tradition,' c. 1820–1977," in *The Invention of Tradition*, ed. E.J. Hobsbawm and Terence Ranger, 2nd edn (Cambridge: Cambridge University Press, 1983), 101–64.

national identity through an encounter with the putative historical and prehistorical sources of the national character. All of these stances, however, were reactions to an uneasy sense that England was in crisis, whether that crisis was perceived as a failure of the imperial, modern, and industrial spirit that had made England a world power, or a reaction against England's wrongful path in the nineteenth century. There was a sense that the very characteristics that constituted English national identity were being denied.

None of these issues is necessarily a marker of an anti-imperialist, anti-industrial stance, nor for a national identity located in the organic village. This is due in part to the historical character of the pastoral mode. From the Greek and Roman poets on, pastoralism has always been expropriated by a wide range of ideological stances, and nineteenth- and twentieth-century Britain was no exception.[7] This is even more true if one agrees with Martin Wiener's premise that the "industrial spirit" was on the wane during this period, especially on the level of cultural representation, in the face of an increasing tendency to place English national values in a rural landscape. This rural national character was in many ways ideologically neutral, and therefore could be deployed by a wide variety of contrasting forms of patriotism. This is possibly one reason for the large number of available positions regarding English national identity current in the first years of the twentieth century, which were, in turn represented as a public, cultural manifestation in contemporary masques.

Ralph Vaughan Williams was one example of a composer during this period searching for an effective musical language that would essentialize a national character and that would communicate that character to the wider public, within and without Britain. *Pan's Anniversary* and other masques written by him show that the composer had little interest in perpetuating clichéd sentiments concerning St George and England's imperial destiny in the occasionally populist musical style of Stanford and Elgar. Indeed, he was enough of an intellectual to consider the possibly deleterious effects of various types of popular music styles of the music hall and playhouse. Vaughan Williams, like many of his generation, still felt that an inclusive, classless national music would emerge from a nationalistically inflected art music rather than from contemporary popular music. At the same time, he felt that it was the duty of the serious composer to produce music that would serve the general population of his or her country. In his fervor regarding the obligation of a nation's music to serve the nation's people, he came close to the more overt calls for national revival active during this period. So when adopting the public, patriotic voice

---

[7] Eric Saylor's *English Pastoral Music: From Arcadia to Utopia* (Champaign, IL: University of Illinois Press, 2017) offers a valuable look at the topic in twentieth-century English music.

by now a very common aspect of the masque genre, Vaughan Williams sought musical representations which resonated with alternative versions of English identity circling around the concept of the organic village. The first years of the century found him immersing himself in the raw materials that could serve as appropriate sources for a new national musical style though his encounters with Purcell, hymn tunes, and folk songs.[8] However, it was the challenge of assuming the public voice offered by the commission to provide the music for *Pan's Anniversary* and his wrestling with the choice of source repertoires that led to a certain consolidation in his views. He was hardly alone in this regard. As the call from some quarters for a national musical style increased during the early years of the twentieth century, many other composers turned to the organic village and its traditional songs in order to break out of the perceived inadequacy that characterized the nationalistic attempts of the previous generation, however ideologically well-intentioned. An academic historicism alone could not offer a national revival, especially when tied to a musical language which continued to speak of an imitative cosmopolitanism. It was time to explore local identities in the music of the "people."

🎶 English Folk Song

Music was obviously a fundamental component in the goals of the folk revival: first through the collection and distribution of folk song; and as an adjunct of the vogue for folk dancing. It was a crucial means by which the antiquarian and scholarly interest in folk culture of the nineteenth century became an active,

---

[8] Vaughan Williams's editorial projects during this period brought him into direct contact with these three historical sources in a way that proved crucial to his development of a bank of appropriate historical sources for an English musical nationalism. These projects are the editing of Purcell's *Welcome Songs* for the new complete Purcell edition, the compilation of the *English Hymnal*, and the first encounters with folk song collecting in the field. Each required a considerable commitment of time and energy, but each paid off by allowing the composer to encounter these respective repertoires in ways which proved extremely fruitful for his development, and which made their presence felt in *Pan's Anniversary*. For a longer discussion of the importance of these projects, see chapter 1 of my dissertation "Composing History: National Identity and the Uses of the Past in the English Masque, 1860–1918" (Stony Brook University, 2004). Roger Savage's essay on Vaughan Williams's involvement in the Purcell Revival is a valuable source for more information: *Masques, Mayings and Music Dramas: Vaughan Williams and the Early Twentieth-Century Stage* (Woodbridge: The Boydell Press, 2014), chapter 4. For Vaughan Williams's own account of his editing of the *English Hymnal*, see "Some Reminiscences of the English Hymnal," in *The First Fifty Years: A Brief Account of the English Hymnal from 1906 to 1956* (Oxford: Oxford University Press, 1956), 2–5.

and at times aggressively didactic, pursuit of the basis for an alternate national identity and source of national renewal. To a certain extent this imperative for a nationalistic cultural transformation had already surfaced as a feature of the early years of the English Musical Renaissance movement. By the late 1890s, supporters of the English Musical Renaissance, as well as many others in the musical establishment, were calling for English music not only to remove the mantle of its continental overlords, but also to re-invent for itself a national musical style. To this end they had turned to the art music of England's past. It now remained for cultural critics outside the movement to convince its leaders that the revival they sought would be found as well in another voice from England's past, folk music.

This gradual shift in emphasis from antiquarianism to incipient ethnomusicology is clearly visible within the early years of the English Folk Song Society. The formation of the society in 1898 marks the beginnings of a second stage in the development of the English Musical Renaissance. The very beginnings of the movement paid homage, at least, to a rediscovery and re-evaluation of the claims of history over modern music. However, the last decade of the nineteenth century saw the beginnings of a link between traditional types of historical narrative and the new interests in folklore linked to the ahistorical narrative of the folk demonstrated in the scholarly writings and research of the period. The formation of the English Folk Song Society in many ways formalized this link, with important figures in the English Musical Renaissance serving as officers and leading members of the new society. Hubert Parry was the first president and Stanford a vice-president, giving an official imprimatur to the society as an extension of the nationalistic goals of the English Musical Renaissance movement.[9] As Parry wrote in his inaugural address, folk songs "are characteristic of the race, of the quiet reticence of our country folk, courageous and content … All the things that mark the folk-music of the race also betoken the qualities of the race, and, as a faithful reflection of ourselves, we needs must cherish it."[10] It is easy to see why accounts of the early years of the society stress the dilettante aspect of its activities, given Parry's purely academic interest in English folk song as reflected in his writings, and the

[9] Other members at least loosely connected to the English Musical Renaissance include J.A. Fuller Maitland, William Barclay Squire, and Sir John Stainer. More on the early history of the English Folk Song Society can be found in Boyes, "The Source is Open to All: Collecting and its Uses in the Revival," *The Imagined Village*, chapter 3. As I have stated previously, however, it is important to note that Parry and Stanford had an approach to folk song that tended towards the vague and abstract. It was for younger men and women in the society to familiarize themselves with folk-song idiom in any depth.

[10] Hubert Parry, "Inaugural Address," *Journal of the Folk Song Society*, 1 (1899), 1–3.

limited ways in which composers like Stanford had used folk song as material for their compositions.[11] But it is important that the society functioned under the auspices of those active in directing the new movement in English music and that its activities were seen to operate within its boundaries. English folk song was a new repertoire, undeniably national, and it offered a possible direction that a search for a national music might usefully incorporate. Since national musical movements in Germany and Russia had already reaped folk song's rich rewards, the older generation in the movement was open to the concept that folk materials might potentially provide a way to invent (or rediscover, as they would prefer to put it) a national identity in music.

However, there were also a number of initial members who had already been active in folk-song collecting, such as Lucy Broadwood and Frank Kidson. These early collectors, who eschewed an academic ivory tower view of folk tradition, had been responsible for the earliest volumes of published folk song. More importantly, they were responsible for the gradual realization by the larger English community that England did indeed have a body of folk song peculiarly hers, a fact that had been denied through much of the eighteenth and nineteenth centuries. Volumes like Lucy Broadwood and Fuller Maitland's *English County Songs*, though it had carefully bowdlerized texts, idealized melodies, and simple piano accompaniment, none the less did poineeringly make its way onto a large number of late Victorian music racks, among other examples of parlor music appropriate for middle-class amateurs.[12] Already these early pioneer collectors felt that they were giving a portion of the nation's heritage back to its people, saving these artifacts from destruction.[13] The

---

[11] It seems clear that Stanford's *Irish Rhapsodies*, for instance, owe less to a genuine desire to resurrect a national folk-song style as a basis for a national musical style and more to an imitation of his much-beloved Brahms and his *Hungarian Rhapsodies*. Stanford and Parry both were huge admirers of Brahms, and both relied heavily on his music in determining their own compositional aesthetic. More apropos, perhaps, is the kind of nationalistic use of folk song espoused on occasion by G.A. Macfarren, which I discuss in my second chapter.

[12] L. Broadwood and J.A. Fuller Maitland, *English County Songs* (London: Leaderhall Press, 1893). Dorothy de Val discusses Broadwood's role in "The Transformed Village: Lucy Broadwood and Folksong," in *Music and British Culture, 1785–1914*, ed. Christina Bashford and Leanne Langley (Oxford: Oxford University Press, 2000), 341–66.

[13] The view that these early folk-song collectors had "saved" the folk-song heritage from certain extinction was perpetuated in accounts throughout most of the twentieth century. However, during the 1980s, a handful of writers challenged the ideological agenda of this phase of the folk-song revival. Underlining the nationalistic, anti-urban, and ultimately anti-working-class attitudes of the collectors, they argued that in a sense these collectors invented a tradition of folk song that was highly colored by their idealism and nostalgia. See in particular

aspirations of such collectors reflect the cultural force gathering momentum during the late nineteenth century; they are the exemplars of the new, active role required by the folk revival during the first years of the twentieth century.

By the first decade of the twentieth century, this revivalist movement was in full swing across the cultural landscape, increasingly replete not only with the rhetoric of keen interest in rediscovering the nearly vanished culture of the folk, but also with a call to plant the seeds of national renewal through reconnecting with a supposed idyllic past located in the organic village. Within the English Folk Song Society itself, demands to make a more aggressive effort to save this rapidly disappearing inheritance of folk music issued from a younger generation of folk-song enthusiasts, including Ralph Vaughan Williams, George Butterworth, Maude Karpeles, and Percy Grainger. Among this group, it was Cecil Sharp who mobilized forces and made the first steps towards proposing folk song as the integral source for the modern, national musical style.[14]

Vic Gammon, "Folk Song Collecting in Sussex and Surrey, 1843–1914," *History Workshop* 10 (Autumn 1980); Dave Harker, *Fakesong: The Manufacture of British 'Folksong' 1700 to the Present Day* (Milton Keynes: Open University Press, 1985); and Georgina Boyes, *The Imagined Village*. For an investigation into how this might have operated within the work of a single collector, see Julian Onderdonk's "Vaughan Williams's Folksong Transcriptions: a Case of Idealization?," in *Vaughan Williams Studies*, ed. Alain Frogley (Cambridge: Cambridge University Press, 1996), 118–38 and his discussion of Vaughan Williams's collecting activities. More recently Dorothy De Val has argued that a more reasoned approach should be taken towards the goals and accomplishments of these early collectors in her essay "The Transformed Village," in *Music and British Culture, 1785–1914*.

[14] Cecil Sharp (1859–1924) was perhaps the seminal figure in establishing and bureaucratizing the revival of English folk song and dance during the first decades of the twentieth century. Though not one of the very early collectors of folk song, once he became involved in the English Folk Song Society in 1903, he quickly motivated the society's younger members to be more active and systematic about their collecting activities. Intensely elitist in his attitudes towards the working classes, Sharp firmly believed that the precious cultural traditions of the past were being lost through the increasing influence of modern mass culture and must be systematically collected to ensure its continuation. For Sharp, however, this was only half of the mission of the folk revival. Sharp firmly believed that folk music and dance had to be an integral part of the national education system, and worked furiously to spread knowledge of these traditions through institutionalized training sessions and schools. For the ideological implications of Sharp's theories, see Boyes, *The Imagined Village*, and J. Porter, "Muddying the Crystal Spring: from Idealism and Realism to Marxism in the Study of English and American Folk Song," in *Comparative Musicology and the Anthropology of Music*, ed. Bruno Nettl and Philip Bohlman (Chicago: Chicago University Press, 1991), 113–30.

The important leap came, however, when folk song became valued as more than a mere collector's item stored in a repository of national inheritance, and instead became the basis for a contemporary musical style. The music provided by Vaughan Williams and Holst for the Stratford masque production reflects this shift in ideology. For it is in *Pan's Anniversary* that both historical and folk music are combined to serve the topical purpose of providing a sound world that will sonorously invent a musical idiom appropriate to the organic village.

❧ A Return to Pan

The text of Ben Jonson's masque *Pan's Anniversary* seems worlds removed from the anxieties and ideologies of modern British imperialist identity at the beginning of the twentieth century. At first glance it seems to be a combination of a literary artifact and a historical relic, with its quaint Renaissance pastoral conventions, its delight in language and fanciful etymology, and the simple certainties of its shepherds. The underlying allegorical symbolism of the masque is redolent of a class hierarchy and monarchical political economy which is so far removed from modern actualities as to incite in an early twentieth-century audience nothing more than a nostalgic fondness for its ancient political system, understood in retrospect to be in its final, albeit glorious, gasp of power. Historically placed, the messages intended by Jonson in his text are no longer relevant to a modern reader, so the text itself is a curious, ideological blank. A piece of history, the masque does not seem to be about history, nor about representing any ideology of history which might speak to the modern audience.

However, to produce a revival of this masque in Stratford in 1905 was anything but ideologically blank. These added ideological properties have little to do with either the content or the signification of the historical artifact itself within its original context as the locus of an Jacobean audience's horizon of expectation. Placed in a new historical context, the work's reception was profoundly transformed as an entire set of meanings died away to be replaced by a set of newly invented ones. Hence, the allegory of Jonson's original, which both referred to and derived meaning from the glorification of an absolute monarch and the social and cosmological ideologies that absolute monarchy supported, was replaced in the Stratford production by signification derived from various traditions of folklore and English village life, as well as Edwardian assumptions concerning Jacobean England.[15] The Jonson

---

[15] This is explored by Roy Strong in his "Illusions of Absolutism: Charles I and the Stuart Court Masques," in *Art and Power: Renaissance Festivals, 1450–1650* (Woodbridge: The Boydell Press, 1984), 153–70. Roger Savage offers a comprehensive look at other Edwardian revivals of works by Jonson in his

text of *Pan's Anniversary* here only served as a base with ideological properties that now attracted more and more associated features in the form of dances, games, music, and spectacle. The version performed in 1905 was arrived at via a kind of additive process – Stratford's *Pan* was in many ways a conglomerate of signifying elements, far different from Jonson's cohesive original text.[16]

A surviving photograph from a rehearsal of the production offers some sense of the disjunctions of the revivalist aesthetic presented to the audience of the Stratford *Pan's Anniversary*. The simple outdoor wooden stage appears both set against and centered in relation to its borrowed scenery, not Jonson's Baroque simulation of a flowery meadow replete with sheep and nymphs, but the imposing edifice of the Shakespeare Theatre, to some "the monstrous erection on the side of the Avon."[17] The building itself is an uneasy mixture of unreal and unconvincing Jacobethan half-timbering and faux thatch and the prosaic hideousness of Victorian brick (Illustration 4.1). This unhappy amalgam really constituted the only scenery for the production, aside from the poplar trees that framed either side of the stage. In this photograph the stage was obviously caught in mid-rehearsal; a motley assortment of chairs

"A Quarry for Profitable Working: Staging the Masques of Ben Jonson in London and Stratford-upon-Avon, 1903–1912," in *Masques, Mayings and Music-Dramas*.

[16] A detailed description of the circumstances surrounding the commission for *Pan's Anniversary* and the music Vaughan Williams chose for the production can be found in chapter 1 of my dissertation "Composing History: National Identity and the Uses of the Past in the English Masque, 1860–1918". Roger Savage also includes a reconstruction of the masque in Appendix One to his *Masques, Mayings and Music-Dramas*.

[17] This designation appeared originally in Gordon Crosse's *Shakespearean Playgoing 1890–1952*, and is quoted in Ian Frederick Moulton, "Stratford and Bayreuth: Anti-Commercialism, Nationalism, and the Religion of Art," *Litteraria Pragensia* 6 (1991): 39–50. The building, completed in 1879, three years after Bayreuth, was designed by the team of Dodgshun and Unsworth, complete with turrets, gables, external strap-like décor, and reportedly a terribly sparse interior and inadequate stage. Kemp and Trewin note the criticism launched at the design from the beginning, quoting one critic who called it "a piece of pinchbeck nineteenth century medievalism" and a "striped sugarstick." When the building burned down in 1926, Bernard Shaw wrote: "Stratford-upon-Avon is to be congratulated upon the Fire." On the other hand, Kemp and Trewin also claim that despite its ridiculous appearance, it "probably excited more affection during its life than any theatre had known." Even Oscar Wilde wrote: "A beautiful building, one of the loveliest erected in England for many years." For a longer treatment of the history of the Stratford festival, see T.C. Kemp and J.C. Trewin, *The Stratford Festival: History of the Shakespearean Memorial Theatre* (Birmingham: Cornish Brothers, 1953). See also Ivor Brown and George Fearon, *This Shakespeare Industry* (Westport, CT: Greenwood Press, 1939, repr. 1969) and Gerald Jaggard, *Stratford Mosaic* (London: Christopher Johnson, 1960).

Illustration 4.1   The Shakespeare Memorial Theatre in the 1920s, Prior to the Fire

stand in a jumble, the orchestra particularly absent, though their trace remains in the metal music stand off to the left. Instead, the music is represented by Ralph Vaughan Williams himself, who appears at the right of the photograph, conspicuously not in period dress, appearing a bit distanced from the costumed masque participants. The bareness of surroundings only heightens the apparent magnificence of the masquers' Elizabethan costumes: young girls – the "maypole sixteen" – in white dresses, men in doublets and hose with fancy trim, and women in ruffs and trains. Another unsettling note is struck by the obviously fantastical costumes of the three rather buxom and matronly women on the extreme right of the photograph, who (one assumes) have been cast in the roles of Jonson's nymphs (Illustration 4.2).

The heightened unreality of the setting in counterpoint to the over-determined authenticity of the costumes presents a conundrum for the modern viewer trying to determine to what extent "historical" truth was valued in such masque or pageant productions. Were history and spectacle meant to overlap? Or was a nostalgic fantasy implied? This indeterminate positioning of the masque between history and fantasy was duplicated in the extended account of the masque's performance appearing in the Stratford newspaper, the *Stratford-upon-Avon Herald*, on Friday April 28, 1905, a week after the première. During the weeks before the production on the day of the Birthday Celebration, the newspaper had included weekly short articles that

Illustration 4.2   Photograph of the Cast and Other Members
of the Production of Stratford's *Pan's Anniversary*

garnered publicity for the event by mentioning the extensive preparations
being made for the upcoming masque – the costumes, the rehearsals of the
dances, and the forces involved. However, almost nothing was said about the
implications of reviving the masque itself, nor did the writer indicate any exact
knowledge about the history of the genre. Indeed, if anything, the articles seem
a bit vague as to exactly the nature of the piece to be performed, as if the writer
was slightly confused about the historical authenticity of a work which seemed
very similar to a commonplace contemporary pageant.

By the time an article was printed that extensively reported on the performance the week after the Birthday Celebrations, someone had obviously done
some research, since half of the extensive account dealt exclusively with the
definition and history of the masque genre up to Jonson's masques for James I,
albeit a slightly jumbled and uncertain description (the complete text of this
article is reproduced in Appendix 4). Citing Ward's *English Dramatic Literature*,
the author traced the genre from its roots in Italian Renaissance entertainments, through its proliferation during the reign of Henry VIII, to the grand
spectacles of the Jacobean masque under Ben Jonson and Inigo Jones. The

author took special care in emphasizing the importance of dance to the genre, probably cued by the amount of dancing presented during the performance. The historical account of the masque in the article was obviously not the work of an expert, since this section of the article reads like a conglomeration of pirated summaries; the article skips over important aspects and confuses the development of the genre from the Tudor court entertainments to the full-blown Jacobean masque. The important thing, though, is that the author thought it necessary to attempt a historical account, justifying the masque's inclusion in the Birthday Celebrations through a reference to history and the authenticity of a validated past. Indeed, the author sometimes apologizes for the slightness of the entertainments and argues a case for the genre's historical and English status through an appeal to history.

But the confusion for the modern reader over whether the performance was an authentic revival of a historical genre or a rehearsal of certain well-worn aspects of folk tradition lingers. After the historical account of the masque, and after a quick mention of the weather and a list of the arrangement committee, the author offers an extended description of the content of the production, highlighting both spectacle and the folk as well as the historical.[18] He begins with a description of the entrance and opening flower speeches of the shepherd and nymphs, followed by a description of the Bidford Morris Dancers who took on the role of the Boeotians. He then mentions the first of the hymns written by Vaughan Williams, characterizing it as one of the most pleasing features of the masque and "exquisitely sweet," echoing Vaughan Williams's program notes by adding that "no attempt was made to reproduce the Elizabethan style." The author continues:

> and then to sixteenth century music the maskers danced their entry in graceful form to extremely fascinating strains. This, however, was only the prelude to an even grander turn, the "Main Daunce (Ye Pavane)," to music arranged for orchestra by Mr. G. von Holst. There was a charming blending of colour, the kaleidoscopic display being improved upon by rays of sunlight, which fell athwart the stage.

The Revels, which were preceded by another hymn and chorus, then commenced, and much hearty laughter greeted the comic element, while considerable admiration was evinced by such effective scenes as, for instance, the "maypole daunce by schole maydens" and the "Dance Ye Galliard,"

[18] None of the people mentioned seems at all connected to the playhouse proper, but instead are representative of the middle-class citizens of the town of Stratford. These include the mayor, the vicar, and various town chancellors. The fact that most of the arrangement committee and the performers were amateur residents of Stratford is actually of integral importance, as I will discuss later in this chapter.

the latter being another of the charming "Elizabethan Daunces in Court enfoldings." This elusive last phrase must have been quoted from the program. Unfortunately it is not explained, though it does tie in with Vaughan Williams's views that art music (and court culture) of the Elizabethan period rested on a close relationship with the folk.[19]

The author was particularly charmed by the little girls' maypole dance, investing it with particular weight as:

> With measured tread the gaily-clad children went round and round and in and out until the plaiting of the streamers was completed, and then with the same childish grace and merry tripping the ribbons were unwound, while the orchestra discourse [*sic*] one of the many English folk-tunes which characterised the revels, including "Selenger's Round", "The Lost Lady", "Maria Martin" and "All on Spurn Point", these also being arranged by Mr. G. von Holst.

What followed was another long and extended scene of incorporated folk traditions not part of the Jonson original. This included scenes of "Old English sports" such as wrestling, fencing, tilting at the quintain, and hippas, from which the audience derived much amusement. The concluding scene of the performance had the Thebans dancing the antimasque to the strains of "Shepherd's Hay."

> With their skins of goats the dancers presented a very quaint appearance, but the scene, though somewhat grotesque, did not lack picturesqueness, and the performers were cheered to the echo as they tripped away into seclusion. A good finale was the hymn by nymphs and chorus: then more dances, a general blending of colour and the revels of the day were ended.

The frenetic pace of the production implied by this journalistic account is remarkable. There is something overdetermined and overwrought about the piling up of scenic elements onto what was originally an understated, tightly controlled, and thematically taut bundle of signifiers contained in the original Jonson text. The author does not question the inclusion of folk traditions in the masque, nor does he make it clear that these were additions to the masque's original text, but instead seems to project the idea that these were part and parcel of the Jonson masque. I would argue that in some sense they were part of the new characteristics associated with the re-invented masque, certainly not the original but the conception of the masque as a conglomerate of history and folk that was beginning to circulate in the years immediate following 1900.

The other striking aspect is the sheer amount of music needed for all of these elements to coalesce. After reading the description of the performance,

---

[19] See chapter 3.

it is a bit easier to understand why Vaughan Williams chose to write only four extended pieces of music for the masque, and to arrange – or to get Gustav Holst to arrange – music for the rest. The repeated strains of the folk songs and the Elizabethan dances, with their regular phrase structure and clear cadential points, allowed for easy variation and development for long periods of time, as original transcriptions will attest. At the same time, their "folky" characteristics, in particular the appearance of repeated rhythmic motives, slight modal inflections, and limited melodic ranges, were an appropriate backdrop for this hodge-podge of folk and historical elements: the re-enactment of the Maypole ritual, folk and Morris dancing, and a procession of traditional, archetypal characters like St. George and Robin Hood. These added elements relate to an ideology of identity which directly connects to history and a nostalgia for the past rooted in a vision of organic community and rural values and are ultimately no less ideologically charged than the elaborate allegorical system underpinning Jonson's rhetoric and Inigo Jones's realization in 1625.

The seeds of this new form of Englishness can be found in the essential elements of the Jonson text, as in the lines reproduced at the beginning of the chapter describing the harmony of the shepherds' community created and maintained by their adherence to the ancient rites given by Pan. This theme of tradition is continually underscored by the drama enacted by the masque. Its opening vignette centers on a group of nymphs preparing for the rituals of Pan's holy day under the supervision of an older shepherd who seems to enact the role of the repository of tradition in this rural, traditional, and timeless society. As the masque continues, tradition is challenged with the arrival of a group of outsiders, Thebans and Boeotians, who threaten the continuity of tradition by their attempt to introduce new dances into the holy-day festivities. The fact that these outsiders are comic, and their boasting self-characteristic antimasque dance is obviously not to be taken seriously, barely camouflages the seriousness of their attempt to do away with the old ways to ring in the new. Their attempt fails, and the shepherds and shepherdesses of the Arcadian community continue with their ordered hymns and dances of praise of Pan.

If the text of the masque supports the centrality of tradition for the maintenance of social harmony, then the historical and folk tropes added to the Stratford production of the masque take on a greater significance than that of mere spectacle. They are the traditions to which the nation must cling, almost in spite of their stereotypical and hackneyed appearance, for such tradition bears the weight of history. It is important, however, to note that clear choices define that tradition and that identity in a certain way, an appropriate historical identity closely related to the English Renaissance and a mythic folk culture. A pervasive musicality envelops this identity, one saturated in the "fascinations" of Elizabethan pavanes and measures and the gay innocence of folk song.

What in this simple story carries such strong ideological resonances in 1905, to the point that a large group of middle-class amateurs would expend a substantial amount of time, effort, and money to present it to the larger public? And what are the implications for the direction of English music and nationalism? The answer to these questions lies in the very fact that the production was by the public and for the public, communicating a message about tradition and the past in a musical and dramatic language that connected the historical and folk materials of that past with a public nostalgic element. In this sense, it was an important feature of this production that members of the community performed these rites of tradition and identity for their own community. Beyond sheer entertainment, there was the increasing belief during this period that this type of participatory musical and dramatic event could serve as the vehicle for social renewal, as if through the process of performing and viewing works that reinforced connections to history and the folk within communities, those communities could be transformed to reflect traditional values. Masques and pageants of the period came to be a crucial component in this belief.

ᔰ The Stratford Movement and Pageant Culture

Interestingly enough, during the years prior to World War I the village of Stratford-upon-Avon had become a focus for the promulgation of social renewal accomplished through the means of communal drama, the epicenter of a growing movement that linked progressive and populist theories of art in society to a nationalistic and nostalgic vision of "Merrie Olde England." The so-called Stratford-on-Avon Movement had many goals, of which only one part was centered on the production of Shakespeare's plays.[20] The theories and goals of this movement were at least partly derived from those of Richard Wagner, especially in the movement's conception of the power of musical drama. They too viewed drama as a kind of *Gesamtkunstwerk*, a "total art work" which linked word, music, and visual art in an aesthetic experience which would reflect and nurture the collective, national spirit of the people. In addition to a Wagnerian conception of the role of drama in society, the movement privileged the idea of folk culture, and its proponents viewed Shakespeare especially, but Wagner too, as achieving sublimity because they had their artistic roots in the folk, which gave their work its intrinsic power. Specific goals of the movement's organization included not only the

---

[20] The group was formally launched in 1909, but this was merely a formality for a group of people who had been actively supporting Stratford's claims as the center of English national identity for several years. Many had been previously active in Stratford's Shakespeare Club, which had sponsored many events throughout the years furthering Shakespeare's pre-eminence.

production of Shakespeare's plays and the advancement of Shakespearean scholarship, but also the promotion of a whole range of traditional and folk activities: Morris and country dancing, traditional games and competitions, folk-song collecting and transmission, village pageants, and plays. Their battle cry was to seed widespread local participation across England, with initiates converging at key ritualistic moments in Stratford. Stratford was to become the new, but more importantly the English, Bayreuth, centered too around its theater, but whose influence would reach out to every English village and town which sought to connect to the past via drama.

The tenets of the Stratford Movement, albeit in their most radical form, are contained in a book published in 1911 under its auspices. Written largely by Reginald R. Buckley, it also included contributions by Frank Benson, Arthur Hutchinson, and Mary Neal.[21] Frank Benson's introduction begins the volume with a description of a May morning in the Bancroft Gardens, and a scene very similar to that of *Pan's Anniversary*:

> It is the first of May. The Dreamer is lying on a smooth lawn by the river-side; part of the garden attached to the theatre buildings. To the right, through a frame of rush and willow, yew and cedar and elm, the spire of the church looks down on the mill where Celt, Roman, Saxon and Dane, Norman and Englishman for centuries have ground their harvest ... But hark! I hear the minstrels play, and after them I know the rout is coming. "Such a May morning never was before," at least within our time. On to the green of the Bancroft dance the singing children of Stratford and the neighbouring villages. Young and old to the number of some thousands follow after to see the final ceremony, to tune their hearts to the rhythm of the final dance, and carry back to their homes the human harmony of the final song ... The queen of the May, a fair little maiden, is seated on a throne of flowers in the midst of her court. The rough spear, entwined with ivy pointing upwards, connects the eternal homage paid by age to youth with the primitive

[21] Reginald R. Buckley, *The Shakespeare Revival and the Stratford-Upon-Avon Movement* (London: George Allen & Sons, 1911). Frank R. Benson was the director of the Shakespeare Memorial Theatre during the period 1885–1911, and was responsible for lifting the festival from a country dramatic series to one of national importance. Arthur Hutchinson, a local historian, provided a brief history of Stratford-upon-Avon and the history of the festival. Mary Neal was the most well-known advocate for folk dance in England during this period, and the founder of the Espérance Movement, which sought to alleviate the plight of the working classes through the efficacy of learning folk dance. She was instrumental in organizing the folk-dance seminars in Stratford. However, soon after the publication of this volume she was involved in a power struggle with Cecil Sharp over the leadership of the folk-dance movement in England, and having lost her position, retired quietly. For more on the debates in the Folk Dance Society during this period, see Georgina Boyes, *The Imagined Village*.

worship from our ancestors to the earth and the sun. Then the Folk-songs of our forefathers ring out blithely on the spring air, and the twinkling feet of the little dancers on the grass catch something of the rhythm of Shakespeare's verse and the music of spheres. ...

The dreamer watches the streams of people scatter ... The bands of teachers troop off to their daily lessons in Folk-song and Folk-dances, or to hear a lecture on Folk-Lore or Shakespeare's girls and their Flowers ... Some, had he questioned them, would have told him that their poet had shown them in the Playhouse how "we English became what we are and how we can keep so."

We obviously have no way of knowing if Benson was alluding to the production of *Pan's Anniversary* six years earlier in this idealized description, though certainly he would have seen it. However, a number of the main tenets of the Stratford Movement were met by the presentation of Jonson's masque in the Bancroft Garden. The site allowed for a large audience, and the fact that the masque was not performed in the Stratford theater proper, with its traditional hierarchy of seats based on ticket price and the ability to pay, spoke of the ideal of a more egalitarian, classless society represented by the audience. The location of the production was also important because it was framed by its by now ideologically burdened landscape, which linked the mythic, pastoral landscape of the masque with Stratford itself, the natural features of which were already being celebrated as the quintessential expression of timeless, rural England by many in Stratford. This is indicative of the important connection being forged between Stratford as a seat of Englishness and the increasingly dominant and endemic cultural trope of pastoralism surrounding of the English southern counties, "the shires," as one of the essential components of English national identity.[22]

In addition, its performers were composed not only of professional actors and musicians, but also of a large contingent of amateurs, hence making the dramatic production a social and inclusionary one. As befitting the head of the Espérance Movement, Mary Neal writes in passionate support of this aspect of the Stratford Movement. Acting as apologist for a belief that the woes of the urbanized working classes of England could be alleviated by a contact with the rural, timeless values contained in folk culture, Neal argues that in "dancing, music, song, and games

---

[22] This point is particularly made by Martin J. Wiener, *English Culture and the Decline of the Industrial Spirit, 1850–1980*. More detailed discussion of the ideologies associated with pastoralism during this period are contained in Jan Marsh, *Back to the Land: The Pastoral Impulse in Victorian England from 1880–1914* (London: Quartet Books, 1982). See also Alun Howkins, "The Discovery of Rural England," in *Englishness: Culture and Politics 1880–1920*, ed. Robert Colls and Philip Dodd (Beckenham: Croom Helm, 1986), 62–88, and W.J. Keith, *The Rural Tradition: a Study of the Non-Fiction Prose Writers of the English Countryside* (Toronto: University of Toronto Press, 1974).

[are contained] those regenerative forces which were helping to restore to the English people their inheritance of joy and of strength, so long held in abeyance through the invading evils of over-crowded city life."[23] She continues:

> The evidences of this awakening are all around us in England today. In cities and in towns young men and women are spending the hours of recreation in singing the folk-songs and dancing the folk-dances evolved from the tillers of the soil, as an expression of race-consciousness in religious ceremonial no less than of joy in everyday work and life. They are also acting and reciting the masterpieces of English literature with tone and gesture which would have been an impossible achievement ten or twenty years ago. Children, too, are being taught in folk-games some of the deepest lessons yet learned by the human race.
>
> And the English country-side is also alive today with this rebirth of our national inheritance of folk-art. In remote villages miracle plays, pageants of history, folk-songs, and folk-dances are studied during long winter evenings to make merry the days when the sun shines and life can be lived out of doors … history and geography have been made living and interesting to the children by dramatising those subjects whenever possible. And not only has this awakening come to the children, but in many villages today ploughmen and sewing-maids, workmen and workwomen, are taking part in drama and dance and song.
>
> There are everywhere signs that the ugliness of cities has reached its limit, that the power conferred by mere money has failed, that commercialism cannot satisfy, and once more men and women are returning to the deeper and more abiding rhythm of life long ago broken by the rush and whirr of machinery. We are relearning the lesson today that the forces which make for evil are apt to be increased both by opposition and by cowardly acquiescence, and that they can be redeemed only by the transmuting power of beauty and of art into willing servants of the best and highest interest of the nation.

Neal's vision of social renewal, and that of the Stratford Movement as a whole, was regenerative only to the point that it was a participatory endeavor. While certainly there was a role for professionals, especially in bringing the greatest works of art to the people and inspiring them to greater heights, the lessons learned had to be taken back into the local realm for musical drama to have its power.

English folk drama, music, and dance were not the only sources of cultural production validated by the Stratford Movement. R.R. Buckley, the editor and primary contributor to the volume, speaks of shrines to Aeschylus and Plato, to Michaelangelo and Beethoven, and that "side by side with the Moralist, the

---

[23] Reginald R. Buckley, *The Shakespeare Revival and the Stratford-Upon-Avon Movement*, 202.

Mystery, and the Miracle play are performed Sakuntala and the Drama of the East." Buckley mentions producing Wagner alongside Shakespeare, performing Elgar with the great choral music of the past.[24] But it is the underlying connections to the folk that for Buckley offer the reasons for inclusion in the Stratford pantheon, since the folk offers the truest expression of national identity, here defined as "Anglo-Celtic." Drama, with its roots in the folk, is a product of the people, an "expression of joy in the community," and as such it not only engenders pleasure, it also serves as an "expression of racial religion."[25] Mary Neal elaborates on this theme, saying:

> To those who have eyes to see and ears to hear it is abundantly evident that there is today an awakening throughout the length and breadth of England. It is an awakening of national consciousness and of national responsibility … The renaissance of this individual consciousness is today in England finding an outward and visible sign in a revival of folk-art in drama, dance music, and song, and love of nature and outdoor life. In legend and folk-tale we are relearning the age-long wisdom of the folk which has always had its roots deep in the traditions of the English people. We are beginning to distrust the generalisations gathered on the surface of the hurrying life of today, and we are looking deeper into the heart of England for some of those qualities without which no nation can fulfil its highest destiny.

It is apparent that many of Buckley's larger theories are derived from Frazer and the Cambridge Ritualists discussed in chapter 3, highlighting their immense currency during the years surrounding the turn of the century. Buckley states that:

(a) The English folk-drama was a ruder form of art closely akin to the Greek, and arose from dances and songs of pagan worship.

(b) That, being allied with the work of the Church, it became Christian.

(c) That, with the awakening of England, first as a response to European learning, and then owing to the national awakening of the country under

---

[24] A broader discussion of the movement, and its connection to Bayreuth, can be found in Moulton, "Stratford and Bayreuth: Anti-Commercialism, Nationalism, and the Religion of Art." Roger Savage has also written about Buckley's nationalist ideologies in "The Edens of Reginald Buckley: Temples and Tetralogies at Bayreuth, Stratford and Glastonbury," in *Masques, Mayings and Music-Dramas*.

[25] Both Benson and Buckley's description of the importance of the folk in establishing a racial commonality and heritage reeks of the worst kinds of racist and imperialist rhetoric current during the period, though stated in the context of a community of races and nations, and its prevalence in this volume implies that this was an important underlying ideology for the movement as a whole. This aspect is explored in more depth in chapter 5.

Elizabeth, the bucolic drama became merged in the wider and deeper drama of Shakespeare.

(d) That folk-customs and plays never died out, and have survived to this day.

(e) That in them we have the forgotten wellspring of English music and drama.

(f) These, being in their essence eminently Shakespearean, are worthy of revival beside the great plays.

(g) And that the living principle of folk-art calls for modern expression, and provides us with the best hope of a contemporary drama.

Several key ideas are contained in this short list. The first two seem directly influenced by Chambers's *The Mediaeval Stage*,[26] with the insistence that there was a direct line of development from primitive dramatic customs to the Greeks, and that this tradition became Christianized, but not essentially changed. Importantly for Stratford, this line continued and reached its peak in the plays of Shakespeare. The last four items revolve around the continued relevance of "folk-customs," shifting from a historical perspective to a timeless one applicable to the contemporary and the modern. For Buckley, at least, they are of one being, one essence, with Shakespeare, and it is here that the future will find its muse. Again, the issue of national identity – that of the historical nation-state rather than the seat of empire – lies at the heart of these statements. It is important to notice that in the fifth statement, it is folk culture that contains the source of national musical and dramatic creativity; it is not just music and drama but "English" music and drama. Neal states it much more succinctly; for her it is an Anglo-Celtic "race consciousness," and only through such a race consciousness that the future of the nation will rest secure.

The Stratford Movement is important in this context not only because of the elevated status of folk culture and the ideologies associated with it, but also because it encouraged its members and anyone interested enough in the movement to propagate the faith, so to speak, in their own communities. Buckley's volume concludes with a practical list for anybody interested in becoming part of the movement. Initiates were encouraged to come to Stratford either for the festival proper or for the summer workshop series, where classes in folklore, folk dancing, and other English traditional activities were offered. However, this was not enough. They were also encouraged to take what they learned back to their own village communities and use them to encourage hometown pageants and other theatricals, for which help would be provided with resources of the Stratford Movement central headquarters. Item iii, for instance, states that members of the movement would further the cause by:

---

[26] E.K. Chambers, *The Mediaeval Stage* (Oxford: Oxford University Press, 1903). See my discussion of this important text in chapter 3.

Writing small dramatic scenes of plays and getting them performed in local centres, and perhaps bringing performers to the Folk Festival to act such village plays; to make centres so that the neighbouring villages can obtain information about performing a play, making and hiring costumes and scenery, with the thousand and one details of a small production, such centres always to be in touch with the general centre at the Festival Association in Stratford-on-Avon.

So practical was this, in fact, that the book includes road and railroad maps, with detailed traveling instructions to help those new to the festival negotiate the wilds of Warwickshire (Illustration 4.3).

The early years of the Stratford Movement and its developing tenets and goals certainly served as the local context for the 1905 production of *Pan's Anniversary*. Congruencies can be seen in the initial choice of a text which stresses the importance of rural traditions, the production's replacement of Jonson's Arcadia with Shakespearean England, the inclusion of hundreds of amateur performers, and the overdetermined mixture of history and folk culture. It would be hard to believe that Ralph Vaughan Williams would not have come into contact with some of the people who would later launch the movement proper. Given that Vaughan Williams supplied a score that contained arrangements of music from both historical and folk sources, and that this was a period in which the composer was actively collecting folk song and enthusiastically supporting the English Folk Song and Dance Society, one could further argue that he may well have felt some affinity to the ideas circulating among the festival's leadership and which would soon be formalized in the Stratford Movement. Certainly by 1913, during his stint as composer-in-residence for the Shakespeare Festival, the composer would have frequently come into contact with the movement. By this point, Cecil Sharp had replaced Mary Neal as coordinator of the summer folk workshops, and through his friendship with Sharp, Vaughan Williams would have been in the thick of Stratford Movement country.

The Stratford Movement is only one example of a group promoting the performance of amateur masques and pageants, and only one example of the cluster of ideologies that subtly or overtly attached themselves to such endeavors. Masques and pageants were being produced all over the country, associated with Christmas and May Day in particular, but frequently also anytime that a village, town, location, or other communal group wanted to celebrate the identity of that community through the representation of iconic subject matter.[27] Not surprisingly, this celebration usually took the form of representing history, since

[27] Roy Judge offers a fascinating history of the growth of the May Day pageant and its connection to the tropes of "Merrie England" in "May Day and Merrie England," *Folklore* 102 (1991), 131–48.

by now English history was one of the key components in the construction of late nineteenth- and early twentieth-century English identity.

Most of these masques were very different from their Victorian predecessors, and unlike *Pan's Anniversary*, most were not revivals of Renaissance masques. Instead, the largest proportion of these masques drew on the characteristics derived from folk traditions laid out in the previous chapter, in essence really only a kind of costumed procession, rather than making any concrete reference to Elizabethan, Stuart, or Restoration models. Topics, rather than any consistent form or formal plan, link masque to masque to create several overlapping categories. For instance, there were masques that reflected the fairy tales and myths of the English countryside – elves, flower fairies, English-style nymphs with a hint of Milton's *Comus*.[28] These were often allied to pastoral subjects not concerned with the supernatural. May Days, the advent of spring, the turn of the seasons and similar festive occasions rooted in the countryside were all popular topics. These could be presented as some kind of timeless present, or could be specific evocations of England's "Golden Age," that fairly unspecific time most usually the England of Elizabeth I, but occasionally a more distant, medieval past. The masques could present historical events or characters explicitly, as in a kind of procession of history. This was sometimes was shown in combination with the pastimes of the common people and sometimes with a specific thread of England's imperial destiny added as well. This encouraged all of these categories or topics to become increasingly linked in the rhetoric of the masque, so that it is difficult to separate out the independent threads. Instead, these works display the tapestry of all that England believed about herself during the first two decades of the twentieth century.

It is difficult to extract a set of consistent characteristics for all of these varieties of masques, but a few very broad generalizations can be made. First, most of the masques consisted of a series of somewhat discrete tableaux organized around a change of scenery or a new central character around which the action for that tableau revolved. These tableaux would involve a sequence of speeches and songs, and then one or two dances. Most masques had arranged music from other sources, whether historical, folk, or popular, though many masques also had music newly composed. And most depended on well-known symbolic, traditional, or historical material, common knowledge rather than newly invented and developed idiosyncratically for the individual masque. At

---

[28] Though not a musico-dramatic work, an important example is Walter Crane's book for children entitled *Flora's Feast*, a book probably seminal to the establishment of the "flower fairy" tradition in English children's literature, a topic certainly taken up by dramatic masques: *Flora's Feast, a Masque of Flowers penned and pictured by Water Crane* (London: Cassell and Co., 1889). For instance, this tradition still operates in Robertson and Ackroyd's *The Masque of May Morning*, discussed in chapter 5.

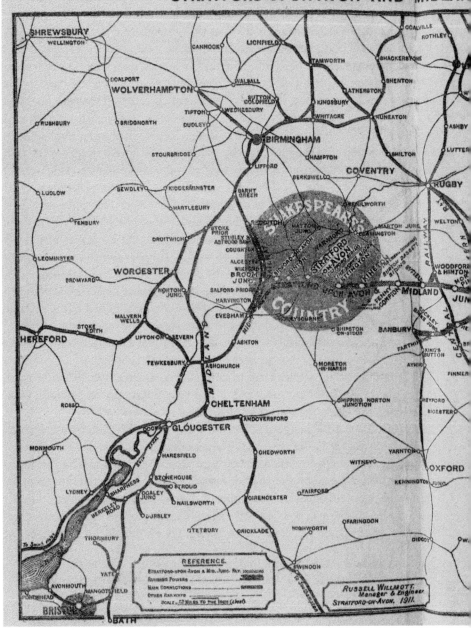

RUSSELL WILLMOTT,
Manager & Engineer.
STRATFORD-ON-AVON, 1911.

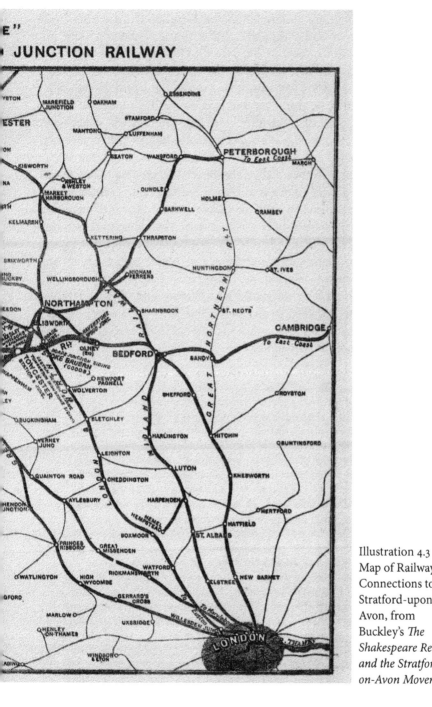

Illustration 4.3
Map of Railway
Connections to
Stratford-upon-
Avon, from
Buckley's *The
Shakespeare Revival
and the Stratford-
on-Avon Movement*

the same time, as one examines the masques in progression from about 1900 to 1930, one sees the symbolic, traditional content introduced in a less invested way, then being taken up and proliferated until it appears again and again, in an "invention of tradition" similar to that described by Eric Hobsbawm.

Despite the multiplicity of these newly invented traditions, most spoke in some way to a modern English patriotism, and to the representation of a national English identity or character. The reasons for this sudden national self-consciousness and virtual "identity crisis" lie in the new challenges to British supremacy, increasing during the second half of the nineteenth century, and culminating in a crisis of national confidence in the first years of the twentieth century in the wake of the Boer War, the increased power of Germany and the United States, and labor unrest at home. The amateur masque or pageant, performed by and for citizens within their own communities, became one of many sites for the representation and hopeful resolution of these questionings of national identity. No matter what the specific topic, this is usually the important underlying theme, in keeping with the function of these amateur masques to educate and uplift the working classes for whom they were designed. Publishing houses like John Curwen and Sons, who traditionally catered to the choral movement and other forms of amateur music making, began to publish masques for just such an audience, a new outgrowth of the "rational recreation" movement.[29]

---

[29] This link is further supported by the fact that masques published by Curwen and others often include Tonic Sol-fa notation, indicating that the performers of these masques were to be drawn from the ranks of beneficiaries of the drive for music education for the masses. As I discussed in chapter 2, the masque was particularly implicated in class relations, in the desire to mold the tastes of the working classes, and in what is usually termed the "rational recreation" or "rational entertainment" movement. As Charles McGuire has succinctly defined it, "rational entertainment was a common nineteenth-century designation for any activity that would keep a member of the working or middle class away from potential morally damaging pursuits." The term was first used in relation to the Tonic Sol-fa movement in the *Tonic Sol-fa Reporter* in the June 30, 1854 issue. The later Victorians were more likely to call it "music for the people." As Dave Russell has pointed out, this movement peaked during the 1840s and 50s, then again during the 1880s and early 1900s, periods when there was an elevated level of friction between the classes, and a higher level of anxiety over the working classes among the ruling classes. Two main themes ran through endeavors to provide "rational entertainment" for the working classes: battling the perceived predilection of the working classes toward excessive alcohol consumption, and the perceived benefit of these entertainments to cement cordial relations between the classes. Charles McGuire's *Music and Victorian Philanthropy: The Tonic Sol-Fa Movement* (Cambridge: Cambridge University Press, 2007) offers an excellent treatment of some of these issues, as does Dave Russell's *Popular Music in England, 1840–1914* (Manchester: Manchester University Press, 1997).

Illustration 4.4   Louis Napoleon Parker, from
Parker's Autobiography *Several of My Lives*

For example, during the same year as Stratford's *Pan's Anniversary*, Louis N. Parker produced the first of his huge open-air pageants in the ruins of Sherborne Abbey in Dorset, involving at least 250 performers and lasting several hours. Apparently Parker had originally called the performance a "Folk-Play," but when the sale of tickets was going badly, Parker (Illustration 4.4) hit upon the idea of entitling the performance a "pageant." The performances were wildly successful, and, according to Parker, launched the national vogue for pageants in England and later in the United States that is such a feature of the period.[30] In 1950, when Parker's grandson wrote his how-to manual on pageant production, he claims that his grandfather's 1906 pageant in Warwick used over three thousand people in its production and drew an audience upwards of forty-five thousand (Illustration 4.5).

For Parker and his many imitators, a pageant was:

A tale of historical happenings, re-enacted if possible in their original setting. It is told in prose and verse, with dialogue, drama, comedy, tragedy, farce, dancing, singing and music, and, most important of all, with spectacle.[31]

Or, as Louis N. Parker described it in his autobiography:

A Pageant is a Festival of Thanksgiving, in which a great city or a little hamlet celebrates its glorious past, its prosperous present, and its hopes and aspirations for the future. It is a Commemoration of Local Worthies. It is also a great Festival of Brotherhood; in which all distinctions of whatever kind are sunk in a common effort. It is, therefore, entirely undenominational and non-political. It calls together all the scattered kindred from all parts of the world. It reminds the old of the history of their home, and shows the young what treasures are in their keeping. It is the great incentive to the right kind of patriotism: love of hearth; love of town; love of county; love of England.

---

[30] Louis Napoleon Parker had a long and successful career as a composer, musician, dramatist, and theatrical producer. He studied at the Royal Academy of Music with Sterndale Bennett, and for many years was the director of music at the Sherborne School, during which he had an active life as a composer. In 1892 he settled in London and began to actively pursue a career as a playwright and stage director for such prominent people as Herbert Beerbohm Tree. He is also credited with the invention of the modern pageant, and wrote and composed several huge pageants during the first years of the twentieth century. Late in his life he wrote an entertaining autobiography, *Several of My Lives* (London: Chapman and Hall, 1928). His grandson, Anthony Parker, also went into the pageant-making business after the Second World War and wrote a valuable how-to manual on the subject: Anthony Parker, *Pageants: Their Presentation and Production* (London: The Bodley Head, 1954).

[31] Anthony Parker, *Pageants: Their Presentation and Production*.

Illustration 4.5   The Cast and Crew of Parker's pageant at Warwick Castle, 1906

The pageant included anywhere from five to ten episodes drawn from the significant events in the history of the locality. Each of these episodes formed an independent entity, with its own look, story, set of performers and, of course, music and dancing. The Parkers even went so far as to recommend that surrounding villages or areas assume responsibility for individual episodes, so that rehearsals and production could be handled in a self-sufficient manner. By 1950, Anthony Parker's pageants had fallen into a pattern of around ten episodes, followed by a ballet, and then ending with a huge spectacular finale. The goals for the pageant were lofty; both Parkers speak frequently of the importance of the pageant in handing down the history and traditions of the past to the successive generations. At the same time, they were pragmatic in their insistence that the pageant not be too highbrow. As Anthony Parker wrote:

> The important thing always to be borne in mind is that the Pageant is, first and foremost, an entertainment. It therefore must have all the essential ingredients of any other dramatic venture; that is to say, interest, contrast, and 'good Theatre'. In addition it depends very largely on Spectacle, it must be moving and exiting, it must introduce singing and dancing, it must have a certain amount of comic relief, it must have charm, and it is founded on fact and tradition.

Given this insistence on the spectacular nature of the pageant, it is not surprising that music played a very important role in pageants such as those produced by the Parkers. Louis Parker himself spent most of his adult life as a music director and composer, so it is natural that he would give music a primary role in his pageants. In his manual, Anthony Parker details at length the position of the Pageant Music Master, who not only must compose or arrange suitable music to support the action of each of the historical episodes, but who must also coordinate assorted choirs and orchestras participating in the event, since they, like the performers and production people, were to be drawn from various local groups. Parker Senior gives a sense of the magnitude of the musical arrangements necessary for these pageants:

> In this tapestry-like fabric are interwoven folk-dances springing naturally out of the episode; and stately dances by courtiers, in which the kings and queens themselves take part; and joyous dances by young people. Shall I ever forget the Rose Dance at Colchester, the Maypole Dance at Sherborne? And the Dramatic Chorus sings, not in the guise of a Choral Society, grinding out a four-part song; but as a part of the people, giving voice to the crowd's emotions, and even breaking into a dance to the list of their own song.
>
> And when the last episode has been acted the Narrative Chorus joins forces with the Dramatic Chorus and together they thunder the Triumph Song: a poem in praise of the town whose history has been displayed. And while this is being sung, the performers of each episode, horse and foot, issue from every point of the compass and form a gigantic circle with all their banners and trophies and insignia ... These form a monumental group in the centre of the picture; and when all are in place the entire body of performers, together with the audience, sing the first verse of the Old Hundredth and lastly the whole of the National Anthem, accompanied by all the bells of all the churches in the town; and on the last line every one of the three or four thousand performers joins in a great salute.
>
> But even yet all is not over. There is no curtain ... so now begins THE MARCH PAST. To a rousing tune the tangle of the final tableau uncoils, and, led by the Narrative Chorus, each episode with its Principals at its head and with its mounted performers, its dancers, its singers, passes by the entire length of the grandstand.

A wide variety of music is implied by Parker's description. L.N. Parker calls for the following musical forces for a pageant:

(a) A full SYMPHONY ORCHESTRA, probably with the winds doubled. A small extra body of players may be required to play in costume on the arena. There must be a full equipment of large-sized tubular bells; and a thunder-machine is a glorious thing to have.

(b) The NARRATIVE CHORUS. This is a male-voice chorus in dignified robes, whose function remotely resembles that of the chorus in Greek drama. In majestic verse and stately music it introduces, links, and explains the episodes. It fills the gaps between them, and so ensures the continuity of the performance.

(c) The DRAMATIC CHORUS: a choir of mixed voices which takes part in the action on the arena. This must be trained not to sing like a choral society standing stiffly in rows, with each of the vocal parts nicely grouped together, but all mixed up, indistinguishable from the "crowd," and acting …

(d) DANCERS. Namely, Folk-dancers (Maypole, Morris, etc.). Dancers of graceful and stately dances, such as corantos, minuets, gavottes, etc, in Court scenes. Children dancers (but not too young!). The number of dancers may be unlimited. The dances (except the Court Dances) must not be too formal; must always convey the effect of being spontaneous. No dance may last more than three minutes; some folk-dances, such as Morris Dances, if protracted, are apt to become desperately depressing.[32]

Obviously, much of the material would have been arranged by the pageant composer from well-known songs and dances appropriate for the time and place of each of the episodes presented during the pageant, whether folk songs or "old" songs associated with the various periods of English history, such as the Agincourt Carol. The Fitzwilliam Virginal Book and Playford may well have been prime sources for scenes requiring Elizabethan or Restoration dance music. This kind of "borrowed" material must have resonated in the memories of the audiences for these pageants, reproducing in a sonic way the idea of the continuity of history that seems such a feature of the pageant.[33]

However, much of the music that Parker describes would have been newly composed by the pageant composer – marches, certainly, but also the music for both the narrative and dramatic choruses. Nowhere does Parker describe exactly what kind of music the mysterious "narrative chorus" would have sung, given its function of maintaining narrative continuity along the lines of the chorus in classical Greek drama, but it seems unlikely that its music could

[32] Louis Parker, *Several of My Lives*, 282.

[33] I have yet to discover any extent list of music for any of Parker's pageants. However, we do know the music that Vaughan Williams composed and arranged for a 1934 pageant written by E.M. Forster for the town of Abinger, similar in style to a Parker pageant (though certainly not with a "cast of thousands"). Music for *The Pageant of Abinger* included the Latin hymn "Angelus ad Virginem," the chant "Coelestis Urbs Hierusalem," the country dance "Gathering Peascods," the metrical psalm-setting "Let God Arise," and the folksongs "Twankydillo," "Seventeen Come Sunday," and "Sweet Nightingale." Vaughan Williams provided one newly composed piece for the pageant, a setting of Psalm 84, "How Amiable are Thy Dwellings."

have been arranged from pre-existing sources. It was important to Parker that the composers for his pageants were drawn from the community producing the pageant, in line with his view that this kind of drama was intrinsically connected to the place and people whose history was being celebrated. In his autobiography Parker pays his respects to the now unknown composers with whom he worked, men like A.J. Tester, Allen Blackall, George Wilby, and Tertius Noble. He writes: "I am happy to say I never asked one of them to omit a single bar of his music. I valued my life too highly."

The size and scope of a pageant produced by Louis Napoleon Parker far exceeded the modest types of local dramatic productions advocated by the Stratford Movement and the bulk of the masques and pageants written and published during this period to fill the needs of schools and churches. But in crucial aspects, the Parker pageants showed themselves to be at one ideologically with other less spectacular forms of the genre. Though on a large scale and certainly somewhat dependent on some professional involvement, the pageants were participatory in their emphasis. The point was for everyone in a town or locale to come together to produce this event for their community, "all classes, all creeds," as L.N. Parker described it. As in the other masques and pageants of the period, there was a moral, an ethical, and/or an educational component to the production, both for those participating and for those attending. All of the various types and styles of masques and pageants during this pre-World War II period stressed community dramatic productions as a way of speaking to a popular base within the community, and through such communication providing a transformative experience for the community that would ultimately have larger ramifications for the formation of national identity and cohesiveness. It must be emphasized that this was a part of broader cultural phenomena at work, tied to complex attitudes towards both the working classes and the character of modern Britain. As an extreme development of the "rational recreation" movement of the late nineteenth century, it sought to allay insecurity in yet one more way through musical-dramatic representations.

&. *Heirs and Rebels: New Directions for the English Musical Renaissance*

In 1912, Ralph Vaughan Williams wrote a seminal article for the *R.C.M. Magazine* entitled "Who wants the English Composer?," in which he described the problems of recognition for the young English composer, offered reasons why it was necessary to have an active English school of modern music, and encouraged English composers to maintain certain moral purposes and artistic goals. He argued that the English citizen needed to hear the nation's own music as the means of realizing "what he himself was dimly and inarticulately feeling and thinking, and that the temper of the age was in danger of passing over him, leaving him untouched and unready."[34] Within its short five pages, Vaughan Williams clearly laid out his social and utilitarian ideals for music. "The composer must not shut himself up and think about art, he must live with his fellows and make his art an expression of the whole life of the community."[35] Throughout this early article, Vaughan Williams asserted that for music to have value, it must come out of experience, both personal and communal. And the raw materials for this communal music lie in the popular music found in the composer's everyday life: certainly folk song, but also the music of the music hall, the barrel organ, the hymn, the choir festivals, the street peddlers, and the factories:

> Have we not in England occasions crying out for music? Do not all our great pageants of human beings, whether they take the form of a coronation or a syndicalist demonstration, require music for their full expression? We must cultivate a sense of musical citizenship; why should not the musician be the servant of the state and build national monuments like the painter, the writer, or the architect?[36]

This theme of the composer's social obligations is a recurring one in Vaughan Williams's writings, and is borne out by the many compositions that the composer wrote specifically for amateur music-making and broad audience appeal both before and after World War I, including *Pan's Anniversary* and the Reigate *Pilgrim's Progress*.[37] A partial impetus for this ingredient of utilitarianism in Vaughan Williams's compositional aesthetic is traceable to the composer's socio-political beliefs. Paul Harrington has convincingly traced the influence of turn-of-the-century English socialism on Vaughan Williams's

[34] Ralph Vaughan Williams, "Who Wants the English Composer?," reprinted in David Manning's *Vaughan Williams on Music* (Oxford: Oxford University Press, London, 2007) 39–42.

[35] Ibid.

[36] Ibid.

[37] It is important, however, not to overstress this element in Vaughan Williams's compositional production, an attitude which has led to much of the problematic reception of Vaughan Williams. Vaughan Williams was also deeply invested in the composition of serious art music, and his forays into more traditionally high-art genres, like the symphony and the concerto, eschew much of the musical rhetoric of populism for a compositional language more influenced by late Romantic and modernist French and German styles. In some sense, there is a split personality to his compositional output, a duality that I feel is indicative of the period's discomfort with the relationship between the arenas of art and popular music.

ideas on the role of art in society.[38] For Vaughan Williams, as for many English socialists of the period, politics of either the practical or the theoretical variety were not an important feature of their socialism. Instead, their socialist beliefs pivoted on a rather vague set of precepts regarding the ravages of capitalism and its role in creating poverty and class distinctions. Vaughan Williams, as well as Holst, was very influenced by the ideas of William Morris, who believed strongly in the necessity of art and beauty to be a part of daily life, whatever a person's class or education. Beyond mere exposure to art and beauty, Morris believed that social transformation would occur when there was widespread participation in the creation of art and beauty, through the hands-on utilization of natural, "real" materials.[39] Echoes of Morris are heard in "Who Wants the English Composer?":

> We must be our own tailors, we must cut out for ourselves, try on for ourselves, and finally wear our own home-made garments, which, even if they are homely and home-spun, will at all events fit our bodies and keep them warm; otherwise, if we pick about among great ideas of foreign composers and try to cover our

[38] Paul Harrington, "Holst and Vaughan Williams: Radical Pastoral," in *Music and the Politics of Culture*, ed. Christopher Norris (New York: St. Martin's Press, 1989), 106–27. Vaughan Williams came by his socialism first through the relatively liberal and progressive views of his extended family, the Wedgwoods, which included his great-uncle, Charles Darwin. For more on their influence, see Byron Adams, "Scripture, Church, and Culture: Biblical Texts in the Works of Ralph Vaughan Williams," in *Vaughan Williams Studies*, 99–117. This trend towards liberalism and socialism was asserted both during his schooldays at Charterhouse, and more importantly, by his circle of university friends at Cambridge, which included G.M. Trevelyan, Bertrand Russell and George Moore. And he certainly was influenced by William Morris's ideas through his friendship with Holst, who belonged to Morris's Hammersmith Socialist Club.

[39] The literature on William Morris and his effect on turn-of-the-century aesthetics is vast. The standard biography remains E.P. Thompson, *William Morris: Romantic to Revolutionary*, revised edn (New York: Pantheon, 1976). Michelle Weinroth outlines Morris's centrality in a particularly English version of socialism in *Reclaiming William Morris: Englishness, Sublimity and the Rhetoric of Dissent* (Montreal: McGill-Queen University Press, 1996), and Anne Janowitz investigates the links in Morris's ideas to English romanticism in "The Pilgrims of Hope: William Morris and the dialectic of Romanticism," in *Cultural Politics at the Fin de Siècle*, ed. Sally Ledger and Scot McCracken (Cambridge: Cambridge University Press, 1995). My own ideas about William Morris's impact during this period were influenced by S.K. Tillyard, who traces the connections between Morris, the Arts and Crafts Movement, and Roger Fry's ideas about early modernism: see S.K. Tillyard, *The Impact of Modernism, 1900–1920* (London: Routledge, 1988). For a broader history of English socialism, see Stanley Pierson, *British Socialism: the Journey from Fantasy to Politics* (Cambridge, MA: Harvard University Press, 1979).

own nakedness with them, we are in danger of being the musical counterparts of savage clothed in nothing but a top-hat and a string of beads.[40]

Two important elements of William Morris's philosophy are reflected in Vaughan Williams's own philosophy. First, for William Morris, the working classes matter; and second, the materials of art matter. We saw in chapter 2 that a concern for the relationship between the working classes and music was an important part of late Victorian musical life: witness both the brass band and choral movements, the Tonic Sol-fa movement, as well as the proliferation of outreach musical education for adults and children of the working classes.[41] Composers regularly provided music for these sorts of performers and audiences, and this included important composers like Parry and Stanford, who contributed to the ideological stance of the early days of the English Musical Renaissance and thereby inculcated within the movement a certain component of social utilitarianism inherited from Victorian attitudes and mores. Furthermore, as we have seen, both the Victorian and the Edwardian masque were particularly implicated in the aesthetic, moral, and nationalistic project of the elite towards the working classes. This manifests itself in the masques' support of a canon of nostalgic topics from English history, and their representation of appropriate attitudes towards those topics.

So, while certain features of English musical life mirrored Morris's writings – already built into attitudes about music during this period and perpetuated within the ethics of the English Musical Renaissance movement – the second aspect above, regarding Morris's theories about the appropriateness of the materials of work, is less easy to correlate. However, it may be argued that the new specificity of younger members of the English Musical Renaissance movement like Vaughan Williams towards the utilization of certain types of music, in their call for the formation of a national musical style, is part and parcel of Morris's attitudes towards creativity and work. Just as the Arts-and-Crafts furniture maker fashions a piece from English oak with a particularly beautiful grain and to a historically traditional design, and just as the bookbinder envelops a canonical English text in a binding of tooled leather in

---

[40] Ralph Vaughan Williams, "Who wants the English composer?."

[41] I have already discussed above the importance of the "rational entertainment" movement within this context. On music education specifically, Bernarr Rainbow has extensively explored the development of music education in Britain during the nineteenth century. For instance, see his "The Rise of Popular Music Education in Nineteenth Century England," in *The Lost Chord: Essays on Victorian Music*, ed. Nicholas Temperley (Bloomington: Indiana University Press, 1989), 17–41. For a valuable dissection of how school children were educated, or not educated as the case may be, into a nationalist British perspective, see Grainger's chapter 3, "*Virginibus puerisque*," in *Patriotisms*.

a Jacobean pattern, so does the composer create a musical work from musical materials that speak to the verities of the past in ways that prioritize the intrinsic worth of those basic elements.

This new attention to the source materials of the national style is certainly only one of many reasons for the folk revival of the first decades of the twentieth century and the sudden interest in folk song around the turn of the century among many British composers. However, it may offer a partial explanation for why folk music suddenly became a means towards a national music, rather than just remaining a sign containing a symbolic association with nostalgic tropes of pastoralism and the "organic village." Folk music joined Tudor and Elizabethan music as the composite musical language that would invoke the English spirit and which would offer the true path towards a national musical expression for British composers. It is an important caveat that this was not the only answer formulated to address the nationalistic, even chauvinistic, call during this period for a native musical product that could compete on the larger European cultural market. Other versions existed in competition with this particular identity based on folk and history. Nevertheless, it did quickly become the most dominant musical ideology of the period, in theory and practice. This is due in no small part to the fact that it was quickly incorporated not only into the framework of composers associated with the English Musical Renaissance movement, but also into the movement's bureaucratic and propaganda wings in musicology, music education, and criticism.

And it was incredibly long-lived; up until his death in 1958, Vaughan Williams continued to exploit the musical rhetoric of the folk for a substantial number of commissions and other works that particularly related to popular and/or amateur use. This despite the fact that an even larger component of his oeuvre, compositions in more conventionally conservative art-music genres, reveal a much more abstracted folk component, if any at all. When one looks at the symphonies or the great choral and orchestral works, how important is folk song?

Obviously, this topic is too large to deal with completely here, and many other writers have attempted to contend with the fraught issue of folk song in Vaughan Williams's music. What I would like to point out is that while folk song is crucial to the type of masque and pageant Vaughan Williams wrote, the fact that he composed works within these genres at all is equally crucial, given their integral connection with active, contemporary tropes of amateur music-making, rational entertainment, and the enlightenment of the working classes. Vaughan Williams's masques, and others of the period replicating topics of the organic village, must be seen in light of the other types of public entertainments designed to offer representations of English national identity that align themselves with the broader ideological implications of the trope.

Folk culture is in many ways a position towards Englishness antithetical to the imperial definition of a national character. While the following chapter will explore how much more complex and blurred is the distinction between folk and imperial definitions, an outwardly simplistic projection of this position clearly fits in with the radical leftist, almost socialist, leanings of Vaughan Williams and many of the second generation of composers who were part of the English Musical Renaissance movement. By creating a national musical style based on history and the folk, the new camp within the English Musical Renaissance movement energized nostalgia as a mechanism for driving home a more revolutionary attitude towards a national musical style, and ultimately, on the broader scale, a new set of cultural politics. Nostalgia may be endemic to the organic village, but for Vaughan Williams and many of his fellow composers, nostalgia and its attendant uses of history ultimately must serve the forward-looking processes of renewal and transformation both in English music and in English society as a whole.

CHAPTER 5

"The Heroic Past and the Earth his Mother": The Reticence of Reception and the Burden of Imperialism

All that can be said is that the *Patria*, the *Heimat*, once lost, has exquisite and destructive power. There may be no consolation, no recompense at all.[1]

I N an essay entitled "Public Poets," J.H. Grainger points to various strands of national definition located in the preface of a popular anthology of patriotic poetry published during the First World War, *Poems of Today: First Series*.[2] The preface elucidates three overarching themes or categories of English poetic patriotic expression:

Man draws his being from the heroic Past and from the Earth his Mother; and in harmony with these he must shape his life to what high purposes he may. Therefore this gathering of poems falls into three groups. First there are poems of History, of the romantic tale of the world, of our own special tradition here in England, and of the inheritance of obligation which that tradition imposes upon us. Then there come poems of the Earth, of England again and the longing of the exile for home of this and that familiar countryside, of woodland and meadow and garden, of the process of the seasons, of the 'open road' and the 'wind on the heath', of the city its deprivations and its consolations. Finally there are the poems of Life itself, of the moods in which it may be faced, of religion, of man's excellent virtues, of friendship and childhood, of passion, grief, and comfort.[3]

These three themes – which might in shorthand be termed the public, the pastoral, and the personal – offer a convenient way of locating differences among expressions of English national identity by where they are essentially grounded or embodied. The voices of nationalism may emanate from English history and history-in-the-making, from the English countryside, or from the hearts and minds of the English people, and each of these sources

[1] J.H. Grainger, *Patriotisms: Britain 1900–1939* (London: Routledge & Kegan Paul, 1986), 3.

[2] Ibid., 66–7.

[3] *Poems of Today: First Series* (London, 1915), vii–viii.

offers a convenient assemblage of defining characteristics for the versions of Englishness that emerge from their collective tropes.

These three themes extend beyond the realm of poetry; in fact, they inform the entire range of cultural production during the late Victorian and Edwardian periods. Witness theatrical works and novels, for instance. These themes are reflected in the three dominant genres of painting exhibited at the Royal Academy exhibits at the end of the nineteenth century – history paintings, landscapes, and portraiture.[4] Even when the subjects of these paintings do not explicitly refer to Britain or the British, these themes are implicit through a discourse that works either by setting up parallels with English topics, or by a contrast with the exotic "other," which too point to English historical, pastoral, or personal identities.

More to the point, this topical trilogy also operated as a set of functional categories in any British musical work that attempted to embody some form of England as a nation, or some conceptualization of the national character or patriotic sentiment. The pastoral impulse, examined in the preceding chapter, was only one component, counter-balanced by equally important expressions of personal subjectivity and stories of the *patria*. The applicability of these three themes becomes manifest in the works of Edward Elgar, probably the most well-known English composer of the period between 1895 and 1910. In the public vein, Elgar composed works on historical English topics such as *Falstaff* and the cantata *Caractacus*, and quintessential invocations of English patriotism in his marches and *Land of Hope and Glory*. His works in the personal vein include characterizations of the richness of friendship in the *Enigma Variations* and the intense religious subjectivity of *The Dream of Gerontius*. And Elgar frequently indulged in the pastoral, as in passages like the "Woodland Interlude" from *Caractacus* and the "river theme" from the First Symphony.[5] The three categories are so applicable to the period they even hold true in the works of Ralph Vaughan Williams, whom critics often cite in stark contrast to Elgar. Indeed, Vaughan Williams's compositions from the

---

[4] For a concise survey of British painting during the period in question, see Julian Treuherz, *Victorian Painting* (London: Thames and Hudson, 1993). Likewise, the collection of essays edited by David Peters Corbett and Lara Perry, *English Art, 1860–1914: Modern Artists and Identity* (New Brunswick, NJ: Rutgers University Press, 2001), looks at many of the same issues of identity that I deal with here.

[5] In a discussion of Elgar and pastoralism, Matthew Riley states that "Elgar's music is not so much *about* a specific place as inspired, or prompted, *by* it." He argues that much of the way in which Elgar tapped into a pastoralist or natural vein of composition was heavily informed by contemporary literary tropes contained in the representation of Nature at the turn of the century: Matthew Riley "Rustling Reeds and Lofty Pines: Elgar and the Music of Nature," *19th-Century Music*, 26 (2002), 155–77.

same period reveal the same triune set of concerns: the historical and public perspective of *The Sea Symphony* and the *Fantasia on a Theme by Thomas Tallis*; the obvious pastoral evocations of *On Wenlock Edge* and the *Norfolk Rhapsodies*; and the personal and subjective contained in his response to Walt Whitman's poetry in *Toward the Unknown Region*, as well as in his many song settings of the period.

It would not do, however, to place too heavy a sense of security on the boundaries of categorization within this trilogy of topics. A closer examination of single works or groups of works reveals to what extent these three domains interacted with and informed each other, complicating any simple attempt to categorize works into thematic groups. It was common for works of this period to slip across these boundaries, appropriating not just one perspective towards the construction of national character but several, again revealing the heterogeneity of national identity during this period. The pastoral is particularly slippery: works can reflect a historical, pre-industrial version of the pastoral, or a pastoral arising from personal subjectivity and meaning, a personal, imaginative landscape.

For the music of the period, whether allied specifically with the aesthetics of the English Musical Renaissance or not, many factors hinder a clear understanding of how components from these three categories of Englishness combine, and ultimately how they should be categorized with regard to the patriotic stances available during the period. An even more essential question is how and how far those patriotic stances are informed by imperialism and the extent to which these three areas of identity are complicit in ideologies surrounding the British Empire. For we certainly cannot deny the inextricable connections between representations of personal and national identity and contemporary British political and social structures that were situated within a complicated imbroglio as a result of Britain's imperial present.

The Edwardian and early Georgian period is often viewed today as a time that displayed the height of a certain type of British patriotic feeling on a national level. This hyper-patriotism supported both imperialist expansion in the non-Western world and, in the West, nationalistic competitiveness and an attempt at ultimate domination over other Western nations. This attitude resulted first in the Boer conflict and came to a catastrophic climax in the events leading to the First World War. But a closer investigation into cultural artifacts which were designed to "do the work" of representing Englishness, so strongly exemplified by the masques and pageants from this period, reveals a far from universally cohesive message about the how, what, and why of English national identity, and the degree and kind of intimacy it had with the imperialist agenda. During our period, patriotism ceased to be a rather blithe union of citizen and nation found throughout most of the nineteenth century, and became instead a contestation between factions of patriots, each of whom was battling to constitute a revised sense of the nation.[6] As Grainger puts it:

> So, what are being sought in Edwardian England are those parts which claim to stand for the whole, which are potentially, if remotely, areas of necessity. Because so much has happened to England, because of the richness and variety of a political order which had absorbed so many political formations and, in insular security, remained free to commemorate all of them, the *patria* has many voices. There is a great buzz about forbears, brothers, land, liberty, journeys, missions about the army and navy, about the near and the far. The patriotic injunction remains simple enough: defend and maintain the given good to which you belong. But the content and boundaries of that good are diverse.[7]

It is these metonymies, these "areas of necessity," which are the sites of contention in the overlapping categories of public, pastoral and personal. And naturally, this clash over sites of identification permeated the arenas of cultural production, negotiating the slippage between reality and fantasy. As Charles Pearson remarked in his *National Life and Character*, nationalism during this period was not merely concerned with preserving what the nation was in the present. It also sought "to recover for it what it has lost, or to acquire what seems naturally to belong to it."[8]

Looking back with eyes open to the implications of the permeable boundaries between these sites of identity, it becomes clearer how the amateur masque and pageant culture that I investigated in my previous chapter manifested a set of "public" ideological concerns which are clearly social, despite its overt

[6] In the eighteenth century, the idea of the patriot and patriotism was essentially understood as a position antagonistic to the present-day realities of the nation as a political unit. A brilliant examination of the concept of patriotism in Britain during this period is contained in Linda Colley, *Britons: Forging the Nation 1707–1837* (New Haven, CT: Yale University Press, 1992). For a more concrete example of how the eighteenth-century conception of the patriot was represented in a masque, see Michael Burden, *Garrick, Arne and the Masque of Alfred* (Lewiston: Edwin Mellen Press, 1994). However, in the nineteenth century much of this antagonism between patriotism and government was resolved into a more complacent union. As Grainger puts it: "It was as if from 1815 the British *patria* in its incontiguity and security had receded from view as an area of necessity. Celebratory of the national life, self-congratulatory rather than perturbed, it had become both too comprehensive and too equivocal actively to serve as a domestic party-political nostrum or programme. It seemed as if Britain pre-eminent had inoculated herself against an 18th-century epidemic." J.H. Grainger, *Patriotisms: Britain 1900–1939*.

[7] Grainger, *Patriotisms*, 23.

[8] Charles H. Pearson, *National Life and Character* (London: Macmillan and Co., 1893), 187.

prioritization of the pastoralist trope. The ideological complexities bound up in imperialist agendas and contained in many of the amateur masques of the period testify to confusions endemic in positing a national identity in any one site. In practice, a conception of these three categories as mutually exclusive is not an Edwardian construct. What binds all of these representations together is the idea of patriotism in its broadest sense, with imperialism and ideologies of race as crucial components.

This chapter focuses on the imperialist and other "public" components in constructions of an English national character in the cultural production of the period.[9] These sources of identity, national and musical, have been framed in the past in ways that heighten the sense of contrast with those explored in chapter 4. However, in discussing this side of English national identity, which seems in such contrast to pastoral and folk identities, I will argue that in essence this component cannot be separated from pastoral constructions. Within the masques of the period, amateur as well as professional, "public" discourse or "public voice" permeated all other representations. Beyond the masque, public voice was a central trope for English music of this period as a whole. I will also argue that within English music and the English Musical Renaissance, it was only subsequent reception that prioritized the pastoral, and to a lesser degree, the personal discourses of identity at the expense of the public. In the process, certain aspects of modernity, including the ideologies of empire and race, were minimized despite their real and potent presence.[10] Ultimately, the distinctions between constructions of musical identity represented by the likes of Elgar and Vaughan Williams had less to do with whether or not these two composers adopted a public voice and much more with how history and nostalgia were to be used in its construction.

This complicates our previous ideas about the distinctions between the identifications based on the empire and modernity, and those based on the organic village explored in the previous chapter. On the one hand, those positions that base themselves on folk and pastoral tropes define themselves as the "other" to modernity, particularly Britain's imperial modernity and the industrial and commercial modernity that was part and parcel of it. However, I would argue that the act of speaking for the nation through the assertion of national character inherently implicates this same modernity, despite where

[9] Martin Clayton and Bennett Zon's edited volume *Music and Orientalism in the British Empire, 1780s–1940s: Portrayal of the East* (Aldershot: Ashgate Publishing, 2007) offers many valuable essays exploring the effects of imperialism on musical production during the period.

[10] As John M. Mackenzie argues in his "Introduction," in *Imperialism and Popular Culture*, ed. John M. Mackenzie (Manchester: Manchester University Press, 1986), 1–16.

that national character is situated, physically or temporally. It is through this intrinsic resemblance in the understanding of the basic "work" of cultural production as essentially nationalistic that we can assert that the public segment of the trilogy of identifications described above ultimately subsumed the others.

In the following pages, I will examine the overtones of race and imperialism informing four versions of the public side of the construction of national identity that are connected to the masque and masque–pageant culture: the Stratford Movement; imperialist masques for children; professionally produced masques and pageants in theaters, including Elgar's *Crown of India*; and reception issues surrounding Elgar's adoption of the persona of the public poet. This collage-like approach mimics the patchwork construction of identity that assembled complementary, and occasionally competing, "areas of necessity" prior to World War I.

ᕍ Stratford and Empire

Stratford-upon-Avon was one epicenter of a movement that sought to constitute a version of Englishness through encounters with the English countryside, English history, and English folk customs embedded in a range of ideologies I have grouped under the heading of the "organic village."[11] The actual Stratford Movement sought to attain social renewal through the means of a performative communal drama. Within this dramatic experience, the English people could encounter both the great works of dramatic art and the folk customs of the nation through controlled aesthetic experiences that would reflect and nurture the collective, national spirit of the people. The inspiration for the concept of a national drama was a specific reaction to the philosophies of Richard Wagner and their concrete realization at Bayreuth, but they easily surpassed the Wagnerian in the range and scope of the movement's goals.[12] The extension of Wagnerian musico-dramatic theories within the context of the Stratford Movement comes via the movement's prioritization of the

---

[11] See chapter 4, "Making the Commonwealth a Harmony."

[12] It is a fascinating aspect of Buckley's essay that outlines this connection to Wagner (see below) that he sees no problem in specifically crediting Wagner as the source of his own belief, and by extension the beliefs of the Stratford Movement, in the necessary racial and nationalistic component of artworks which have the power to effect social transformation and renewal. That Wagner is concerned with the promotion of a specifically Germanic racial consciousness is negated in Buckley's context by the prioritization of the Anglo-Celtic. It is so obvious to Buckley that, given the opportunity, an Anglo-Celtic Wagnerism will far outdo the original.

folk and folk traditions of all sorts, expanding on Wagner's own ideas of the importance of myth.

The connection with Wagner is an important one because the Stratford Movement not only tapped into Wagner's theory of the *Gesamtkunstwerk*, but also into the racial foundations that support such contemporary appropriations of the language of myth and the folk. It is not surprising, then, that the writings of the Stratford Movement are permeated with racial discourse, as are most English writings that deal with folklore, ethnography, and myth from the *fin-de-siècle*. And this concern with race and definitions of "otherness" extends far beyond the obvious realm of the folk. Race, along with gender and class, constitutes a trilogy that serves as the essential focal point for many modern critical approaches to Victorian and Edwardian cultural production. A large critical bibliography currently exists which demonstrates that issues of race and "otherness" saturate every aspect of cultural production during Britain's "long" nineteenth century, only intensifying as the ideologies of empire were increasingly threatened at the close of the century.[13] An important aspect of this critical discussion is the realization that racial ideologies are bound to all discourses of the period, whether they are overtly about empire or not, particularly in dominant literary genres, and especially in the novel. In an atmosphere redolent with racial discourse, even positions that declare themselves to be contra-imperial and situated firmly in "Little England," like those associated with the folk revival, reveal the boundary confusions endemic to public versus pastoral debates.

A re-examination of the rhetoric associated with the previously discussed Stratford Movement offers a good entry point into the ways through which the discourses of race and imperialism could pervade ostensibly simple surface expressions of pastoralism and the folk revival. For while the movement outwardly spoke of England's villages, countryside, and local customs, it did so in the name of a more global perspective, connecting with England's mission to lead the nations culturally, as well as politically and economically, in a glorification of the "Anglo-Celtic" race. Additionally, though the movement projected the idea that it spoke as one with the "Little England" of the inhabitants of village and countryside, in many ways the methodology espoused by the movement replicated British colonial agendas across the seas.

---

[13] The current bibliography on imperialism and post-colonial theory is immense. A valuable account of postcolonialism from both a historical and theoretical perspective is Robert Young's *Postcolonialism: an Historical Introduction* (Oxford: Blackwell Publishers, 2001). For a more general overview of orientalism throughout arenas of cultural productions, see John M. MacKenzie, *Orientalism: History, Theory and the Arts* (Manchester: Manchester University Press, 1995).

Returning specifically to an important source of period rhetoric discussed in chapter 4, *The Shakespeare Revival and the Stratford-on-Avon Movement*, the organizers of the Stratford Festival and its extension into the Stratford Movement felt that the tenets of their cause represented a veritable "racial religion," as Mary Neal explicitly termed it.[14] Frank Benson, in his panegyric to the Stratford May Day "vision" of the dreamer that forms his introduction to *The Shakespeare Revival*, quoted in chapter 4, includes a scene in his "vision" that makes manifest a Shakespearean cultural imperialism:

> Among the crowd are many people from over-seas; blood brothers of the race, fellow subjects from distant parts of our Empire, friends from foreign countries all the world over … The Spaniard, the Bohemian, the African, the Asiatic recognize in many of the dances some primitive ceremony still in vogue among their own folk to this day … The Indian Prince, guest of honour on this occasion, expresses his pleasure at being present with words full of meaning. "I will take back to my country the story of your song and dance and your Shakespeare Festival, that my people may have more joy in their lives, and that your folk and my folk may better understand each other's religion." As said an Eastern in a bygone age, "Your people shall be my people, and your gods my gods."[15]

At the end of his "vision" the dreamer sees a temple of art, a "college of humanity," dedicated to the genius of the Anglo-Celtic race, but with side shrines to the approved products of other nations:

> Stratford, Warwickshire, the British Empire, and America join in an informal conference of the Anglo-Celtic confederation. With their differences adjusted in a world of art, music and literature their common race possession, they will realise, as they join hands with the subtle strength of India, the triumph of the Aryan Empire, which seems on this night of May to be drawing near with the dawn, for the pilgrims who have realised Shakespeare's message of strong and strenuous self-control. For them the blending of East and West and the reconciliation of Black and White can be left to the coming years.
>
> > "From the four corners of the earth they come
> > To kiss this shrine, this mortal breathing saint,"
>
> bringing in their train the fervour of the Romance nations, the discipline of the Teuton, the primitive vigour of the Slav, the enterprise of the Scandinavian, the mystic reverence of the Oriental.[16]

[14] Reginald R. Buckley, *The Shakespeare Revival and the Stratford-Upon-Avon Movement* (London: George Allen & Sons, 1911).

[15] Ibid., xiv–xv.

[16] Ibid., xviii–xix.

But it is Buckley, the book's editor and author of its longest multi-sectional essay, "The Nature of Drama," who obsessively hammers home the connection between the goals of the Stratford Movement and the ideas of nationalism and racial religion. Picking up on a previous dispute with the music critic Ernest Newman, who at this point was arguing for a cosmopolitan and anti-nationalist path for English music, Buckley expounds for pages upon the necessity of a racial component in great works of art, especially English ones. He links Shakespeare and Wagner as twin poles of genius that reveal the necessity of the nationalist and racial configurations of myth and folk in works designed to address the double task of cultural renewal and the edification of English society.[17] Buckley moves between what is specifically Anglo-Celtic, and larger racial issues of Aryanism that bond the English with Wagner's Teutonic expressions:

> Mr. Newman being the cleverest of the anti-nationalists I gave him a definition of the Englishman. I repeat it here … The English are a mixture of many races, pure in one respect. We are Indo-Europeans, and are kindred of the Celtic, Teutonic, and Indian Stock … Not only have armed invaders fought their way into the family circle, but each county has moulded its type and its dialect, throwing up defenses against the common enemy, Cosmopolitanism. And when I walk along a London street, seeing Parsees, Kaffirs, Frenchmen, Jews, Germans and Spaniards, London does not seem less English. These barriers of race are everywhere in evidence. Each face flies its own flag.
>
> Mr. Newman held that all this talk about nationality and race feeling was a pose, that Reason, the sharp-tongued goddess, had broken down these sentimental barriers. When Shakespeare drew Shylock he showed his race feeling … But when Shakespeare created Othello it was a very different matter. The character is drawn as an Englishman, and only colour marks the difference. The cleverest critic cannot acquit Shakespeare of the natural race feelings common

---

[17] Obviously, this is not a stance with which Wagner himself would have agreed. Rather, it displays Buckley's attempt to appropriate Wagner's ideologies into an "Anglo-Celtic" context, thereby diffusing Wagner's Germanic nationalism. We also have to remember Wagner's enormous popularity in England during these years, and so Buckley's desire to "anglicize" may also be an attempt to latch onto some of that popularity. Ernest Newman himself was the first English biographer of Wagner, George Barnard Shaw was an avid "Wagnerite," and many an English composer, music critic and music lover made the pilgrimage to Bayreuth. For more on this topic, the classic treatment remains Anne Dzamba Sessa, *Richard Wagner and the English* (London: Associated University Press, 1979). Emma Sutton offers a closer look at Wagner as a signifier of identity at the end of the nineteenth century in her *Aubrey Beardsley and British Wagnerism in the 1890s* (Oxford: Oxford University Press, 2002).

to all men. We love Wagner none the less because his art sprang from the soul of the people and was based on folk-tales.[18]

For Buckley, the quintessential musical expression of the English race lies in her choral music, and Buckley devotes a section of his "The Nature of Art" to the role of choral music in the Stratford Movement. In it he argues that choral music has to move from the imprisoning venues of the concert hall and choral societies and into a stronger relationship with a racial communal drama that is at the heart of the Stratford Festival. Stating that drama and choral music spring from the same root, and that in Shakespeare "music and speech were as one," Buckley seeks to remove from choral music the taint of the urban and the commercial and, instead, plant it in the true heart of England, thereby reaffirming its importance to the racial religion. In return, Stratford brings yet one more communal expression of the people into its "temple of art," one linked to drama by its ability to "blend the emotions of the multitude":

> I believe that, by incorporating in the scheme representative [choral] works such as I have outlined, new blood and new energy would be drawn into the Movement. The Choral North would come to the Avon banks, and their picked festival choruses could speak to our hearts in a language that we understand ... Instead of working separately with their own publics and methods they would regard Stratford as a clearing-house of English Art, and of Art more than English ...
>
> Australia, rich in singers and poets; New Zealand, truly a land of zeal, would be there. Indeed, from the Seven Seas would come the tribes to be sealed at Stratford.
>
> The unity of race which has marked out Judaism among the nations, would set the Anglo-Celtic peoples, the Indo-European race at common cause ...
>
> And as you read it, especially Indians, who do not know that kinship between our Arthurian cycle with your Ramayana, remember before the cosmopolitan spirit has widened the breach.
>
> Nationalism not only reaches to the heart of India, and finds a homeland on every shore of the Seven Seas, but goes deep down into the past, the first gleaming hopes of the race before we became tribes, before we began to forget each other as do brothers who lived long in distant lands.
>
> The Movement has reached a stage which demands development. Imperial Federation is in the air, yet never was there a time when Little England was so essentially the homeland of a great people.[19]

Apart from Buckley's grandiose dreams of an Anglo-Celtic and Indo-European world coming to worship at the shrine of the racial art, closer

---

[18] Buckley, *The Shakespeare Revival and the Stratford-Upon-Avon Movement*, 104–5.

[19] Ibid., 173–5.

to home, in Little England itself, the goals of the Stratford Movement cannot be separated from imperialist and colonialist ideologies. Even the domestic outreach programs promulgated by the movement that sought to encourage national drama in the towns and villages of England take on a colonial agenda, as the initiates of Stratford intrude into the pastoral countryside, enacting the missionary concern of the white settler bringing culture to the native. Buckley and his fellow leaders of the movement assume the ideology of a colonial settler, one of self-rejuvenation and social renewal. This is combined with an implied attitude in which the superior conquering race rescues the native population from its own degeneration, restoring to the natives their lost heritage, which they can no longer be trusted to maintain.[20] It is in these agendas that the Stratford Movement reveals its full immersion in a very "modern" concern for issues of identity and nationhood, despite the nostalgic implications of its prioritization of history and the folk. And the pastoralist stance that is seemingly at the heart of the movement's search for an English national identity is inextricably intertwined with public and modern expression of nationalism and race. As Buckley himself put it: "It is the modernity not the medievalism of Shakespeare that has made the Festival possible."[21]

﷽ Masques in the Mix

The example of the Stratford Movement demonstrates how organizations within amateur masque and pageant culture were heavily infused with racial and imperial cultural discourses of the period that were deeply embedded in their preferred local, pastoral and historical topics. Similarly, a closer look at particular examples of amateur masques and pageants reveals the means by which this entire genre spoke in some way to a modern English patriotism, steeped in imperialism and the nation's perceived destiny to regenerate the world. No matter what the topic, patriotism is usually the underlying theme, in keeping with the function of these amateur masques to educate and uplift the lower classes for which many

---

[20] Georgina Boyes cogently argues that a fundamental principle underlying the collecting of folk song and other traditions was the essential belief by the upper classes that the working classes, urban and rural both, had degenerated from a purer state in the past, and could no longer be trusted to be the repository of folk culture. It needed to be extracted from them and held in trust for the large community by collectors who were more fit to see the markers of the pure past of the folk: Georgina Boyes, *The Imagined Village: Culture, Ideology, and the English Folk Revival* (Manchester: Manchester University Press, 1993).

[21] Reginald R. Buckley, *The Shakespeare Revival and the Stratford-Upon-Avon Movement*, 153.

of them were designed.[22] Many, if not most, exploit the trope of the historicized folk explored in chapter 4 that was so vital to the masque and pageant culture during this period. A substantial number, however, also appropriate a more public rendition of history to communicate public versions of national identity. These circulate around the inclusions of kings, battles, and conquests, as well as British cultural superiority in science, economics, government, and literature.

A Mayday masque written and composed in 1904 by Arthur Poyser[23] offers a good example of how imperialistic rhetoric was grafted onto pastoral and historical tropes. The masque displays the now-stereotypical version of a country May Day, familiar in all its musical incarnations since Sterndale Bennett's 1858 cantata *The May Queen*:[24] time and location fuzzily unspecific,

[22] This is not to say that all manifestations of imperialism in popular types of entertainment, such as music-hall shows, were designed by the ruling classes for a reluctant working-class audience. New evidence on concert attendance and performance data shows that not only were these types of entertainment patronized by members of all classes, but that the working classes were enthusiastic supporters of the imperialist sentiment. For a general discussion of this issue, again see John M. Mackenzie's "Introduction," in *Imperialism and Popular Culture*. Dave Russell discusses the relationship between working and ruling classes in the realm of popular music in *Popular Music in England, 1840–1914*, 2nd edn (Manchester: Manchester University Press, 1997). However, as demonstrated in my fourth chapter, the amateur masque and pageant movement manifested still a heavy reliance on the ideologies of "rational recreation" above that of other popular fare.

[23] Poyser's introduction is noteworthy on one level because it is one of the few available descriptions from this period that attempts to define the modern masque genre as it had come to be conceptualized in the early twentieth century: "The term 'Masque' is used to differentiate this class of performance from the Operetta which necessitates the provision of a stage, scenery, proscenium, fittings, etc. and from the cantata, a term usually applied without action, costume, or scenery. The 'masque' occupies a place between the operetta and the cantata, combining certain features of both, and yet requiring no stage accommodation whatever. All that is necessary is a tolerably large hall – the larger of course the better – a clear floor space, a wide door at one end of the hall for the entrance and departure of processions, a small platform for the stationary chorus, a supply of costume and necessary properties such as a maypole, queen's throne, etc. ... The Masque of Maytime can also be produced with excellent effect in the open air, on a large level lawn with raised banks all around, or on a village green." At the British Library, the masque is bound in a multi-work miscellany of a variety of operettas and cantatas. Poyser's introduction, however, claims a status for his masque somewhere between the two, definitely staged – he goes on to offer extremely detailed advice on costumes and blocking – but not requiring the accessories that mark a theatrical production.

[24] For more on the trope of the May Day in Victorian musical-dramatic works, see chapter 2. For an overview of the importance of May Day as a trope in all kinds of civic festivities, see Roy Judge, "May Day and Merrie England," *Folklore* 102 (1991), 131–48.

with solo and choral songs, as well as incidental music and dances that both at times self-consciously utilize a folksy pastiche. The final tableau presents a maypole dance, followed by the traditional combat between St. George and the Dragon. The topic of St. George – the quintessential embodiment of both the chivalric British defense of the good and British ascendancy and victory in conflict – offers a convenient segue to the patriotic content of the final song:

> Let voices sing of England's fame
> Of gallant deeds. Of fearless men.
> Let Warrior's Sword and Poet's pen
> The Might of British realms proclaim.
> St. George and England be the cry,
> Let Britons o'er the Empire wide
> Take up the olden strain with pride
> And for that land ne'er fear to die!

It is the perfunctory nature of this transition from pastoral to imperial that is so striking, since the transition from the folk to the realm of "Warrior's Sword and Poet's pen" is so little prepared by the quaint pastoral idiom that dominates most of the masque. In retrospect, the lack of preparation for this sudden patriotic expression clearly indicates that one is to understand that the patriotic, indeed imperialistic, message has been implicit all along, ineffably tied up in the vision, the meaning, of representations of the past in the masque. The timeless verities of the pastoral trope as located in the folk traditions of the English countryside speak to the imperial present, the "olden strain" confirming Britain's attempt to extend British virtues, political, religious, and moral, to the rest of the world.

Yet another example from several years later offers a similar instance of the imperial component present in much of the masque writing for amateurs, both before and immediately after World War I. In 1918, the Hon. Mrs. Edith Gell published a masque entitled *The Empire's Destiny: A musical peace masque for young people*. In the preface of the Mowbray and Co. edition, Mrs. Gell succinctly sets forth goals for her masque that reflect the complex ideology resonating through much of the masque repertoire written during the early years of the twentieth century. It is so remarkably open about its "larger project" that the preface is worth reproducing in its entirety:

> The cordial welcome accorded to *The Empire's Honour*[25] and the urgent requests received by many quarters for a new masque prove that there is a wide-spread desire for the return of the old pageants which lent so much colour to daily life.

---

[25] A masque previously written by Mrs Gell in 1915 during World War I.

The thousands of performers of *The Empire's Honour* have revealed unsuspected talent even in remote villages, both on the dramatic and musical side. It is of the first importance that these gifts should be developed, so that by degrees every parish may have the means in its midst of dispelling dreariness and the woeful dullness which is the very parent of evil, without recourse to artificial and often stupidly vulgar entertainments.

There is no more wholesome recreation for young people of all classes than taking part in representations which seek to place before actors and audience alike, noble ideals in popular form. The representations give scope for individual development and expression ... the qualities of perseverance, patience, co-operation, unselfishness which go to make a successful performance are none the less valuable because they are fostered indirectly. It is hoped that a time will come when each county will have a series of such musical masques for performance, embodying the chief historical events within its bounds ... performers who, reverently setting forth great ideas, have helped to form a sound public opinion, thus contributing their quota of service to the building up of "an empire, God-commissioned to regenerate the world."

Several important strands find their way into this brief introduction. Most obviously, Gell firmly roots her attitude towards the value of the masque within the domain of social utility that we have seen has been continuously present in a certain type of masque since the middle of the nineteenth century and which became full-blown in the pageant culture described in chapter 4. While Gell does say that these masques are appropriate for "young people of all classes," her call to "remote villages" and "parishes" reveals her particular concern for the social edification of the lower classes, urban and rural, and in particular those who would otherwise fall into danger of pursuing "artificial and stupidly vulgar entertainments." Gell also situates her masques in a relationship to history: her masque is in the style of "the old pageants which lent so much colour to daily life." This past, however, is vague and unspecific, more a "simpler, better time" than any true historical period, and the modern is not subjected to the overt criticism that is frequently found in other recursions to the past. The obvious reason for this lack of nostalgia is that Gell is actually advocating for a particularly modern view of Englishness in this introduction, and one that bears a close analogy to the "public," the first of the three patriotic themes mentioned in the introduction to *Poems of Today*. Gell's proposed series of local masques that will inspire the public by the illustration of historical events, resonates with the "poems of History, of the romantic tale of the world, of our own special tradition here in England, and of the inheritance of obligation which that tradition imposes upon us."[26] But it is the

[26] *Poems of Today*, vii.

call to empire and to Britain's God-given destiny which make this masque so timely. A work like "The Victory Song" (Illustration 5.1) encourages children to make the imperatives of empire a religious obligation, and to think of their Englishness as a vocation to "stand with Right and Brotherhood."[27] This text is projected musically with the diatonicism and square rhythms that by the first decade of the twentieth century have become important hallmarks of the English patriotic march idiom, popularized first by Sullivan and solidified into yet another "invented tradition" by Elgar.

Unmistakable extensions of pageant culture discussed in the previous chapter, these masques are just two examples from the huge corpus of musico-dramatic works written specifically for children's productions in schools and Sunday schools that proliferated during the first decades of the twentieth century. These masques draw on all of the themes present in the masques for adults, though they are far simpler in most aspects such as theme and topic, music and dance, and other items related to stage production. As in the adult masques and pageants, the pastoral element is very much visible throughout this repertoire. For instance, a masque such as *The Masque of May Morning*, by W. Graham Robertson and Arthur Akeroyd, published in 1908, offers yet another version of a child's version of the May Day masque–cantata popular since the middle of the nineteenth century. Characters include Winter, Snowdrop, Primrose, April, and May, with choruses of the Snow and May Dew Gatherers. Akeroyd's music is actually quite extensive, but the songs are easy and tuneful, with choral parts for treble and alto. Each phase in the transition from Winter to May is characterized by a solo song from a main character, a chorus, and opportunities for dancing. In this masque, the pastoral trope is uncomplicated by the appearance of imperialist ideologies.

Perhaps more typical is a volume of masques by Alice Buckton entitled *Masques and Dances*, published in 1904 in two volumes, in which the pastoral idioms and morals about the cogency of folk tradition intermingle with the messages of empire and modernity. This collection contains several masques first published in the magazine *Child Life*, based on actual fairy tales or fantastic, moralistic stories geared for simple, student productions, each with some simple songs printed at the end for interpolation if desired. "The Garden of Many Waters" is the most elaborate of these masques. The Spirit of the Hour comes across a beautiful garden tended by two child gardeners. Impressed with its beauty, the Spirit searches for its creator among such allegorical characters as Commerce, Science, Law, Poetry, and Philosophy, each duly

---

[27] Also note the mission for England's women, to give birth and raise a "noble race" of British subjects! For more on how women's reproductive roles are tied to nation-building, see Nira Yuval-Davis, *Gender and Nation* (London: Sage Publications, 1997).

THE EMPIRE'S DESTINY

The Victory Song

Illustration 5.1 Gell, *The Empire's Destiny*, "The Victory Song"

celebrated in turn, but none of these can take credit. The puzzle is solved in the last tableau, which shows a peasant family. The presentation of each of the allegorical characters affords an opportunity to present the importance of these aspects to British national life. Ultimately, it is again the character of the pastoral country folk that is England's greatest asset, and the achievements of modernity cede their precedence to the representations of the historicized folk. However, unlike many of those masques, there is an implicit message in this masque and others like it: while versions of national identity may be rooted in the folk, the inflorescence of those roots leads England into its own particular mission of modernity.

While most of the music of Buckton's masques is somewhat featureless and typical of what one would expect for plays written for and performed by children, she specifies some historical incidental music to impart an air of pastness to "The Garden of Many Waters." She recommends a prelude that would use "music in an old style such as a Sarabande or 'une Fête à Trianon' by Henri Roubien, resolving itself into the old Pavane music of Henri III, 'Belle, qui tiens ma vie'!" The specific period or style of music is hardly an issue here; it is instead just the "old style" that is of crucial importance to underlining the central image of the "Golden Age" pastoral and its inhabitants. "Belle, qui tiens ma vie!," for instance, a song contained in Arbeau's *Orchesographie*, had by this time made its way into volumes of "old" songs in easy arrangements for piano.[28]

Pieces like this are fairly innocuous. However, children's masques often contained a quite virulent form of imperialist rhetoric. Here the message, because less sophisticated, was sometimes particularly blatant.[29] A remarkable and quite extensive masque for children from this period is G.T. Kimmins' *The Masque of the Children of the Empire* published by Curwen in 1909. The masque has a huge list of characters:

> The Prolocutor robed in a doctor's cap and gown, as in the Old Morality Plays, with ink horn and pen … brings forward 10 centuries, each is introduced and lays offerings at the feet of Britannia.

---

[28] The first English editions of *Orchesographie* seems to be that of Peter Warlock in 1925, who used the songs as a basis for his *Capriol Suite*. But editions were published in Germany and France during the late nineteenth century, and selected songs were quickly assimilated into a bank of readily accessible Renaissance songs.

[29] J.S. Bratton offers a fascinating look at imperialist content in children's literature in "Of England, Home, and Duty: the Image of England in Victorian and Edwardian Juvenile Fiction," in *Imperialism and Popular Culture*, ed. John M. Mackenzie, 73–93.

The centuries are the tenth through the nineteenth, and each is accompanied by "suitable music." They are followed by the procession of "Daughter Nations" – each in characteristic dress and each with its own standard-bearer – who also give offerings to Britannia. The "laying of offerings" is indicative of the governing agenda of this masque. Instead of the nostalgic prioritization of the past, the symbols of the past and the imperial present together continuously replicate their subservience to the all-encompassing *patria*, as it exists at present, as one after another they lay their offerings at Britannia's feet.

Part II of the masque involves "The Revels," the quintessential component of the masque genre from the period, and usually an excuse for a free-for-all type of spectacle combining song, dance, and elaborate pageantry. Here the Revels consists of a series of English, Irish, Scottish, and Welsh dances, with detailed instructions included on the choreography of the folk dances and possible folk songs to use for each of the dances. Clearly even the folk can be subsumed in a representation of a modern and progressive vision of Britannia.

The masque concludes with these lines:

> Hear ye, good people, links with all the ages!
>
> Take ye my thanks across the whirl of time.
> Rich the inheritance – great the varied stages
> By which ye brought this nation to its prime.
> Prize ye the history linking Past and Present;
> Value the bond which binds us each to each;
> Grant that the chain between us ne'er be lessened,
> Nor dimmed the glory which the Past doth teach.
> Rather let one and all link hands in token,
> In pledge that History's tale be understood.
> Past, Present, Future, all in the unshaken,
> Linked in one vast, living brotherhood.

> *Prolocutor:* Fare well! The Centuries so closely woven
> With all the rich great history to be –
> Remember now the ages long forgotten,
> And in this Masque the truth of History see.

The publication itself is unique. The first noticeable characteristic is the amount of space and effort devoted to describing how amateurs could get their production to "look right," with as much correct historical and ethnographic costume as is possible. This includes not only descriptions but also amusing photographs of children dressed up in appropriate costumes (Illustration 5.2).

The cover of the printed masque emphasizes the imperial agenda. A drawing in a style reminiscent of a children's book illustration shows a semi-circle of

Britannia
With her six Daughter Nations, and Child of the Empire.   [After 19th Century.

The Ten Sovereigns
With Britannia, Father Time, and Prolocutor.

Illustration 5.2   Costumes from Kimmins' *The Masque of the Children of the Empire*

children dressed in the costumes of Britain's empire posed respectfully before the figure of Britannia. The message clashes violently with the mantle of innocence projected by the style of the drawing (Illustration 5.3).

Masques like those of Gell and Kimmins inculcated a whole generation of English children into a particular view of history that created imperatives for the present and future. To be English and the inheritors of English history was to be responsible for continuing a whole range of traditions bound up with Christian duty, the defense of British liberties, and the code of chivalry symbolized by the ever-present St. George. Above all, to accept these imperatives was linked in kind to the perpetuation of empire. Duty and defense were not just local in their conception; they expanded outward in ever-widening

THE MASQUE OF THE
CHILDREN OF THE EMPIRE
(Curwen's Edition, 5735.)

By

G. T. KIMMINS.

Illustration 5.3   Cover Illustration from Kimmins'
The Masque of the Children of the Empire

circles, forming the moral bedrock of the Pax Britannica. Because the ideologies of duty and empire had such an important position in the cultural discourse of the period, subtlety was never the issue, either ideologically or aesthetically. These amateur children's masques were clearly designed to do the work of disciplining young minds into the Englishness of obligation, an obligation made manifest by the example of history.

Though I have been focusing almost exclusively in both this chapter and the last on the amateur masque, the masque was not only a genre for amateurs during this period. Theatrical, professional productions continued in the tradition of those types of masques performed during the mid- and late nineteenth century, whether as independent, occasional works, or as scenes inserted into musical theatrical pieces, and they too could operate as laborers in the field of empire-building on the homefront, this time to an audience steeped in the modernity of the contemporary theater and the musical hall. Like the amateur masques, several of the professional masques of the first years of the twentieth century display similar pressures and concerns to represent Englishness and English identity. Building on Victorian tropes – pastoral and historical – that were traced in chapter 2, the professional masque grafted onto these familiar forms of representation the patriotic and imperialist ideologies so prevalent in these years of heightened chauvinistic rhetoric and Boer War jingoism. We have already seen that the public ideologies of the period supported nationalistic representations of the *patria* and identity throughout the entire range of cultural production during this period. Within the music halls and professional musical theaters, it became clear that these kinds of works were not only ideologically apropos, but also financially profitable.[30] As a genre historically associated with patriotic themes, to which Arne's ever-present "Rule Britannia" was a testament, the masque seemed ideally suited as a genre for the expression of such sentiments within the very public, professional musical theatrical scene. Also, due to the increasing presence of amateur masque productions in communities around England, masques were increasingly presented by professional actors and producers for various kinds of benefits and charity performances on the public stage, a function which fits in neatly with its history as an occasional genre.

The Masque of War and Peace, presented in London on February 13, 1900, typifies these professionally-produced masques. Written by Louis N. Parker and composed by Hamish MacCunn,[31] the performance was organized and directed by the famous actor and theatrical producer Herbert Beerbohm Tree for the benefit of the widows and orphans of deceased members of Her Majesty's Household Troops (Illustration 5.4).[32]

---

[30] More on imperialism and the music halls during this period can be found in Penny Summerfield, "Patriotism and Empire: Music-Hall Entertainment, 1879–1914," in *Imperialism and Popular Culture*, ed. John MacKenzie, 17–48.

[31] Hamish MacCunn (1868–1916) was a respected and prolific composer of stage and orchestral works at the turn of the century, many drawn from Scottish sources and stories. He wrote one other masque–pageant, *Pageant of Darkness and Light*, with a text by Oxenham. For more on this masque and on MacCunn in general, see Jennifer Oates, *Hamish MacCunn (1868–1916): A Musical Life* (Farnham: Ashgate Press, 2013).

[32] Parker writes about the masque in his autobiography, *Several of My Lives* (London: Chapman and Hall, 1928): "I was busy devising a masque at Lady Arthur Paget's invitation, to be played at Her Majesty's for the benefit of the Widows of the Household Troops … It was all very amusing. Poor Hamish McCunn wrote the music, and the cast we got together was, at any rate from the social point of view, absolutely stupendous; we had what I believe is called a galaxy of beautiful women, headed by Miss Muriel Wilson … The Masque was performed on February 13, before a house all diamonds. The Prince of Wales (Edward VII) sent for Tree, McCunn, and myself and we went in great trepidation to the tiny octagonal room behind the royal box. The Prince was very cordial. When we were dismissed, the

Illustration 5.4   Program Cover for *The Masque of War and Peace*

Appropriately enough, given the context and purpose of the performance, the masque's theme glorifies the British soldier and the empire he defends. The text continuously emphasizes the superiority of British soldiers and the necessity for war and conflict to right wrong and to bring Christianity and British moral values to the world. Explicit is the idea that the British soldier is merely the representative abroad for the English people, whose duty it is to support external military efforts on several levels. Chivalric and missionary ideals were crucial components in popular ideologies of the British Empire during this period, hard-wired into how Britain's citizens formed narratives of

three of us backed simultaneously towards the very narrow door behind us. There we got jammed. I, being in the middle, got jammed worst. My collar broke away from its mooring and flew up under my ear. The Prince laughed; the Princess laughed; their entourage smiled discreetly; and when we had at last squeezed through the door we disliked each other for quite five minutes."

the imperatives of empire.[33] These ideals play an important part in this masque, as they do in many other representations of the British military overseas.

Linking its very modern, imperial message with representations of history, the masque communicates its message through a textual reliance on stock allegorical figures and a musical underpinning of arranged old favorites and new pieces relying on nostalgic tropes. The allegorical characters include many familiar to the masque genre: War, Glory, Victory, Rumour, Peace.[34] A few of the allegorical figures are updated in telling ways. London, for instance, is a Cockney, and Neptune a British Sailor. The Yeoman makes his appearance, representing the sturdy English countryman of times past and present. The historical and nostalgic gambit is played specifically at the point in the narrative when Peace appears. Peace is summoned through the newly composed madrigal "Come smiling Peace," where textual allusions to the "Merrie Olde England of Yore" overlay the musical association of the madrigal with the Elizabethan period.

The point could be made that a masque like the one I have just described and others like it, as well as the amateur masques discussed previously, are relatively unimportant works, clearly occasional in nature and designed to appeal to as wide an audience as possible through spectacle and platitudes. Neither canonical nor aspiring to high art, the crudity of their patriotic sentiment and the simplicity of the music that supports it can be explained away by their functionality and the resultant horizon of expectations. However, this type of overt patriotism and imperialistic nationalism also permeated a large section of the art music of the period, reaching the borders of the English Musical Renaissance and forcing many of the realignments noticeable in the movement during the first years of the twentieth century.

❧ Elgar, "The Crown of India", and the Paradox of Patriotism

Research into Edwardian musical nationalism and the problem of imperialism in music during the period 1895–1915 has most recently focused on the figure of Edward Elgar. Elgar was in many ways the most popular and successful English composer of the years prior to World War I. A composer virtually unknown

---

[33] The most complete treatment of this subject still remains Mark Girouard's *The Return to Camelot: Chivalry and the English Gentleman* (New Haven, CT: Yale University Press, 1981).

[34] The V&A Museum's Lafayette Negative Archive has a wonderful series of portraits of the notable society women who participated in the masque which were originally photographed by the Lafayette Studio and published in the *The Queen* (issue of February 17, 1900).

for much of his early musical career, his *Enigma Variations* catapulted him to fame in 1899. The variations were followed by a series of works that solidified his position as England's premier composer. This occurred first within what was perceived as the particularly English genre of the oratorio through the successes of *The Dream of Gerontius* and *The Apostles*, and his fame was assured by his first symphony and a score of smaller but no less popular works. The link between the composer and expressions of Edwardian nationalism comes in a large group of works that Elgar wrote for public, national, and often royal occasions.[35] Pieces such as the *Pomp and Circumstance* marches and the song "Land of Hope and Glory" that was adapted from one of these seem to embody quintessentially the chauvinistic and imperialistic character of England before the World War I. These works, and works that exploit a very different and widely varying set of personal, pastoral, and literary themes, have consistently been seen as containing the very essence of an English national character in music – as having the expression of "Englishness" at their very heart.

The explicitly nationalistic, patriotic, and often imperialistic strands in Elgar's oeuvre, however, posit a complex set of dilemmas for the established narrative of English musical history during the period, which, as I have been arguing throughout this chapter, actively sought to deny the public component of representations within this narrative in favor of the pastoral, despite the public sphere's very real presence. The reception of Elgar throughout the twentieth and early twenty-first century has been characterized by ambivalent attitudes towards the kinds of overt patriotism and public voice clearly heard in his works, and these attitudes have relegated him to a fairly odd relationship with the narrative of the English Musical Renaissance. As both insider and outsider to the dominant groups within English music during this period, Elgar's public voice seems to sit in an uneasy alliance with the dominant pastoral discourse of Vaughan Williams and other English Musical Renaissance composers.

But what is this public voice that Elgar sought to project in his explicitly patriotic music, those pieces in which he consciously expressed a musical representation of the *patria*? Within often paradoxical and conflicting personas projected across his oeuvre, his patriotic and imperialistic works implicate Elgar in the appropriation of the persona of the public poet. Elgar has been compared to Rudyard Kipling *ad nauseam*, rightly and wrongly.[36] I would

---

[35] A good overall look at this aspect of Elgar's oeuvre is Charles McGuire's "Functional Music: Imperialism, the Great War, and Elgar as a Popular Composer," in *The Cambridge Companion to Elgar*, edited by Daniel Grimley and Julian Rushton (Cambridge: Cambridge University Press, 2005), 214–24.

[36] The latest, and perhaps most extensive, contribution to this continuing trope in current Elgar reception appears in Jeffrey Richards's *Imperialism and Music: Britain 1876–1953* (Manchester: Manchester University Press, 2001), 51–2.

emphasize, however, that within the set of terms by which these two men can be compared it is the relationship to the figure of the public poet that is perhaps the most fruitful. Kipling, of course, was not the only Edwardian poet whose verse spoke in this voice. Much of the "public" poetry of the period by such authors as Alfred Austin, William Watson, and Henry Newbolt testifies to the appeal of such a persona during a time of the questioning of national identity. As Grainger has put it in a valuable account of the "public poet" during the first years of the century:

> They reminded, reassured, mobilized, sang praises and identified enemies within an objective, easily recognized world. Far from illumining their own subjective wholenesses, they were content to tell men what they already knew. … The poet repeatedly affirmed sentiments and told the tale again and again. As the public poet of a wide successful *imperium* he was not bardic. Bards are for lost or submerged *patriae*. Yet like the bard he looked for the heroic, the singular in the familiar story, emphasizing not freedom broadening down from precedent to precedent, not the long slow march of everyman, but deeds that made the realm and Empire … The public poet invoked, exhorted, clearing not muddying the springs of action.[37]

This aspect of explicit and consistent repetition in Grainger's description of the poet who rehearses over and over what the people already implicitly know and feel about England has its counterpart in Elgar's music. Even at the beginning of the twenty-first century, there is a strongly traditional attitude toward his works that finds in them the embodiment of a particular kind of England and Englishness, whether one perceives that national identity to be suspect or not.[38] It is useful to think of Elgar as articulating one aspect of his role as a composer through the period's valid and pervasive notion of the respected public poet speaking in the voice of a unified nation.[39]

---

[37] J.H. Grainger, *Patriotisms: Britain 1900–1939*.

[38] This point was reasserted at conference on Elgar and Vaughan Williams at the British Library in late March 2003. Not only did paper after paper raise the issue, but the concluding round-table discussion also focused on why and how Elgar and Vaughan Williams seem to project Englishness.

[39] It is important to emphasize here that the voice of the public poet was only one of the many personas adopted by Elgar, both in his life and works. I will discuss below how conflicted and paradoxical was Elgar's projected self-identity. It is enough here to say that the negation of personal subjectivity that is in some way demanded by the utterances of the public poet was a source of personal conflict for a composer whose work seems to be in many ways replete with autobiography and self-representation. And few Elgar scholars today, influenced by seminal work by Michael Kennedy, Jerrold Northrop Moore and Byron Adams, would argue that Elgar could ever project a sort of unitary identity.

Elgar's one composition in the masque genre, *The Crown of India, an Imperial Masque*, typifies the kind of Elgar work that lies at the center of the problematic reception of the aspect of his adopted compositional persona represented by the "public poet." The masque was written at the request of the impresario Oswald Stoll, who was planning an elaborate production in March 1912 at the London Coliseum to celebrate King George V's Delhi Durbar of December 1911.[40] Stoll pulled out all the stops for this lavish and expensive production, allotting a budget of over three thousand pounds for fabulous costumes and elaborate sets, and for the hiring of popular actors and actresses, including Nancy Price in the role of "India" – all to a script by Henry Hamilton. Music was to be a crucial element in the production, and it was natural that Stoll would commission England's most famous living composer and recent recipient of the Order of Merit, Edward Elgar, to provide songs, marches, and other incidental music for the pantomimes and processions of the masque.[41]

The Crown of India offered a representation of British colonial power and imperial ideologies at their historical peak. The masque contained two scenes, or tableaux: "The Cities of Ind" and "Ave Imperator!" The first tableau opened on the following scene:

> A Temple typifying the legends and traditions of India. At the back is a view of the Taj Mahal at Agra. In front of it and occupying the entire scene is a semi-circular amphitheater of white marble, its boundary defined by tiers of steps at the summit of which is a semi-circle of sculptured and fretted seats of marble, for the Twelve Great Cities of India … After a musical prelude, the curtain rises on darkness, upon which a faint steel-blue light gradually dawns, warming by degrees to amethyst, which slowly changing to rose, is finally succeeded by a golden glow.[42]

India summons and then introduces each of her twelve daughter cities, excepting Calcutta and Delhi, characterizing each as they present themselves.[43]

[40] As Corissa Gould has described, King George V's Delhi Durbar was a huge media event, exciting intense public interest in Britain. Part of the king and queen's royal tour of India, the durbar was an updated version of a Moghul court occasion, when princes would assemble to pay homage to the ruler. As an "invented tradition," in Hobsbawm's terms, this kind of translated ceremony was perfectly geared for the imposition of a new British ruler on Indian soil. For more on the fascinating impact of the event on the imaginations of the British people, and how this was fueled by emerging media technologies, see Corissa Gould's "Edward Elgar, *The Crown of India*, and the Image of Empire," *The Elgar Society Journal*, 13, 1 (March 2003), 25–35.

[41] Jerrold Northrop Moore, *Edward Elgar: A Creative Life* (Oxford: Oxford University Press, 1984).

[42] Henry Hamilton, *The Crown of India* (London: Enoch and Sons, 1912), 3.

[43] Lucknow's presentation, for instance, invokes the Indian Mutiny of 1857, and her subsequent forgiveness by a merciful British imperial overlord.

India is in turn panegyrized in a big aria by Agra in terms that solidify her position as queen of the East. Calcutta and Delhi then enter, arguing about which of them is the chief daughter city of the realm. Delhi supports her claim with a "March of the Mogul Emperors," followed by Calcutta's retort of a song offered by a group representing the East India Company, the "John Company." The first tableau ends with a triumphant appearance of St. George, singing "The Rule of England," joined at the refrain by everyone on stage:

> Wherever England flies her flag
> O'er what her sword hath won,
> Her claim to keep, to rule, to reap,
> She rests on duty done.
> Her title strong, no tyrant brag,
> Of frowning fort, nor fleet,
> But Right upheld, and Rancour quelled,
> Wrong beneath her feet.

> Lift aloft the Flag of England,
> Her it is to lead the Light,
> Ours to keep her yet the Kingland,
> Keep her ancient Honour bright,
> Her manhood ever glorious,
> Her Valour still victorious,
> Lift aloft the Flag of England
> Break the Wrong, and make the Right!

> Of old I trod the Dragon down
> And yours it is today –
> The Dragons great of Greed and Hate
> And Ignorance to slay.
> So ne'er shall England lose renown,
> Nor ever love shall lack,
> But Freedom stand at her right hand
> Beneath the Union Jack.

> Lift aloft the Flag of England, *etc.*

> Oh, sons of Merry England born!
> Oh, Knights of good Saint George!
> Still may your steel from head to heel
> Be bright from Honour's forge.
> Still be your blades for England worn,
> Dear Land that hath no like!

And for her Fame and in her Name
Unsheath the sword and strike!

Lift aloft the Flag of England, *etc.*

The second tableau displays India leading her cities to offer homage to the new British emperor, and the crowning of Delhi as India's new capital city. The masque ends with the standard rendition of "God Save the King," with slightly rewritten words to match the occasion:

God save the Emperor,
Hear now, as ne'er before,
One India sing:
Send him victorious,
Happy and glorious;
Long to reign over us,
God save the King!

The masque provided for plenty of pageantry and spectacle in the various entrances, progressions, and marches, and a good dollop of the exotic in such numbers as "Dance of the Nautch Girls," "Warrior's Dance," and "The March of the Mogul Emperors." Not content to fill the stage with the various person-ifications and the dance participants, Stoll crowded in courtiers, soldiers, attendants, pages, natives, and a multitude of etceteras, offering a visual display of the public's colonialist fantasies of India as an exotic dreamland firmly controlled by the ubiquitous British military and commercial presence.

Elgar created a score full of a variety of stage musics – introductions, melodramas to support speeches, songs, interludes, and marches – in a broadly general style that is reminiscent of his 1903 *Coronation March* in its reliance on repetition with little development.[44] More importantly, at certain points Elgar's music reflects the stereotyped characteristics of the orientalist mode so prevalent among late nineteenth- and early twentieth-century musical repre-sentations of non-Western locales.[45] In England these characteristics had long

---

[44] Moore points out the link with the *Coronation March* in his brief discussion of *Crown of India* in *Edward Elgar: A Creative Life*, 630. Elgar's music for *The Crown of India* has been published as Volume 18 of the *Elgar Complete Edition*, ed. by Robert Anderson (Elgar Society Edition/Novello, 2004).

[45] The uses of exoticism were not foreign to Elgar. In his *Elgar's Oratorios: The Creation of an Epic Narrative* (Aldershot: Ashgate Publishing, 2002, 201–4), Charles McGuire points to the appropriation of Jewish melodies and other more conventional orientalist features Elgar used to set the chorus of the temple dancers in the oratorio *The Apostles*, again using the juxtaposition of Western and non-Western musical idioms for ideological purposes.

been fully exploited in light orchestral program music of the type frequently played in venues such as the Crystal Palace; in the music of the theater, serious and comic; and above all in the huge corpus of parlor song settings of exotic, orientalist lyrics. In *The Crown of India*, the standard elements of exoticism emerge in the clear identification of certain types of music exclusively with either the "Eastern" or the "Western" characters. Representations of the Indian elements of the masque utilize complex rhythmic figures that juxtapose slow and fast motion in rapid alternation. Also conventionally, the "Indian music" is extremely chromatic and harmonically unstable. Pentatonic melodies figure extensively, as do accompaniment patterns that feature open fifths, again the basic hallmarks of exotic musical discourse. These characteristics are most apparent in the "March of the Mogul Emperors." The march is in a 3/2 meter, not a meter to which one can march properly.[46] Ostensibly set in B minor, Elgar abandons the diatonicism usual in his marches, replacing it with a restless and rapid movement through remote key areas. The theme uses diminished fifths and chromatic passing notes, which adds further to the harmonic instability. The utilization of ostinati patterns is also quite apparent. Given the locale and the identities of most of the allegorical characters, this orientalist idiom dominates most of the masque. However, there is a telling musical contrast in the few sections that represent elements associated with England – St. George and John Company. John Company enters to a markedly European *tempo di menuetto*, as opposed to the exotically inflected marches that fill much of the masque. Its music is predominantly diatonic and in a major key that sounds bright and confident after the modal mixture of the Indian pieces. St. George's song "The Rule of England," the most important item in the score both in its length and its placement at the center of the work, shares many characteristics with the John Company music, with relatively square rhythms and limited chromaticism. The melody of the refrain, "Lift aloft the Flag of England," is a clear reference to a patriotic march, easy to sing and obviously designed to have a wide appeal when published and marketed by itself.

Once the score was completed, Elgar threw himself actively into the performance aspects of the production. He conducted music rehearsals with the cast, both chorus and solos, to a large extent playing the piano accompaniment himself, and then prepared the pit orchestra. During the first two weeks of the masque's run, Elgar conducted two performances a day, and often ran additional rehearsals as needed. The effort exhausted him and, by

---

[46] Corissa Gould rightly suggests that this odd meter may have been designed to suggest the incompetence of the Mogul emperors – their lurching march would have contrasted with the orderly regular marching of the Westerners. Corissa Gould, "Edward Elgar, *The Crown of India*, and the Image of Empire," 30.

its end, brought on an ear condition that required several months of rest and relaxation.

Many might, and probably did, think it beneath a composer of Elgar's stature to waste valuable composition time and energy on such populist, commercially motivated music. Responding to such an implied line of questioning during an interview with a reporter writing for *The Standard*, Elgar provided at least a public answer to the issue:

> Sir Edward Elgar would commit himself to no special opinion regarding his first definite contribution to the programme of a big music-hall. 'It is hard work, but it is absorbing, interesting,' he said, during a pause in the proceedings. 'The subject of the Masque is appropriate to this special period in English history, and I have endeavoured to make the music illustrate and illuminate the subject.'[47]

This response strikes us as a thinly veiled attempt to give the commission a little dignity and merit by projecting Elgar's patriotic sensibilities. In his account of the years 1910–12, Moore clearly lays out the Elgars' financial difficulties during this period, chief being the move into Severn House, a large and expensive house in Hampstead. Moore quotes a letter from Elgar relishing the effects of the sizeable income derived from potboilers like *The Crown of India*:

> When I write a big serious work e.g. Gerontius we have had to starve & go without fires for twelve months as a reward: this small effort allows me to buy scientific works I have yearned for & I spend my time between the Coliseum & the old bookshops ... also I can more easily help my poor people [his brother and sisters' families] – so I don't care what people say about me – the real man is only a very shy student & now I can buy books ... I go to the N. Portrait Gallery & can afford lunch – now I cannot eat it. It's all very curious & interesting & the *people* behind the scenes so good & so desperately respectable & so honest & straight-forward – quite a refreshing world after Society – only don't say I said so.
>
> My labour will soon be over & then for the country lanes & the wind sighing in the reeds by Severn side again & God bless the Music Halls![48]

The monetary rewards of popular commissions like the masque obviously held their appeal, but this is certainly not the whole story. As Corissa Gould has argued, Elgar had no qualms about turning down commissions that he did not feel suited his temperament, musical and ideological.[49] Furthermore, during the run of the production, Elgar's wife Alice repeatedly brought

---

[47] March 1, 1912, quoted in Moore, *Edward Elgar: A Creative Life*, 629.

[48] Letter to Frances Colvin, 14 March 1912, quoted ibid., 630.

[49] Corissa Gould, "Edward Elgar, *The Crown of India*, and the Image of Empire."

friends and family to the Coliseum to see it. She wrote proudly in letters and diaries of the glories of the production and her husband's music in a way that strongly conflicts with the idea that either of the Elgars was embarrassed by the composer's participation in the production. Moreover, the quotation above implies Elgar had more than a grudging respect for the people involved in the production, rather than regarding them with the expected sense of superiority and condescension. More importantly, however, *The Crown of India* was not an isolated example of popular patriotic music among Elgar's works, though it was his first work specifically written as a commission for the venue of a large music hall. The quotations above have an air of ambiguity about them; in his interview with *The Standard*, the reporter had to press him for comments on the work, and in his letter to Colvin, he attempts to justify his participation in this popular event as a necessity, knowing that people are judging him negatively because of it.[50] Yet, Elgar's seemingly paradoxical, enigmatic attitude towards these works and the values they embody reflects a personal uneasiness with English national identity and his relationship to it that in many ways is symptomatic of the country as a whole during the first years of the twentieth century.

Elgar did not disdain feeding the English public's appetite for popular types of art music that had been an important aspect of the English musical scene for over a hundred years, and which remained a part of serious music-making during the Edwardian period with the likes of the Crystal Palace concerts and Henry Wood's Promenade concerts. Unlike the music of the early English Musical Renaissance characterized by the works of Stanford and Parry, which often carried about it the high-brow air of academe, Elgar's music drew a foundation of support, often impassioned, from the middle-class and provincial musical audience, which was at the height of its power at this very moment and to which the immense popularity of a work like *The Crown of India* attests. While his music was sometimes labeled vulgar, as much a reference to his lower-middle-class family origins as to the music itself, Elgar, as a composer without a regular income, knew where his future as a composer lay. At the same time, his music straddled the line between popular and high forms of art music, in the contrast between *The Crown of India* and the two symphonies, for example, thereby allowing him to retain the title as English music's reigning king within both spheres. He frequently placed his music at the service of royalty and the state, writing pieces such as "Land of Hope and

---

[50] This letter is patently self-deluding anyway, as Byron Adams has pointed out to me. Elgar was only temporarily dabbling in science during this period, he very rarely sent money to his family, and over and over again his attitude throughout this period of his life reiterates that he cared very much about what other people thought of him.

Glory," the *Crown of India*, the *Imperial March*, and many others that were enormously popular during the period before 1920. Works such as these seem to distill the very essence of Edwardian England in music. While less explicitly nationalistic, other works such as *King Olaf*, *Caractacus*, and *Falstaff* also tangle with the fabrication of Englishness in a more cultural, less political way.

Given both their popularity and their centrality to views of the composer and to the versions of national identity they seem to represent, these Elgar works raise many questions. To question Elgar is in many ways to question the constructions of Englishness during this period. The disjunction between what his music seems to say and what he says about his music echoes the nation's ambivalence regarding national identity. A natural step to understanding the cultural significance of Elgar's patriotic music would be to start with the composer himself, examining biography, writings, and reception history in an attempt to both align and distinguish Elgar from his contemporaries. However, attempts to place Elgar's patriotic output in some kind of biographical context are constantly frustrated by paradoxical and contradictory views of Elgar sketched in the literature on the composer. Again, it is tempting to trace this confusion to the man himself, and further, to the confusion over representations of national identity in English society as a whole. More importantly, however, this confusion is one more sign of how the sanctioned narrative of the renaissance of English music, in the process of being formulated during the period 1895–1915 and replicated again and again for most of the twentieth century, was increasingly fixed on the pastoral and personal aspects of the patriotic triumvirate, at the expense of the public. Elgar's own discomfort with the position of such an overtly public patriotic work like *The Crown of India* in his compositional output offers a hint of what was to come in the subsequent histories of the English Musical Renaissance.

Within a century of writings on the composer, two main camps of opinion regarding Elgar clearly emerge, though within these two camps significant differences exist, which is natural given the passage of time, fashion, and reaction. Significantly, the main tenets of these two portraits hinge on the status of the patriotic works and Elgar's view towards them. At the most basic level, one side takes these compositions at face value, accepting the idea that they reflect the motivation of an uncomplicated patriotism and nationalism that in this sense can seem an important feature of Elgar's character and personality. Elgar reception along this vein is very much connected to the vicissitudes of the reception of late Victorian and Edwardian nationalism as a whole. Thus a modern critic like Meirion Hughes can assert that Elgar's loss of status during the 1920s and 30s was in many ways tied to the younger generation's rejection of the snobbishness, conservatism, and imperialistic forms of patriotism that characterized their view of the pre-war period.[51] As Hughes aptly puts it, "there seems no room for doubt that Elgar was, quite willingly and consciously, both a cultural warrior and political figurehead."[52]

The other camp of Elgar scholarship challenges this acceptance of Elgar's imperialism as uncomplicated and unmediated by other issues and is defensive of his reputation as a composer above the imperialist fray in the face of increasing questions regarding Elgar's involvement with the ideologies of imperialism and racism. In this camp, the standard method of excusing Elgar's overtly patriotic works describes them as commissions and always-needed moneymakers. Furthermore, some analyses of the composer attempt to find within the works themselves evidence of Elgar's ambivalence towards the rampant imperialism and jingoism of the pre-World War I period in England.

An important part of this strand of Elgar reception seeks to recuperate Elgar by aligning him more closely with the English Musical Renaissance movement, and the "pastoral" and "personal" basis for English nationalism that were by the early twentieth century fixed and essential characteristics of an English national musical style. Biographers like Michael Kennedy and, most recently, Lewis Foreman, reposition Elgar, turning him from a public composer to a private one, creating a personal identity that questions and undermines his public persona. This offers yet one more instance of how many of the leading

[51] Meirion Hughes, "The Duc d'Elgar: Making a Composer Gentleman," in *Music and the Politics of Culture*, ed. Christopher Norris (New York: St. Martin's Press, 1989), 41–68. This view was already in evidence by the 1930s, expressed, for instance, by Constant Lambert in *Music Ho! A Study of Music in Decline* (New York: Charles Scribner's and Sons, 1936). Another important discussion of this issue can be found in Jeremy Crump, "The Identity of English Music: The Reception of Elgar 1898–1935," in *Englishness: Culture and Politics 1880–1920*, ed. Robert Colls and Philip Dodd (Beckenham, Croom Helm, 1986), 164–90.

[52] This view of Elgar is easily supported. Many writers, both among Elgar's contemporaries and in more modern scholarship, have documented Elgar's extreme class-consciousness. After his marriage to a woman considerably above him in social status, Elgar spent the rest of his life trying to transcend his lower-middle-class origins by adopting all of the outward trappings of the country gentleman, to the point that he avoided discussion of his compositional activities because he could not reconcile them to his adopted persona. Elgar also was extremely devoted to the royal family, playing his connections to them by seeking from them dedications, awards and commissions, angling for first his knighthood and then a peerage. Additionally, he was rabidly conservative in his political and social views; the Labour Party's overthrow of the Conservative Party in 1905 led to suicidal thoughts and was one factor in Elgar's personal crisis during the years 1905–06. Finally, his regular production of patriotic works like *The Crown of India* seems to indicate that Elgar supported the assertive Edwardian brand of English nationalism and of British holdings overseas.

writers on the English Musical Renaissance have a deep-seated reluctance to accept the public persona as a component of canonical English composers of this period. Kennedy ends his recuperation of Elgar by equivocating on patriotism itself:

> It would be a distortion if I were to suggest that Elgar was not in many ways a representative figure of his time. He was innately conservative and patriotic, he respected and loved tradition and he enjoyed honours ... we forget today what a patriot is. Newspeak and the twisting of language to political ends have equated it with naked militarism and aggression. Elgar loved his country because he loved its rivers and trees and cathedrals and lanes and the pageantry of the streets of London. He loved Shakespeare and the other poets. He loved its prose. He wanted to share his love, through music, with his fellow-countrymen, to give them something they might love.[53]

Given Kennedy's own allegiance to the pastoral and personal narrative of English music during this period, it is not surprising that he can only read Elgar in these terms, ones that necessarily implicate him in the dismissal of Elgar's persona of the public poet. If Elgar is to fit into the mainstream of an English musical destiny, he must be seen to gain meaning and identity from the twin sources of England's countryside and England's cultural history, not from racist and imperialist stances like those reflected in *The Crown of India*. This glorification of Elgar's love of a certain kind of England, however, does not necessarily place him firmly within the boundaries of the more liberal cultural tendencies of the time. Nor does it smooth away the antagonisms between Elgar and the ideals of the English Musical Renaissance, a group that was gaining dominance just as Elgar began to consciously express some kind of "public voice." Instead, it could be asserted that Elgar was against many of the core constituents of the historical aesthetic espoused by this movement. In a chapter entitled "The English Way of Life," Martin Wiener argues that all sides in the debate over national identity, whether looking inward towards the recovery of a lost ethos or outward to empire and domination, evoked the elements of pastoralism and English rural life to support their agendas. It is not pastoralism *per se*, but the purposes of pastoralism, that differentiate versions of English identity.[54]

What fuels the Elgar debate is his very status within the English Musical Renaissance, and the various strains of revisionist history-making that

[53] Michael Kennedy, "Elgar the Edwardian," in *Elgar Studies*, ed. Raymond Monk (Aldershot: Scolar Press, 1990), 107–17.

[54] Martin J. Wiener, *English Culture and the Decline of the Industrial Spirit, 1850–1980* (Cambridge: Cambridge University Press, 1981).

surround views of this crucial period – crucial on both the musical and the politico-social level. The more central point, however, is not which of these versions of Englishness "Elgar the Edwardian" subscribed to, but the fact that he subscribed to all three, in a way that is marked by ambivalence and lack of clarity. To a certain extent this paradoxical nationalism was consciously projected and manipulated by the composer.[55] Crucially, though, it is remarkable how this personal paradox echoes a comparable paradox on the national level, and how conscious and unconscious mythmaking enter such representations on every level.

❧ Elgar and the Uses of History

It is noteworthy that *The Crown of India* was Elgar's only masque, despite the popularity of the genre during this period and Elgar's involvement with the types of national identity that were circulating within it.[56] Realistically, during this period masque compositions were usually the result of a commission, and not too many masque productions could hope to lure a composer of the stature of Elgar to provide music for what was essentially an occasional piece with limited subsequent performance. However, the increasing association of the masque genre with the representation of history and the utilization of historically inflected musical materials, at least in masque compositions for amateurs, may also have limited the masque's appeal to the composer. Elgar's, above all, was a modern, progressive version of national music, and throughout his career he was rarely drawn to materials of English musical traditions, either in genre or technique.[57] As a composer he was not willing to abandon the

[55] In particular, Byron Adams has cogently laid out the puzzling aspects of Elgar's character in an essay on the *Enigma Variations* that specifically deals with Elgar's homoeroticism. Byron Adams, "The 'Dark Saying' of the Enigma: Homoeroticism and the Elgarian Paradox," *19th-Century Music*, 23 (2000), 218–35.

[56] The only other closely related work was *The Pageant of Empire*, written to open the immense British Empire Exhibition at Wembley in 1924. For this he supplied a few vocal pieces and a march that ultimately was replaced by the *Imperial March*. Beyond this pageant, *The Spirit of England*, *The Banner of Saint George* and countless marches and songs form an impressive group of patriotic works in Elgar's oeuvre.

[57] One could argue that, of course, Elgar was integrally involved in two historically English musical genres, the cantata, and more importantly, the oratorio. There is a distinction to make here, though. For Elgar and his contemporaries, the oratorio was a contemporary genre, continually developing and open to the most advanced musical trends. There was never a question of resurrecting the earliest phases of the oratorio genre, nor was there the Elizabethan connection that characterized the historical genres serving as a bank of source materials for composers like Vaughan Williams. In this sense, the oratorio was a modern genre.

claims of a universal, cosmopolitan musical language continually developing and expanding in its resources, whether those resources were continental or not, for a more insular and parochial set of compositional tools. In this sense, Elgar still reflects the confidence in progress and development that was such a feature of the Victorian, as opposed to the Edwardian, spirit.

This is one important area of clear differentiation between Elgar and many of the other composers of the period, especially those within the fold of the English Musical Renaissance – their validation of the claims of history over modernity. In many ways, Elgar stands apart from the people and ideas that formed the core of the English Musical Renaissance movement, though in subsequent revisions of the history of the movement, Elgar seems to have been placed as the crucial "next step" in the narrative of English music in the late nineteenth and early twentieth centuries.[58] More to the point, Elgar seems to have understood, and demurred from, the relationship between Englishness and history being posited within the official narrative of the English Musical Renaissance even during its early days. Suspicious of what he saw as a fairly suspect and perhaps dangerous conglomerate of sources and ideology, Elgar continued to uphold the cause of modernity, with its overt statements of imperialism, against the formulations of history and the folk in the creation of an English school of music.

Several obvious elements of his background and training led Elgar to feel disenfranchised from the musical establishment that steered the English Musical Renaissance movement. Raised in the provinces, from a lower-class family, with no formal higher education or musical training, he was already distanced from the gentry-based London and Oxbridge backgrounds of those at the head of the English Musical Renaissance. It took Elgar a long time to break into the English musical world. Even at the height of his popularity he did not forget that his support through the years came from outside the musical establishment, and continually reiterated what he saw as his outsider status. However, his background and upbringing may very well have profoundly influenced his attitudes toward the aggregate of ideologies that connected modernity, progress and imperialism during the late Victorian and Edwardian periods.

Martin Wiener identifies two broad attitudes towards progress, modernity, and English identity that he aligns along a North versus South axis.[59] The "North" in his construction, basically from the Midlands northwards,

---

[58] See Michael Trend's *The Music Makers: Heirs and Rebels of the English Musical Renaissance, Edward Elgar to Benjamin Britten* (London: Weidenfeld & Nicholson, 1985), for instance.

[59] Martin J. Wiener, *English Culture and the Decline of the Industrial Spirit, 1850–1980*.

represents the claims of capitalism and imperialism, with its industrial development and dependence on the supports of technology and development. This attitude was further associated with provincialism and the lower classes, regardless of actual personal wealth. Along these lines it is easy to see how Elgar could associate himself with the "North," and this ideological association might explain his support of the claims of modernity over history. The alternative position in Wiener's construction, the "South," represents opposite values of history, tradition, Merrie Olde England, and a humanist rather than technological tradition, all values assimilated by the English Musical Renaissance. Elgar's further distance from social ties that bound many of the English Musical Renaissance composers was emphasized by religious and political factors. First, Elgar was a practicing Roman Catholic at a time when Roman Catholicism was barely tolerated among mainstream English society. A work like *The Dream of Gerontius*, setting an explicitly Catholic text by Cardinal Newman, openly declared his religious sensibilities. Second, Elgar was politically a staunch conservative, or Tory, in marked contrast to the much more liberal political views held by many of the main figures within the English Musical Renaissance, including Parry and Stanford.

Of course, once Elgar's popularity was assured, the English Musical Renaissance reached out to embrace him, fully aware that his accomplishments had to be seen to advance the cause of a unified approach to an English national style of music.[60] On a certain level, consistent with his personal mission to leave his origins behind him and gain a higher social status, Elgar accepted the overtures of the English Musical Renaissance nationalists. But, as in so much of Elgar's motivations, this too was a conflicted and paradoxical move. Given the opportunity to create an alternate school of composition in opposition to the English Musical Renaissance, and, through extension, an alternate identity for a modern English national music, Elgar set himself further apart from the ideological fold of the English Musical Renaissance and articulated a different relationship to both the past and the present.

---

[60] Hughes and Stradling describe how, after the popularity of the *Enigma Variations*, the leaders of the English Musical Renaissance attempted to assimilate Elgar into their milieu, first through the granting of an honorary D.Mus. degree from Cambridge, which came through the offices of Stanford. Parry and Stanford then both put him up for membership at the prestigious Athaeneum Club, a sure indicator of inclusivity: Meirion Hughes and Robert Stradling, *The English Musical Renaissance 1840–1940: Construction and Deconstruction*, 2nd edn (Manchester: Manchester University Press, 2001), 50–52. For more on these and other figures' attitudes towards Elgar, see Jeremy Dibble's "Elgar and His British Contemporaries," in *The Cambridge Companion to Elgar*, 15–23.

⁊ The Birmingham Lectures

The opportunity to attempt a different, modernist formulation for a national musical style came in 1905, when Elgar was offered the newly endowed Peyton Chair in Music at the University of Birmingham. Charles Peyton had offered funding for the position with the stipulation that it would be offered to Elgar alone. Elgar was not enthusiastic about the position, feeling that with his lack of academic credentials he was not qualified for the job, and justly worried that his very busy schedule would be further stressed by the addition of new responsibilities. However, with the creation of the position at stake, and with persuasive arguments of friends and colleagues in Birmingham, Elgar accepted the post.[61] Much of this pressure came from men like Granville Bantock and Joseph Holbrooke, younger composers who similarly shared Elgar's outside status with regard to the London-dominated English Musical Renaissance, and who looked to Elgar as a mentor. Surely they hoped that the establishment of an academic music department situated in the Midlands, led by England's most famous composer, might create a rival compositional school to that led by Parry and Stanford in London. The fact that relations between Elgar and Stanford in particular were always strained lent impetus to the idea that Elgar spearhead a different sort of national musical school.

In proportion to his sizeable salary, Elgar's duties were not particularly heavy. He began to organize a music library for the university, getting friends and patrons to donate volumes and sets of music he felt were important for the fledgling department to own. He initiated the formation of several performing groups within the university. His role was mainly to publicize the university and department, and to use his influence to further the first steps of the newly formed department. Most importantly, he was to offer a series of lectures on music for students and interested members of the community. Percy Young places these lectures within a long tradition of adult lectures for the purpose of uplifting the lower, less educated classes, and it seems that, in the minds of the university administration and patrons, such a series of lectures would tie in well with Elgar's main function as a means of focusing publicity and goodwill.[62]

Elgar's lectures certainly did attract public attention, but this took the form not of placid goodwill, but instead of heated controversy both locally and in

---

[61] See Percy Young's introduction and commentary to Edward Elgar, *A Future for English Music and other Lectures*, ed. Percy M. Young (London: Dennis Dobson, 1968) for a detailed look at the background to Elgar's acceptance of the Birmingham post and his subsequent work for the department. See also Jerrold Northrop Moore, *Edward Elgar: A Creative Life*.

[62] Percy Young, "Introduction," in *A Future for English Music and other Lectures*.

London. In most of the seven lectures he offered during 1905 and 1906, Elgar managed to attack English composers, performers, and critics alike, though throughout the uproar he continually claimed to have been "misquoted" in the newspaper and journal reporting of the lectures. Each lecture generated heated pro-and-con correspondences in the press, and more than one leading musical personality, including Stanford, felt called to defend himself against the insinuations of the lectures. Elgar leveled most of his negative comments at the London musical establishment, those he felt had marginalized him all his professional life. At the same time, he maintained throughout the lectures that his concern was not for himself but for young English composers and musicians and the lack of opportunities that the current situation in England provided for them.

The lectures themselves are somewhat disjointed and undeveloped. This seems due to a combination of three factors: Elgar's lack of experience in giving lectures of this sort, the minimal amount of time he allotted to their preparation, and the fragmentary condition in which they survive, as Elgar improvised whole sections while delivering the lectures.[63] However, a central theme among all the lectures was the necessity for young English composers or musicians to find what is essential and important in their own personal compositional style to create a musical language that would impact the world around them. Elgar, like most people involved in music during this period, was extremely concerned with the state of English music at the beginning of the twentieth century and wished to articulate how English music might choose to define itself. But there is an important difference between Elgar, with his modernist and progressive stance, and other composers of the period, particularly those associated with the English Musical Renaissance group; Elgar denied the claims of history and historical consciousness, and instead validated the modern world and a continental, advanced musical language. Elgar clearly laid his views on the line in the inaugural lecture, aware that this, of all his lectures, was the one that would receive the greatest attention on the national level:

> In looking for a practical starting point for anything that may be usefully considered in relation to present day music, I think it unnecessary to go back farther than 1880 …
>
>   Some of us who in that year were young and taking an active part in music – a really active part such as playing in orchestras – felt that something at last

[63] Percy Young's edition is a particularly valuable tool for examining Elgar's thought processes with regard to these lectures. The pages of the edition offer several columns, one reproducing the final text, one Elgar's notes and addenda, and the last Young's editorial comments.

was going to be done in the way of composition by the English school. A large number of compositions during the twenty years following were brought before us, and the whole atmosphere of English music was changed … An interest hitherto unknown was taken in the work of our native composers. Some of us who were accustomed to play the works of Beethoven, Weber and – to come down to the most modern man of that date, Wagner – while we were anxious to believe all that a friendly Press told us about the glories of the new English school, could not help feeling that the music given us to play, was, not to put too fine a point upon it, rather 'dry'. I am not going to criticise these works in detail: it is not necessary. Happily for us some still live and give their quota of joy and satisfaction: the great portion are dead and forgotten and only exist as warnings to the student of the twentieth century. It is saddening to those who hoped so much from these early days, to find that after all that had been written, and all the endeavour to excite enthusiasm for English music – 'big' music – to find that we had inherited an art which has no hold on the affections of our own people, and is held in no respect abroad.[64]

In the notes to the draft of this lecture, at the point where Elgar briefly discusses Richard Strauss's comments on English composers during the late eighteenth and nineteenth centuries as imitators, Elgar scribbled the following:

There are enough and to spare of essayists and lecturers giving us useless accounts of men and things whose importance died with them. Mr. Gladstone once said this age "will be looked upon as 'AN AGE OF RESEARCH'" – I wish he had said useless research.

Yes: research is a good thing in its way: but most of our musical enthusiasts reciting the deeds of the 16th and 17th centuries are as usefully employed as blind men might be, groping in a churchyard at night trying to read epitaphs in a forgotten tongue … Few of them ever had a separate existence: there was no true birth and the umbilical cord was never severed & the wretched infant led a miserable life attached to its parent … This has been the inevitable end of manufactured music: we were told our men were giants, equal to Brahms, and we find that our best are only equal to the Grimms and the Reineckes of Germany.[65]

A little later in the inaugural lecture proper, Elgar continues:

What, then, is and can be an English School of Music? It is easy to go back to the days of Purcell and revel in the glories to those days and earlier, when England led the world in the matter of composition; but such thoughts have no practical

---

[64] Inaugural Address, March 16, 1905, ibid., 33.

[65] Ibid., 42.

value on the music of the present day, which in this University is all we have to consider.[66]

Elgar finds hope not in the growth of English music during the preceding twenty years, and certainly not in the more distant past, but in the contemporary world of younger composers, despite their inexperience, their imitation and their occasional "vulgarity":

> But there seems to be hope that the younger school of England is at last coming to its own ... The honours for the last year at the Musical Festivals, which still, unhappily, furnish practically the only opportunities of producing new large works – the honours have fallen, save with one exception, to the younger men. They have provided us with serious music and they have given us something earnest and something sincere.[67]

Elgar attacks the figures of the English Musical Renaissance establishment clearly in the following excerpt. From his perspective, the source of their ultimate failure is their goal to root the modern in the historical:

> It is not difficult to deal with the men of whom I have spoken who sit by the wayside and say: "This is the end of art and the way ends here." They say this when they mean that they see no farther and that their wings have drooped and their souls (if they have them) are tired. It is easy to leave them by the wayside. More difficult to deal with and more clogging to any real progress in art are those formalists who say: "we are modern and we are in the race": when, as a matter of fact, they are quite out of any running for any artistic prize: – the men who go about assuming that they are most modern, and singing revolutionary songs to the wrong tune. It is all very well to sing "Ca ira, ca ira – but the effect is quite lost if it is chanted to the Old Hundredth and excites nothing but pity for the performer.[68]

In these excerpts, as well as throughout the Birmingham lectures, Elgar's language is redolent with the language of progress, and of the modern. Moreover, he overtly carries imperialism into the cultural sphere, into the competition between countries, and into the national and worldwide marketplace. This is an identification with values that are not at all typical of the educated, cultured, above all upper-class English personage, who at this point in history was increasingly uneasy with commercialism, progress, and the empire. It certainly does not reflect the values of the English Musical Renaissance, neither of the generation of Parry, Grove, and Stanford, nor

[66] Ibid., 51.
[67] Ibid., 49.
[68] Ibid., 41.

of the younger generation represented by Vaughan Williams, despite their cultural nationalism.

In speaking of Kipling as a public poet, Grainger says that, for Kipling, "the foe was an England in which men had become the disinterested spectators of their own history." This holds true for Elgar as well. Anxious that English music would become a rehearsal of a dead and buried past in the name of a national musical style, he asserted time and time again that hope for English music lay in its engagement with the demands of modern music – yes, even if that music came from Germany or France. The English nature of the music would come in the themes explored by the English composer rather than the actual musical materials of the past. This obviously holds up in many examples in his own body of works. Pieces like *Falstaff* and *Caractacus* exploit thematic tropes of Englishness in musical language saturated with Wagner and linked to Strauss, consciously avoiding historical parody or folk-like nostalgia. In this sense Elgar allies himself with the Victorian composers explored in chapter 2, who tapped into the literary and historical sources of Englishness at the same time that they continued to be musically driven by modern and progressive continental trends.

However, it must have been clear to Elgar that England no longer situated itself in the same self-identity in 1905 as it did in 1865, either nationally or musically. His oft-cited comment "I write the folk songs of England" reveals a consciousness of the change in the air, despite his own deep-seated convictions that these new uses of history would not lead to a viable national musical style. It is important to reiterate, though, that it is not history as a topic or an expression of English patriotism that Elgar seeks to leave out of his formulation for English music, but rather a reliance on the musical tools of history to avoid the confrontation with modernity and relapse instead into the pointless and unprofitable exercise of musical nostalgia.

❦ Conclusion

Both this and the previous chapter show how, despite the increasing dominance of historical and pastoral strands in the narrative of the English Musical Renaissance and its attendant sites of viable musical Englishness, the claims of modernity were inherent in the expression of a public voice and a public discourse. This public voice was explicit in the messages of nationalism and imperialism, inextricably bound during this period with "our own special tradition here in England, and of the inheritance of obligation which that tradition imposes upon us" mentioned in the preface to *Poems of Today* quoted earlier.[69] It was also explicit in the persona of the public poet

---

[69] *Poems of Today*, vii–viii.

adopted by a few composers, particularly Edward Elgar. Yet this public voice was equally powerful in the implied messages of the pastoral and the folk movement investigated in chapter 4. I would argue that this component is intrinsic in all works of the period, due at least in part to the intense public and modern concerns surrounding identity and its sources during the first years of the twentieth century. While distinctions can be made between how and where identity is to be situated, the search for that identity, and the role of history in that identity, is above all a modern and public issue to which many spoke in many guises. It is through this underlying conceptualizing strand, which defined the basic "work" of cultural production, including music, as essentially a "patriotic" enterprise, that we can assert that, in its search for a national musical style, much English music of the period was overwhelmingly concerned with public discourse.

Quickly, however, with the approach and the ultimate catastrophe of World War I, overt expressions of a public voice within English music became increasingly suspect and discouraged. After the war, modernism focused on a different set of concerns, and patriotic and societal enthusiasms of the pre-war period quickly became either antiquated or changed radically to speak to a very different England by necessity. These changes, then, will serve as the focus of my conclusion.

CHAPTER 6

"A typically English institution": The Masque after the First World War

The masque is a typically English institution. We have never taken kindly to grand opera, delightful as an importation brought to the country by young noblemen on the Grand Tour and set up with all the [pomp] of Italian music and Italian composers and their sopranos and prima donnas as a fashionable entertainment. It has never, and I believe, never will endear itself to the heart of the people. They much prefer the ballad opera which is in a language they could understand ... For masques the great poets of the land were pressed into service – witness Milton's Comus and Ben Jonson's Pan's Anniversary – and the finest musicians.[1]

IN very broad terms, this investigation has traced how ideas of history and nostalgia mapped onto contrasting, and eventually competing, formulations of English national identity, musical and beyond, in Victorian and Edwardian England. Using the masque genre as a case study, we have seen how an historical imagination increasingly combined with a didactic ideology of social renewal as this period progressed. The tradition of the masque was "re-invented," to tweak Eric Hobsbawm's concept,[2] from a genre that had links to its seventeenth- and eighteenth-century predecessors in form and content, to one which, by 1900, was radically different in appearance from masques of the past, though still considered to be a continuation of this musico-dramatic tradition. The masque was framed as a "typically English institution," or so Vaughan Williams mused in the marginalium quoted above, through the establishment of the genre's "true" nationalistic roots located in the English Renaissance and English folk traditions. Its re-invention came about as a result of two tendencies in cultural and musical ideology during the second half of the nineteenth century. The

---

[1] Marginalium written by Ralph Vaughan Williams on sketches for his ninth symphony in 1953–4, British Library Add. 50376. There seems to be no obvious reason why Vaughan Williams would have made a note about masques on the symphony sketch – possibilities include thoughts towards an article or lecture, or perhaps he was contemplating a new masque composition. Whatever he was thinking, it never materialized, frustratingly.

[2] The concept, of course, comes from Eric Hobsbawm, "Inventing Traditions," in *The Invention of Tradition*, ed. E.J. Hobsbawm and Terence Ranger (Cambridge: Cambridge University Press, 1983), 1–14.

first was the increased reliance on the topos of the Tudor, Elizabethan, and Jacobean periods as an "English Golden Age" within actual musico-dramatic works of the period, a topos that exploited the appearance of a visual and aural reality as a spectacular component to appeal to audiences across a wide range of backgrounds and classes. The second was the increased historiographic interest in English music and drama of the past, an interest prompted by the fundamental concern of establishing evolutionary patterns that connected the present to appropriate versions of the nation's relatively distant past.

Once this "re-invention" had occurred, and the masque was established as a tradition with these sorts of associations, it came to be used to assert contrasting kinds of English identity. On the one hand, Victorian and Edwardian masques continued to exploit the political and dynastic forms of English identity that had been established within the court masque very early in its history and which were solidified on the public stage by works like Dryden and Purcell's *King Arthur* and Arne's *Alfred*. By the turn of the twentieth century, masques that reflected these sorts of English identity were heavily invested in the representation and validation of the nation as modern and progressive, with all the attendant and often conflicting ideologies that clustered around this image of Great Britain during the first decades of the twentieth century. On the other hand, identities that utilized a set of concepts that went hand in hand with the emerging folk revival and the concept of the "organic village" sought to replace a vision of England as situated in modernity and progress with one that mediated present-day realities through an idealized past. Masques exploiting folk traditions and pastoral idioms certainly had their roots in the scenes of May Days and village fairs prevalent in late Victorian literary, dramatic, and musical works. However, at the turn of the century this kind of spectacle overshadowed by historical nostalgia became wedded to ideologies of social renewal. By reconnecting to a past located in a folk and a Jacobethan aesthetic, many believed that England could rediscover a historical national identity that would solve the looming problems of the contemporary nation. A multitude of masques, therefore, were written as communal activities, seeking involvement from local amateurs in an effort to reactivate the past through participation at a local level in representations which were permeated with nostalgia for a lost national identity.

In the decades surrounding 1900, the campaign for an English national music participated in current national debates about identity, replicating possible solutions as the musical community began its own search for appropriate versions of musical Englishness. Often the ways through which this identity was defined were constructed via a relationship to history and England's musical past. Towards the end of the nineteenth century, in the wake of other kinds of English nationalisms, there was a new awareness of

England's native composers and performers, and a concern to raise the quality of English music to a level that could compete with music from the continent. A new generation of composers was thrust into the public's eye, and the new nationalist movement in music was quickly identified, sometimes termed the English Musical Renaissance. By 1900, many English composers began to reformulate their understanding of a national music as one not only of increased compositions and performances, but also one built on a national musical language whose rhetoric insisted on its derivation from inherently English sources, though the actual compositional style was of course greatly influenced by continental music, such as that by Sibelius or Debussy. In the push for this kind of reconceptualization, certain kinds of sources and certain kinds of ideological stances became prioritized within the emerging narrative of an English national music dominated by those associated with what came to be called the English Musical Renaissance. While certainly a not a uniform set of precepts during the years prior to World War I, the musical language championed by English Musical Renaissance composers and ostensibly derived at least in part from historical and pastoral kinds of English identities increasingly hid more overtly public and modern manifestations of English music, such as those exemplified by Edward Elgar. The masque was one genre in which this debate of national identity was contested in a very real way. By World War I, the genre was implicitly understood to be about English identity, despite the variations of Englishness that were represented across the multifarious examples of the period.

Masque composition did not stop after World War I; if anything, productions of masques and pageants increased during the period 1920–1940. Many of these masques were similar to those produced before the war, written for and performed by amateurs within local, community-oriented productions, with subjects that oscillated between the pastoral, historical, and imperial. Organizations like the English Folk Dance Society, whose popularity soared after the war, sponsored regular productions of masques and pageants that sought to reify certain now-iconic folk and pastoral scenes. Villages and towns competed to produce pageants celebrating local and national history in efforts to raise money for worthwhile charities.[3] And with the increase in tourism to historical sites made easier by the upsurge in automobiles, castles and stately homes regularly produced masques and pageants as part of their tourist appeal.

---

[3] This "pageant culture" is wickedly satirized in E.F. Benson's *Mapp and Lucia*, but more sensitive uses of pageants in novels from the period can be found in Cowper Powys's *Glastonbury Romance*, among others. Especially noteworthy is Virginia Woolf's *Between the Acts*, which perhaps grew from her experiences working on Vaughan Williams and E.M. Forster's *The Pageant of Abinger*.

Again, Vaughan Williams offers an instructive example of these trends in masque writing. *Pan's Anniversary* was not an isolated feature among his compositions, and he continued to write masques and related stage works throughout his life, mostly for amateur productions.[4] Many of the later masques incorporated music similar to that of *Pan's Anniversary* and the Reigate *Pilgrim's Progress* pageant: arrangements of hymns, sixteenth- and seventeenth-century dance music, and folk song. These sources quickly solidified into a consistent bank of music for his commissions for amateur and populist kinds of music-making and formed the basis for the compositions and arrangements he provided for the 1911 *London Pageant*, and the 1912 and 1913 seasons of the Stratford Shakespeare Festival, which was by then also the home of the English Folk Dance Society's summer school. All of these earlier masques, pageants, and other occasions for which he provided incidental music essentially follow a fill-in-the blank approach to providing accessible vocal, instrumental, and dance music as called for by the script or scenario.

Vaughan Williams returned to masque and pageant writing in the 1920s, when he was well-established as one of Britain's leading composers. There is a marked change in his overall approach to writing masques and pageants during the years between World Wars I and II. He continued to provide music throughout his life for groups like the English Folk Dance Society, in which he continued to have an active presence. Even after 1920, most of his works in this vein featured arranged music similar to that of *Pan's Anniversary*. Examples include the *Pageant of Abinger* (1935), with text by E.M. Forster; the *English Folk Dance Society Masque* (1935), essentially a two-movement arrangement of well-known Christmas carols; and *England's Pleasant Land* (1938).[5] As late as 1950, Vaughan Williams contributed music for the *Solemn Masque of Charterhouse*. Though first written for a professional ballet company and only later performed by amateurs, *On Christmas Night*, very loosely based on Dickens's *Christmas Carol* though more generally an evocation of "Christmases Past," should be considered with these others, containing as it does a procession of his arrangements of Christmas carols, folk tunes, and country dances. These post-war works reflect the full development of Vaughan Williams's ideas of the social utility of music, enumerated again and again throughout his writings. These ideas harken back to ones clearly stated in his early article "Who wants the English Composer?," where he wrote, "the composer must not shut himself up and think about art, he must live with his fellows and make his

---

[4] The best source for details on these masques and pageants is Michael Kennedy, *A Catalogue of the Works of Ralph Vaughan Williams*, 2nd edn (Oxford: Oxford University Press, 1996).

[5] This last work incorporated early sketches from the composition of the composer's fifth symphony.

art an expression of the whole life of the community."[6] With this philosophy Vaughan Williams reflected the aims and goals of many of his friends and fellow workers in such organizations as the English Folk Dance Society and their emphasis on the need for a social renewal of the English people through an encounter with their national roots via participation in various folk arts. These were all ideas that were intrinsically part of the educational outreach aspect of the English Folk Dance Society after World War I, and were ones with which the composer obviously sympathized.

However, Vaughan Williams also wrote several other masques during these years that reflect a set of concerns somewhat removed from his masques for amateurs and the other amateur masques of the period. These concerns were a reaction to new forms of modernism emanating from the continent, particularly the neo-classical compositions by Stravinsky and many others. In the years surrounding 1900, the historical and folk ideologies of the English Musical Renaissance had wrestled with an opponent characterized by advanced and progressive continental musical styles. These styles of pre-War War I modernism could be seen as opposed to the main ideological concerns of the English Musical Renaissance because of their cosmopolitanism and perceived anti-historical and anti-folk stances. However, during the 1920s and 30s, modernist neo-classical music could not be so easily dismissed, given neo-classicism's engagement with the vestiges of historicism. For English composers desirous of working within a modernist aesthetic and at the same time remaining loyal to the historical and folk narratives by now well established as English musical identity, neo-classicism offered many possibilities.

And so, under the influence of these new modernist trends, categories within the masque genre divorced themselves from the forms of the amateur masque–pageant and underwent a profound transformation in the period after World War I. The masque was a natural candidate for inclusion in a set of English neo-classical genres within poetry, modern dance, and musical drama, given its historical identity, its ties to Renaissance drama and folk traditions, and its traditional utilization of Renaissance and Baroque dance forms.

An obvious direction for further research would be to take an in-depth look at masques written after World War I, including notable examples by Constant Lambert and Benjamin Britten,[7] an investigation for which I do not

---

[6] Ralph Vaughan Williams, "Who wants the English composer?," reprinted in *Vaughan Williams on Music*, ed. David Manning (Oxford: Oxford University Press, 2007), 39–42.

[7] Constant Lambert, *Summer's Last Will and Testament* (1928), Ernest Moeran, *Overture for a Masque* (1949, albeit only a concert overture), Benjamin Britten, "The Norwich Masque" in *Gloriana* (1953) and songs for *This Way to the Tomb* (1945). Other twentieth-century masques include Tippett's *The Mask of Time* (1982), Martin Shaw's *Master Valiant* (1936) and Harrison Birtwistle's *The Mask of Orpheus*

have space here. Again, though, it is instructive to focus briefly on Vaughan Williams's participation in this neo-classical masque form. He composed two masques that fall into this category: *Job, a masque for dancing* (1930) and *Bridal Day* (1938). To these one might add the ballet *Old King Cole* (1923), though Vaughan Williams did not explicitly entitle it a masque. On the most basic level these masques were also expressions of a nationalist sentiment, in that Vaughan Williams hoped that they would further his dreams and aspirations for a truly national English modern dance style. The motivation for these goals was held in common with friends and fellow members of the English Folk Dance Society, especially Cecil Sharp. In 1919, both Sharp and Vaughan Williams had contributed to an issue of the journal *The Music Student* devoted to folk dance.[8] In their articles, both men expressed their wish that the public's fascination with continental ballet, as exemplified in all its decadent extremes by Diaghilev's *Ballets Russes*, would be replaced by a love of English folk dancing. For both men, several aspects of folk dancing held obvious appeal: its national character, its ties with England's past, its use of natural movement (both men loathed the *en pointe* dancing of the classical prima ballerina), and its communal nature symbolized by the various non-hierarchical yet synchronized patterns of the folk dances themselves. Sharp goes on to advocate that these aspects of folk dancing could valuably be extended to form a particularly English form of art dancing on stage, beyond strictly folk dancing:

> Their aim, which, it must be confessed, is an ambitious one, is to rescue the Dance from the slough into which it has fallen in the course of the last two centuries and re-instate it as one of the fine arts; and the way in which they propose to affect this reformation is to do for the Dance what the Florentine reformers in similar circumstances did for Music 300 years before, viz., to revert to the art of the folk and build afresh.

Ten years later, in a republication of Sharp's music to *A Midsummer Night's Dream*, the preface cites Vaughan Williams's masque or ballet *Old King Cole* as a first move in this direction.[9]

(1986), Peter Maxwell Davies's *Le Jongleur de Notre Dame* (1978) and *Blind Man's Bluff* (1972), and Malcolm Arnold's *Song of Simeon* (1959). The interesting play of words between "masque" and "mask" in some later masques points to some of these interesting shifts, and a self-consciousness about tensions inherent in the genre.

[8] *The Music Student*, 11, 12 (August 1919). Sharp's writing was adapted from an earlier preface he had written for a production of *Midsummer Night's Dream* in 1914 at the Savoy, in which he contributed arrangements of historical Elizabethan and folk musical pieces. Interestingly, this created quite a lot of discussion: half the audience liked the "new" music, the other half clamored for a return to the "traditional" Mendelssohn!

[9] *Bridal Day* or *Epithalamion* also falls into this category. In its first form it was a masque, though Vaughan Willimas subsequently recast it as a cantata in the 1950s

Vaughan Williams's most ambitious work in the masque genre is *Job, a masque for dancing*, and the complexities of this masque go far beyond a mere desire to stimulate a national dance style.[10] It bears little resemblance to his other masques in that it does not incorporate any folk song or dance, nor any speaking, miming, or vocal music, solo or choral. Apart from its title, the composition works almost completely as a ballet, similar in many ways to ballet works by contemporaries like Stravinsky, a connection probably somewhat deliberate on Vaughan Williams's part, given that the work was originally written for a proposed production by Diaghilev's *Ballets Russes*.[11] Formally, its only gestures towards the historical generic content of the masque

after the work was given a belated first production on television, a production Ursula Vaughan Williams says they both detested and of which there is an interesting account in her *R. V. W.: a biography of Ralph Vaughan Williams* (London: Oxford University Press, 1964). It too was originally to have been an English Folk Dance Society production. Its relatively late date of composition, 1938, well after the composition of *Job*, as well as the quality and complexity of the work, sets it somewhat apart. This is due primarily to a text which had literary merit (the libretto for the work was adapted from Spencer's *Epithalamion* by the then Ursula Wood, who was an accomplished poet) which obviously inspired Vaughan Williams both in the richness of its language, the seriousness of its artistic aims, and its reflection of contemporary neo-classical trends.

[10] *Job, a masque for dancing* is a rich and complicated work, and there is no space here to offer a detailed account of the piece. A good overview of the composition of *Job* and an analysis of the work can be found in Patricia Wiles, "A study of 'Job, A Masque for Dancing' by Ralph Vaughan Williams" (dissertation, Texas Tech University, 1988). For a more critical look at issues surrounding its composition, see in particular Alison McFarland, "A Deconstruction of William Blake's Vision: Vaughan Williams and *Job*," *International Journal of Musicology* 3 (1994), 339–71. Further important research can be found in Frank Ries's "Sir Geoffrey Keynes and the Ballet *Job*," *Dance Research*, 2 (Spring 1984), 19–34.

[11] An interesting aspect for further exploration would be the influence of Stravinsky on *Job*. The question is an intriguing one. Eventually Diaghilev turned the work down, but certainly the idea of that type of ballet production must have influenced Vaughan Williams, at least in the early days of the work's composition. A letter from Vaughan Williams to his librettist Gwen Raverat after his meeting with Diaghilev survives at the Fitzwilliam Library in Cambridge: "My dear Gwen: I amused myself with making a sketch of *Job* – I never expected Djag wd look at it – and I'm glad on the whole – but it really wdnt have suited the sham serious really decadent and frivolous attitude of the R.B. toward everything – can you imagine *Job* sandwiched between *Les Biches* and *Cimaroisiana* – and that dreadful pseudo-cultured audience saying to each other 'My dear, have you seen God at the Russian Ballet.' No – I think we are well out of it – I don't think this is sour grapes – for I admit that it wd have been great fun to have had a production by the R.B. – though I feel myself that they wd have made an unholy mess of it with their over-developed calves. Yours affectionately, R. Vaughan Williams"

are the dances from Renaissance and Baroque models: the "Minuet of the Sons of Job and their Wives," and the "Pavane and Galliard of the Sons of Morning," and again, these kinds of dances are quite typical of neo-classical works of the period. Its designation as a masque, therefore, owes more to ideological concerns rather than formal characteristics.[12]

Twenty-five years after Ralph Vaughan Williams initial foray into the "new" Tudor genre of the masque, by 1930 it was no longer so imperative for English composers to define themselves and English music as a whole with the same kind of oppositional, "us or them" stance towards imported music from the continent, nor was it so necessary to fight to establish appropriate sources for a national musical language. The English Musical Renaissance was active and prospering, and English music had finally gained some respect from the English public. English folk song was no longer an obscure, misunderstood body of music, but was widely disseminated by professionals and amateurs, and formed the basis of music education in the English school system. The music of the sixteenth and seventeenth centuries in England was thoroughly researched and edited, and as well was regularly performed. Vaughan Williams now was part of the older generation, and already on his way to acquiring the stereotyped persona of the quaint pastoralist that continues to plague him to this day, despite many forays into modernist compositional idioms in works like *Job*, his fourth symphony, and *Donna Nobis Pacem*. In 1930 he had other battles to fight, and fight them he did, from the position of power granted him by his huge popularity and acclaim.

The ideological aspects, then, that encouraged Vaughan Williams to make *Job* a masque rather than a ballet or other modernist dance work are tied to a different set of principles, and offer an explanation for why the composer was so relieved that Diaghilev turned down his proposed dance work as "too English." For, despite the historicity of much of the new neo-classical spirit, Vaughan Williams's goals were still to uphold the ideology of difference that was inherent in his lifelong espousal of a national music. He worked, therefore to embed neo-classicism within English musical style rather than be absorbed into it.

So we return to the question of what, for Vaughan Williams, is masque-like about *Job*. Several basic connections are to the subject matter of the masque. First, the source, topic, and scenario of his dance work must have held associations for the composer that resonated with what he believed about the relationship between poet and composer in the masques of the past. The link

[12] Yet from certain perspectives one can see shadows of the court masque glimmering behind *Job*. Satan's scenes could be described as a type of an antimasque, and the pavane and galliard as stand-ins for the revels as Satan is cast down. By extension, Elihu becomes the divine agent, who through the symbolic dance of the "Pavane of the Sons of the Morning" enacts the restoration of cosmic order and harmony. My thanks to Roger Savage for suggesting this interpretation to me.

here is the status of his sources: the Authorized Version of the Bible, and the paintings representing the peculiar English visionary character of William Blake. Second, because Keynes and Raverat's scenario was based on a pictorial source, Blake's illustrations, as much as on a textual one, *Job* proceeds in tableau-like units that were characteristic of both historical and contemporary masques. Other connections relate to the status of the dance in the masque. Dance was always the crucial component of the seventeenth-century masque, and from a certain perspective the other aspects of a masque in many ways exist to justify the presence of dance in the narrative. Taking into account my description of Vaughan Williams's visionary goals for his dance work, this underlying history of validating English dance forms within the masque would hold obvious attraction. The composer connected to this dance aspect of the masque through the inclusion of dances that borrow from the Renaissance and Baroque.

Finally, most masques, either those of the past or of Vaughan Williams's own lifetime, contained some kind of exhortation or moral instruction through allegorical, symbolic, or blatantly direct means. Vaughan Williams's designation of *Job* as a masque was meant to emphasize the seriousness and moral purpose of his own work, in marked contrast to the supposed frivolity and decadence of 1920s continental ballet. Foremost, obviously, were the messages contained in Blake's system of social and religious beliefs reflected in his illustrations of the Job story. These were joined and mediated on several levels by the Keynes and Raverat scenarios and the composer's own interpretative strategies. At the same time, however, the purpose of calling *Job* a masque was all about asserting difference along national lines, even when those differences were not apparent on the levels of musical content or style. True, to a certain extent Vaughan Williams was declaring his desire for a national dance style based on folk dance in the same way that he declared a national musical style based on folk music. This necessarily forced the composer to seek to incorporate signifiers of Englishness, of which the masque title was an important one.

Vaughan Williams's placement of *Job* into the masque genre through the subtitle *A Masque for Dancing* invokes a concept of the masque at its most abstract position, as a potent exposition of English identity that operates almost completely without the inclusion of obvious characteristic generic elements. This is possible only because the masque's Englishness was completely understood by the 1920s. Gone are the debates, implicit and explicit, about what topics are appropriate for the masque, or what kinds of music it should include. The process of re-invention outlined in the preceding chapters of this book had reached its fulfillment. The masque designation alone works as a component of English identity; its re-invention is complete.

Appendix 1: Chronology of Masque Compositions During the Nineteenth Century

Date	Composer/Author	Title	First Performance
1809	James Fisin/William Congreve	*Judgement of Paris*	unknown
1825	Gesualdo Lanza/William Earle	*The Spirits of Dew*	unperformed (?)
1840	George Alexander Macfarren/George Macfarren Sr.	*An Emblematic Tribute on the Queen's Marriage*	Drury Lane, London
1840	Henry Bishop/J.R. Planché	*The Fortunate Isles*	Covent Garden, London
1852	Edward Loder/George Sloan	*The Island of Calypso*	Covent Garden, London
1862	Arthur Sullivan/Shakespeare	*Masque for The Tempest*	Leipzig, Crystal Palace
1863	George Macfarren/John Oxenford	*Freya's Gift*	Covent Garden, London
1864	Arthur Sullivan/Henry Chorley	*Kenilworth, a masque*	Birmingham Festival
1865	Henry Baumer/J. Watkins	*The Triumph of Labour*	Industrial Exhibition, Greenwich
1871	Arthur Sullivan/Shakespeare	*Music for the Masque from The Merchant of Venice*	Prince's Theatre, Manchester
1887	Anonymous	*Masque of Flowers*	Gray's Inn, London

Date	Composer/Author	Title	First Performance
1889	Alfred Cellier/B.C. Stephenson	Masque scene in *Doris*	Lyric Theatre, London
1891	Charles Villiers Stanford/Robert Bridges	"Adam's Vision" in *Eden*	Birmingham Music Festival
1897	Arthur Sullivan	"May Day" scenes 2 and 3 in *Victoria and Merrie England*	Alhambra Theatre, London
1899	Arnold Dolmetsch/Walter Crane, *et al.*	*Beauty's Awakening: A Masque of Winter and Spring*	Guildhall, London
1900	Hamish MacCunn/Louis N. Parker	*Masque of War and Peace*	Her Majesty's Theatre, London

Appendix 2: Chronology of Masque Historiography Prior to 1930

Date	Composer/Author	Title	Publisher
1821	Gascoigne, George	*Gascoigne's Princely Pleasures*	London: J.H. Burn
1823	Nichols, John	*The Progresses of Queen Elizabeth*	London: private printing
1828	Nichols, John	*The Progresses, Processions, and Magnificent Festivities of King James the First*	London: private printing
1831	Collier, John Payne	*History of English Dramatic Poetry and Annals of the Stage*	London: J. Murray
1842	Cunningham, Peter	*Extracts from the Accounts of the Revels at the Court, in the Reigns of Queen Elizabeth and King James I*	London: Shakespeare Society
1847	Rimbault, Edward	*Ancient Vocal Music of England*	
1848	Cunningham, Peter	*Inigo Jones: A life of the Architect*	London: Shakespeare Society
1882	Soergal, Oscar	*Die Englischen Maskenspiele*	Halle: private printing
1885	Macfarren, G.A.	*Musical History Briefly Narrated and Technically Discussed with a roll of the Names of Musicians And the Times and Places of their Births and Death*	Edinburgh: Adam and Charles Black
1890	Fleay, F.G.	*A Chronicle History of the London Stage, 1559–1642*	London: Reeves and Turner
1890	Latham, Morton	*The Renaissance of Music*	London: D. Stott
1891	Fleay, F.G.	*A Biographical Chronicle of the English Drama, 1559–1642*	London; Reeves and Turner

Date	Composer/Author	Title	Publisher
1895	Davey, Henry	History of English Music	London: J. Curwen & sons
1896	Naylor, Edward	Shakespeare and Music: with illustrations from the Music of the 16th and 17th centuries	London: J.M. Dent & Co.
1897	Evans, H.A.	The English Masque	London: Blackie & Son
1899	Art Worker's Guild	Dedicatory Epistle and Prologue to Beauty's Awakening	The Studio (Summer, 1899)
1899	Ward, Adolphus	A History of English Dramatic Literature	London: Macmillan and Co.
1900	Lorrain, Jean	Histoires de Masques	Paris: Société d'éditions littéraires et artistiques
1900	Thorndike, Ashley	"Influence of the Court Masques on the Drama"	PMLA, 15 (1900), 114–20
1902	Brotanek, Rudolf	Die Englischen Maskenspiele	Vienna: W. Braümiller
1902	Greg, W.W.	A List of Masques, Pageants &c, supplementary to a List of English Plays	London: Bibliographic Society
1902	Parry, C. Hubert	The Music of the Seventeenth Century	London: Oxford UP
1903	Chambers, E.K.	The Mediaeval Stage	Oxford: Clarendon Press
1906	Prendergrast, A.H.D	"Masques and Early Opera," in T.C. Southgate, ed., English Music, 1604 to 1904: Being the Lectures Given at the Music Loan Exhibition of the Worshipful Company of Musicians, Held at Fishmonger's Hall, London Bridge, June–July 1904	London: Walter Scott Pub. Co.

Date	Composer/Author	Title	Publisher
1907	Walker, Ernest	*A History of Music in England*	Oxford: Clarendon Press
1907	Castelain, Maurice	*Ben Jonson: L'Homme et L'Oeuvre*	Paris: Hachette et Cie
1907	Cunliffe, John	"Italian Prototypes of the Masque and Dumb Show"	*PMLA*, 17 (1907), 140
1908	Baskerville, C.R.	"Sources of Jonson's Masque of Christmas and Love's Wellcome at Welbeck"	*Modern Philology*, 6, 2 (Oct. 1908)
1909	Reyher, Paul	*Les Masques Anglais*	Paris: Hachette and Cie
1910	Dowden, Edward	"The English Masque" in *Essays Modern and Elizabethan*	London: J.M. Dent & sons
1911	Forsyth, Cecil	*Music and Nationalism: a study of English Opera*	London: Macmillan
1912	Lawrence, W.J.	"The Mounting of the Carolan [sic] Masques" in *The Elizabethan Playhouse*	Stratford: Shakespeare Head Press
1913	Sullivan, Mary Agnes	*Court Masques of James I; Their Influence on Shakespeare and the Public Theatre*	London: J.P. Putnam's Sons
1923	Chambers, E.K.	*The Elizabethan Stage*	Oxford: Clarendon Press
1925	Nicoll, Allardyce	*British Drama; an Historical Survey from the Beginnings to the Present Time*	London: G.G. Harrap
1926	Steele, Mary	*Plays and Masques at Court*	London: Oxford UP
1927	Welsford, Enid	*The Court Masque*	Cambridge: Cambridge UP
1928	Dent, Edward J.	*Foundations of English Opera*	Cambridge: Cambridge UP

Appendix 3: Chronology of British Masque Compositions, 1901–50

Date	Composer/Author	Title	Publisher
1901	Keith Huntington/H. Kenilworth	*King Alfred, a masque*	London: J. Williams
1902	Edward German	*Masque for As You like It*	London: Novello
1902	Alfred Redhead/H. Kenilworth	*Sweet and Twenty, a masque for the new century*	London: J. Williams
1903	Edward German/Basil Hood	Masque from *Merrie England*	London, Chappell and Co.
1903	C.W. Smith (arr.)/Ben Jonson, Milton	*Hue and Cry after Cupid*, from *Comus*	Unpublished
1904	Henry Hadow/Robert Bridges	*Demeter*	performed Somerville College, Oxford – music unpublished
1904	Alice Buckton	*Masques and Dances*	London: C.F. Hodson & Son
1904	Arthur Poyser	*A Masque of May-time*	London: Curwen
1905	Ralph Vaughan Williams/Ben Jonson	*Pan's Anniversary*	Unpublished
1908	Arthur Akeroyd/W.G. Robertson	*Masque of May Morning*	London: Boosey and Hawkes
1908	Wm Henry Bell/Ben Jonson	*Vision of Delight*	Unpublished
1908	William Nicholls/J. Flecker	*The Masque of the Magi*	London: Bayley & Ferguson
1909	Gustav Holst	*Vision of Dame Christian*	London: St Paul's Girl's School (private printing)

Date	Composer/Author	Title	Publisher
1909	T. Tertius Noble/James Rhoades	*The York Pageant*	York: Banks & Son
1911	Wm Henry Bell/Ben Jonson	*Christmas His Masque*	Unpublished
1911	Frederic Corder/F.H. Markoe	"The Masque Imperial" from *The London Pageant*	London: Bernrose & Sons (text only, ed. Sophie Lomas)
1911	George Clutsom/R. Lother	*King Harlequin*	London: Chappell and Co.
1912	Edward Elgar/H. Hamilton	*The Crown of India*	London: Enoch and Sons
1912/13	Patrick Geddes	*Masque of Learning and Its Many Meanings* (two parts)	Edinburgh: P. Geddes and Colleagues
1914	Granville Bantock/Helen Bantock	*The Great God Pan*	London: Novello
1914	Alfred Bisdee/F. Converse	*The Holy Night*	London: Curwen
1914	Agnes Lambert	*The Masque, Love and the Dyad*	London: Boosey and Hawkes
1915	Edith Gell	*The Empire's Honour*	London: Mowbray and Co.
1917	Kitson Clark/Mrs. H. Porter	*Masque of Patience and Hope*	London: Wells, Gardner, Darton & Co.
1917	Thomas Dunhill	*The Masque of the Shoe*	London: Year Book Press
1917	Joseph Holbrooke (based on E.A. Poe)	*The Masque of the Red Death*	London: J. and W. Chester
1918	Cecil Forsyth/H.J. MacLean	*A Masque*	Birmingham
1918	Mrs. Gell	*The Empire's Destiny*	London: Mowbray and Co.
1919	Leslie Heward/Ben Jonson	*The Witches Sabbath*	London: Goodwin & Tab

Date	Composer/Author	Title	Publisher
1919	E.D. Rendell	Charterhouse Masque	London: Weekes & Co.
1920	Alec Rowley	Punchinello, a Masque of Shadows	London: Ashdown
1924	Richard Chanter/Marjorie Woolnoth	Masque of Midsummer	London: Curwen
1926	Alexander Brent-Smith	The Masque of A Fox	London: Elkin and Co.
1926	Ralph Vaughan Williams/after Charles Dickens	On Christmas Night	London: Oxford UP
1929	Mabel Dolmetsch	Masque of Ishak and Tohfa	Haslemere
1930	Ralph Vaughan Williams/after William Blake	Job, a masque for dancing	London: Oxford UP
1932	Walter Leigh/Herbert Farjeon	Masque of Neptune	Unpublished (?)
1935	Ralph Vaughan Williams	English Folk Dance Society Masque	Unpublished
1935	Anthony Bernard/C.A. Clay	The Cherry Tree	London: Winthrop Rogers
1936	Martin Shaw/B. Baron	Master Valiant, a choral masque	London: Oxford UP
1937	Constant Lambert/Thomas Nashe	Summer's Last Will and Testament	London: Oxford UP
1938	Ralph Vaughan Williams/Ursula Wood after Edmund Spenser	The Bridal Day	London: Oxford UP
1949	Ernest Moeran	Overture for a Masque	London: Jos. Williams

Appendix 4: Review of
Pan's Anniversary from the
Stratford-upon-Avon Herald, April 28, 1905

N OT the least important event in the programme on Monday was the presentation of the masque entitled "Pan's Anniversary, or the Shepherd's Holiday", as given at the Court of King James. Since the announcement was made of its production at this year's festival much as been written on the interesting subject. In Ward's "English Dramatic Literature" we read that early in the reign of Henry VIII (1512–13), in connection with Court functions, there was introduced, a "new species of entertainment from Italy", the "mask", which appears to have differed from the earlier "disguisings" by the circumstances of the dancers wearing masks as well as costumes. Such a "mask" is that described by Cavendish in his "Life of Wolsey" and introduced with great effect by Shakespeare into his "Henry VIII". Inasmuch as moralities were represented at Court and exercised their influence upon its taste, the degree of action introduced into the disguising and masks varied considerably; at times decorations or properties (the term is ancient) were employed; and on special occasions those various kinds of entertainment were, no doubt, combined with exhibitions of a very elaborate description. At Henry VIII's Court, we accordingly hear of many kinds of more or less dramatic entertainments – of a Latin satirical play, in which Luther and his wife were derisively introduced; of morals acted by the King's players and the children of the chapel royal; of "interludes" comprising a morrice-dance presented by ladies and gentlemen of the court; of masks and disguisings of various sorts; on one occasion (in 1520) even of "a goodly comedy of Plautus", doubtless in Latin. In reference to the creative activity of Ben Jonson in what can hardly be regarded as a branch of dramatic literature proper, it has been pointed out that there is no intrinsic difference between the latter and earlier species of entertainments customary at the English Court and in the great homes of the nobility. The mask is, properly speaking, nothing more of less than a dance with masks and dance always remained its central point – the pivot, so to speak, on which the structure turns; but in other respects it is quite as elastic as the entertainments which it to some extent superseded. The distinction between a mask and a disguising is, therefore, no essential difference, and though not, properly speaking, falling under the designation of masks, may be classed with them as to all intents and purposes homogeneous. The degree in which a mask mixed the elements of declamation, dialogue, music, decoration, and scenery was determined by no minor law, but merely by the circumstance of each particular case. In its least elaborate form from a literary point of view, it nearly approached the pageant so consistently favoured by the citizens of London; where the characters were more carefully worked out, where something like a plot kept the whole together, and where something like an action was introduced, it trenched to some extent upon the domain of the drama. Ben Jonson was the most successful, as he was the most prolific, author of masks. Of his numerous compositions of this kind many hold a permanent place in our poetic literature, and taken together they furnish an extraordinary proof of the fertility and versatility of his poetic genius. He was conscious enough of his success in this direction. Next to himself, he said, only Fletcher and Chapman could write a mask. Fortune favoured him in placing on the throne a patron whose learned tastes caused him to view with peculiar favour this species of entertainment. It is the last infirmity even of a higher order of scholarship than James I possessed to pride itself on its readiness in perceiving allusions; and allusiveness is the very atmosphere of the mask. But the love of splendour which characterised the age, and the great advance which the decorative arts were making at this time were, of course, the principal cause of the favour extended to those amusements. Lastly they gratified the sense of aristocratic exclusiveness (this will, of course, not apply to the pageant which still continued in vogue), and to the nobility they supplied constant occasions for emulating on another in extravagant and costly flattering of a prince, the top of whose bents in this respect it was not easy to reach. In regard to the characteristics of his masks, Jonson showed and almost inexhaustible inventiveness, (drawing his devices partly from classical story) in which instances he loves to give in his notes chapter and verse for the sources of his erudition), partly from later legend or history. The construction of his masks was the least part of the labour; but this head he (apparently in deference to the taste of the king), in his later masks, almost invariably adopted an ingenious innovation which furnished him with admirable opportunities for the display of his comic genius. This was the "anti-mask", which has been defined as a species of parody which the poet himself occasionally adds to his invention and generally prefixes to the serious entry. It thus, as Schlegel observes, supplies an antidote to the excess of sweetness with which the flattery contained in the mask itself might be liable to cloy the audience. And it furnishes Ben Jonson in particular with opportunities for the introduction of many humourous characters, lightly but vigorously drawn, and even of comic situations worthy of his dramatic powers. The execution of these masks is more than adequate, and frequently rises to a high level. Jonson's lyrical gift, which has been unjustly depreciated, here finds many opportunities of displaying itself with remarkable ease and grace. It cannot be said of him that he raised the mask to the highest poetic level of which this species of production is capable – this was reserved for a genius of a very different order, but it would be an erroneous judgment which should undervalue the learning, the ingenuity and the creative vigour which he, in these masks, most abundantly displays. The combination of these qualities, with much true eloquence and lyrical beauty, gives a lasting value to many of these inventions of his fancy, called for by a taste artificial indeed, but neither degraded in itself nor degrading to the poet who ministered to its demands. So much for the history of the masque.

Fitful gleams of sunshine strove for the mastery of the fleecy clouds, and a stiff breeze swept the waters of the Avon as the public trooped into the Bancroft gardens, which formed the locale of the performance. The weather was, of course, an important factor in an outdoor gathering such as this, and considering the unfavourable climactic conditions which had prevailed previously many fears were entertained that the spectacular effects of the masque would be marred by the fickleness of the April weather. Fortunately however, no rain fell, and save only for the cold breeze which rendered things just a trifle uncomfortable to players and audience the prevailing conditions were as favourable as once could expect thus early in the season of sunshine. The Bancroft formed an ideal situation for the representation. 'Neath the shadow of the Memorial theatre a stage had been erected. The tall budding poplars were a natural scenic background, and on either side the trees, bursting into new foliage, formed the "wings". Palms and other plants complete the scenic effect, which were greatly enhanced by the magnificent Elizabethan costumes which stood out in strong contrast to the light and dark greens of Spring's garb. The arrangements were in the hands of a committee appointed by the Shakespeare club, consisting of the Mayor (Councilor G.M. Bird) the Vicar (the Reverend G. Arbuthnot), the chaplain of the Guild (the Rev. Cornwell Robertson), Aldermen W.G. Clobourne, W. Pearce, R. Latimer Green, Councillors R.C. Cox, E. Deer, G.W. Everard, A.S. Flower, T. Kitchen, Messrs J. Palmer, A. Andrew, G. Boyden, F.E. Callaway, E.A. Deer, J.R. Eccles, S.F. Ellis, H.T. Hickling, F. Sigwick, and W.E. Waithman. The secretarial duties were entrusted to Mr. F.W. Evans, and very capably he discharged them. The reserved portion of the seating accommodation was entirely occupied, while without the enclosure a long throng assembled, it being estimated that from three to four thousand persons entered the garden.

"Pan's Anniversary" or "The Shepherd's Holyday" (1625) was the last mask witnessed by King James. It opens very prettily with a catalogue of flowers. A trio of nymphs enter carrying prickles or open wicker baskets and strewing several sorts of flowers before the altar of the god. Each sings as she performs her task. One carries a basket of violets which she showers upon the ground to these lines –

> Drop, drop your violets: Change your hues,
> Now red, now pale, as lovers use!
> And in your death go out as well
> As when you lived, unto the smell!
> That from your odour all may say,
> This is the shepherd's holyday.

There is, says a writer of "Shakespeare's Predecessors", no crabbed erudition here, but rather a faint evanescent scent of Shelley's lines upon the violet.

When the nymphs have done singing an old shepherd, who is a prominent figure throughout the masque, and who was on this occasion most ably impersonated by Mr. H.T. Hickling, addresses the gathering thus:

> Well done, my pretty ones! Rain roses still,
> Until the last be dropped, then hence and fill
> Your fragrant prickles for a second shower.
> Bring corn-flag, tulips and Adonis' flower,
> Fair ox-eye, goldy-locks, and columbine,
> Pinks, goulands, king's-cups, and sweet sops-in-wine,
> Blue harebells, pagles, pasnies, calaminth,
> Flower-gentle and the fair-haired hyacinth;
> Bring rich carnations, flower-de-luces, lilies,
> The checked and purple-ringed daffodilies,
> Bright crown imperial, king-spear, hollyhocks,
> Sweet venus-navel and soft lady-smocks;
> Bring, too, some branches forth of Daphne's hair,
> And gladdest myrtle for these poets to wear,
> With spikeward weaved and marjoram between,
> And stained with yellow-golds and meadows-green,
> That when the altar, as it ought, is dressed,
> More odour come not from the phoenix nest,
> The breath there of Panchaia may envy,
> The colours China, and the light the sky.

With many musicians and singers seated about Pan's alter, "The Fountain of Light", the foregoing picturesque lines were given with much dramatic effect by Mr. Hickling, and in passing it may well be wondered when the poet had sent this shepherd with this flourish off the stage whether he could himself have pointed out each herb amid the prodigality of quaint named blossoms in some actual garden. The effect, however, is rich and those who care to reconstruct old English flower-beds in their imagination may learn from some herbal guide what goldy-locks, and goulands, sops-in-wine and pagles, lady-smocks, calaminth, and purple-ringed daffodilies really were. But to proceed. This pretty ceremony over, a fencer, portrayed by Mr. Edgar Waithman, steps in upon the scene and inquires the reason of the merry-making, and challenges the shepherd as to the superiority of the sports. This little altercation over, the Boeotians enter and dance the anti-masque, the Bidford troop of morris dancers, conducted by Mr. E. Salisbury, filling this section of the programme with much distinction, their antics evoking much applause. The first of four hymns to Pan follows here. Assuredly the musical section was one of the most pleasing features of the Masque. The music was especially composed by Dr. R. Vaughan Williams, but no attempt was made to reproduce the Elizabethan style. The compositions were, however, exquisitely sweet both in regard to solos and choruses. In the rendering of the latter by the Choral Union, the members of which had been trained by Mr. H.J. Caseley, there was a times a little irregularity due to the fact that the chorus was flanked on either side of the stage instead of en masse. This division resulted in uncertainly of movement in the attacks, although this defect could have been obviated by a closer attention to the conductor's baton. With pleasing effect the hymn was sung by the three nymphs (the Misses Cissie Saumarez, Elaine Sleddell, and Kate Cordingley), and then to sixteenth century music the maskers danced their entry in graceful form to extremely fascinating strains. This however, was only the prelude to an even grander turn, the "Main Daunce" (Ye Pavan), to music arranged for orchestra by Mr. G. von Holst. There was a charming blending of colour, the kaleidoscopic display being improved upon by rays of sunlight which feel athwart the stage. The revels, which were preceded by another hymn and chorus, then commenced, and much hearty laughter greeted the comic element, while considerable admiration was evinced by such effective scenes as, for instance, the "Maypole Daunce by schole maidens" and the "Daunce Ye Galliard", the latter being another of the charming "Elizabethan Daunces in Court enfoldings". In regard to the Maypole Dance it was evident that Shakespeare's instructions had been followed to the letter – "The children must

Be practis'd well to this, or they'll ne'er doo't."

The little maidens carried out this quaint custom of Merry May Day very prettily indeed, and as they tripped around the pole, holding in their hands the brightly-coloured ribbons, the spectacle was indeed picturesque. With measured tread the gaily-clad children went round and round and in and out until the plaiting of the streamers was completed, and then with the same childish grace and merry tripping the ribbons were unwound, while the orchestra discourse [sic] one of the many English folk-tunes which characterised the revels, including "Selenger's Round", "The Lost Lady", "Maria Martin" and "All on Spurn Point", these also being arranged by Mr. G. von Holst. The loud and prolonged plaudits which had greeted the efforts of the juveniles having subsided, the attention of the audience was directed to "The place appointed for the wrestling": in other words, the old English sports began. These consisted of fencing, wrestling, tilting at the quintain, hippas, &c. The two former incidents elicited a fare share of praise, but this tilting evoked much mirth as one by one the seekers after distinction came in contact with the weighted end of the quintain, and thus came to grief much to the amusement of the audience. The concluding stage of the performance was now entered upon as the Thebans danced the anti-masque "Shepherd's Hay". With their skins of goats the dancers presented a very quaint appearance, but the scene, though somewhat grotesque, did not lack picturesqueness, and the performers where cheered to the echo as they tripped away into a seclusion. A good finale was the hymn by nymphs and chorus: then more dances, a general blending of colour, and the revels of the day were ended. After paying their adieus to the audience the players to continued applause disappeared amid the foliage behind the scenes.

Concerning the "role of Player", generally speaking favourable opinions have been expressed. It was no fault of the performers that those at good distance from the stage could not hear them. They were speaking in the teeth of a strong wind which carried the sound of their voices in an opposite direction. Those who had the good fortune to be within hearing distance are, however, by no means stingy in their praises. Without a doubt the solos of the two Bensonian ladies and Miss Cordingley were greatly admired, as also was the portrayal of the Shepherd by Mr. Hickling, who possesses considerable histrionic ability, and is to congratulated on his apt treatment of a somewhat difficult role. As an elocutionist Mr. Edgar Waithman has long ago won his laurels, and the expectation in regard to his impersonation of the Fencer were certainly not misplaced. Of the other performers the masquers were: Maysters John Palmer, Ralf Salter, George Randall, Harry Donisthorpe, Francis Harris, William Harding, Patrick Thompson, James Simmonds; Mistresses Nora Ball, Amy Harris, Nelly Berry, Daisie Marics, Beatrice Berry, Winnie Morgan, Lillie Harding, and Ada Morgan. The Maypole dancers were: Isabel Tompkins, Nellie Callaway, Kate Willey, Connie Bennett, May White, Agnes Morby, Lily Baker, May Kendrick, Edith Duncombe, Dorothy Hunter, Rose Hudson, Essie Morby, Nellie Taylor, Dorothy Hirons, Rita Bailey, Nora Goldring. According to the programme, these were "graciously taught under the direction of Dame Mary Fenn, by Mistress Emma Greening and Mistress Florence Grundy". The whole production was under the direction of Dr. Vaughan Williams, who is to be congratulated on the harmonious compositions from his own pen, and also on the standard of efficiency attained before the public. The orchestra consisted of players from the Theatre (Mr. G.W. Collins) band, with augmentations from the Choral Union and the Town Band. The whole performance was a decided success, and we venture to think that the committee who thought within themselves, "Let us devise some entertainment for them" amply met the wants of the hosts of Shakespearean devotees and other trippers to the town. We might add that Mr. E.A. Deer superintended the erection of the stage and the general arrangements on the ground.

Bibliography

Poems of Today: First Series. London, 1915.

Adams, Byron. "The 'Dark Saying' of the Enigma: Homoeroticism and the Elgarian Paradox." *19th-Century Music* 23 (2000), 218–35.

———— "'No armpits please, we're British': Whitman and English Music, 1884–1936." In *Walt Whitman and Modern Music*, edited by Lawrence Kramer, 25–42. New York: Garland Publishing, 2000.

———— "Scripture, Church, and Culture: Biblical Texts in the Works of Ralph Vaughan Williams." In *Vaughan Williams Studies*, edited by Alain Frogley, 99–117. Cambridge: Cambridge University Press, 1996.

Anderson, Benedict. *Imagined Communities: Reflections on the Origin and Spread of Nationalism.* rev. edn. London: Verso, 1991.

Austin, Linda M. *Nostalgia in Transition, 1780–1917.* Charlottesville, VA: University of Virginia Press, 2007.

Bailey, Peter. *Leisure and Class in Victorian England: Rational Recreation and the Contest for Control, 1830–1895.* London: Routledge & Kegan Paul, 1978.

Banfield, Stephen. *Sensibility and English Song: Critical Studies of the Early Twentieth Century.* Cambridge: Cambridge University Press, 1985.

Banister, H.C. *George Alexander Macfarren.* London: G. Bell and Sons, 1891.

Barker, Simon. "Images of the Sixteenth and Seventeenth Centuries as a History of the Present." In *Literature, Politics and Theory: Papers from the Essex Conference 1976–84*, edited by Peter Hulme Francis Barker, Margaret Iversen, and Diana Loxley, 173–189. New York: Methuen, 1986.

Barone, Anthony. "Modernist Rifts in a Pastoral Landscape: Observations on the Manuscripts of Vaughan William's Fourth Symphony." *Musical Quarterly*, 91 (2008), 60–88.

Barthes, Roland. *Mythologies.* Trans. by Annette Laver. New York: Hill and Wang, 1972.

Beer, Gillian. "Speaking for the Others: Relativism and Authority in Victorian Anthropological Literature." In *Sir James Frazer and the Literary Imagination*, edited by Robert Fraser, 38–60. London: Macmillan Press, 1990.

Bellman, Jonathan, ed. *The Exotic in Western Music.* Boston: Northeastern University Press, 1998.

Benoliel, Bernard. *Parry before Jerusalem: Studies of his Life and Music with Excerpts from his Published Writings.* Aldershot: Ashgate, 1997.

Biddlecombe, George. *English Opera from 1834 to 1864 with Particular Reference to the Works of Michael Balfe.* New York: Garland Publishing, 1994.

Bolton, H. Philip. *Scott Dramatized.* London: Mansell Publishing, 1992.

Booth, Michael R. "The Social and Literary Context." In *The Revels History of Drama in English, Volume VI: 1750–1880*, 1–58. London: Methuen & Co., 1975.

——— *Victorian Spectacular Theatre, 1850–1910*. London: Routledge & Kegan Paul, 1981.

Boyes, Georgina. *The Imagined Village: Culture, Ideology, and the English Folk Revival*. Manchester: Manchester University Press, 1993.

Bratton, J.S. "Of England, Home, and Duty: the Image of England in Victorian and Edwardian Juvenile Fiction." In *Imperialism and Popular Culture*, edited by John M. Mackenzie, 73–93. Manchester: Manchester University Press, 1986.

Broadwood, L. and J.A. Fuller Maitland. *English County Songs*. London: Leaderhall Press, 1893.

Buckley, Reginald R. *The Shakespeare Revival and the Stratford-Upon-Avon Movement*. London: George Allen & Sons, 1911.

Burden, Michael. "Britannia versus Virtue in the Harmony of the Spheres: Directions of Masque Writing in the Eighteenth Century." *Miscellanea Musicologia*, 17 (1990), 78–86.

——— *Garrick, Arne and the Masque of Alfred*. Lewiston: Edwin Mellen Press, 1994.

——— "The Independent Masque 1700–1800: A Catalogue." *Royal Musical Association Research Chronicle*, 28 (1995), 59–159.

——— *Purcell Remembered*. Portland, OR: Amadeus Press, 1995.

Burton, Nigel. "Oratorios and Cantatas." In *The Romantic Age 1800–1914*, edited by Nicholas Temperley, 214–43. London: Athlone Press, 1981.

Butler, Martin. *The Stuart Court Masque and Political Culture*. Cambridge: Cambridge University Press, 2008.

Cannadine, David. "The Context, Performance and Meaning of Ritual: The British Monarchy and the 'Invention of Tradition', c. 1820–1977." In *The Invention of Tradition*, edited by E.J. Hobsbawm and Terence Ranger, 101–64. Cambridge: Cambridge University Press, 1983.

Chambers, E.K. *The Mediaeval Stage*. Oxford: Oxford University Press, 1903.

Chan, Mary. *Music in the Theatre of Ben Jonson*. Oxford: Clarendon Press, 1980.

Clark, Kenneth. *The Gothic Revival: An Essay in the History of Taste*. New York: Harper & Row, 1974.

Clayton, Martin and Bennett Zon. *Music and Orientalism in the British Empire, 1780s–1940s: Portrayal of the East*. Aldershot: Ashgate Publishing, 2007.

Cole, Suzanne. *Thomas Tallis and His Music in Victorian England*. Woodbridge: The Boydell Press, 2008.

Colley, Linda. *Britons: Forging the Nation 1707–1837*. New Haven, CT: Yale University Press, 1992.

Crump, Jeremy. "The Identity of English Music: The Reception of Elgar 1898–1935." In *Englishness: Culture and Politics 1880–1920*, edited by Robert Colls and Philip Dodd, 164–190. Beckenham: Croom Helm, 1986.

Culler, A. Dwight. *The Victorian Mirror of History*. New Haven, CT: Yale University Press, 1985.

Davey, Henry. *History of English Music*. London: J. Curwen and Sons, 1895.

Davies, Robertson. "Playwrights and Plays." In *The Revels History of Drama in English, Volume VI: 1750–1880*, 147–269. London: Methuen & Co., 1975.

Day, James. *'Englishness' in Music from Elizabethan Time to Elgar, Tippett and Britten*. London: Thames Publishing, 1999.

—————— *Vaughan Williams*, edited by Stanley Sadie. *The Master Musicians*. Oxford: Oxford University Press, 1998.

Deane, Seamus. "Imperialism/Nationalism." In *Critical Terms for Literary Study*, edited by Frank Lentricchia and Thomas McLaughlin, 354–68. Chicago: University of Chicago Press, 1995.

Dent, E.J. *Foundations of English Opera*. Cambridge: Cambridge University Press, 1928.

de Val, Dorothy. "The Transformed Village: Lucy Broadwood and Folksong." In *Music and British Culture, 1785–1914*, edited by Christina Bashford and Leanne Langley, 341–66. Oxford: Oxford University Press, 2000.

De Van, Gilles. "Fin de Siècle Exoticism and the Meaning of the Far Away." *Opera Quarterly*, 11, 3 (1995): 77–94.

Dibble, Jeremy. "Elgar and His British Contemporaries." In *The Cambridge Companion to Elgar*, edited by Daniel Grimley and Julian Rushton, 15–23. Cambridge: Cambridge University Press, 2005.

—————— "Parry as Historiographer." In *Nineteenth-Century British Music Studies*, edited by Bennett Zon, 37–51. Aldershot: Ashgate, 1999.

—————— "Parry, Stanford and Vaughan Williams: the Creation of Tradition." In *Vaughan Williams in Perspective*, edited by Lewis Foreman, 25–47. London, Albion Press, 1998.

Dingley, Robert. "Meaning Everything: The Image of Pan at the Turn of the Century." In *Twentieth-Century Fantasists: Essays on Culture, Society and Belief in Twentieth-Century Mythopoeic Literature*, edited by Kath Filmer, 47–59. New York: St. Martin's Press, 1992.

Dodd, Philip. "Englishness and the National Culture." In *Englishness: Culture and Politics 1880–1920*, edited by Robert Colls and Philip Dodd, 1–28. Beckenham: Croom Helm, 1986.

Downer, Alan. *The Eminent Tragedian William Charles Macready*. Cambridge, MA: Harvard University Press, 1966.

Easthope, Antony. *Englishness and National Culture*. London: Routledge, 1999.

Elgar, Edward. *A Future for English Music and other Lectures*, edited by Percy M. Young. London: Dennis Dobson, 1968.

Evans, Herbert Arthur. *English Masques*. London: Blackie and Son, 1895.

Ewbank, Inga-Stina. "'These Pretty Devices': a Study of Masques in Plays." In *A Book of Masques for Allardyce Nicoll*, ed. T.J.B. Spencer and Stanley Wells. Cambridge: Cambridge University Press, 1967.

Fearon, George and Ivor Brown. *This Shakespeare Industry*. Westport, CT: Greenwood Press, 1939, repr. 1969.

Fischler, Alan. "*Oberon* and Odium: the Career and Crucifixion of J.R. Planché." *Opera Quarterly*, 12, 1 (1995), 5–26.

Fiske, Roger. *English Theatre Music in the Eighteenth Century*. London: Oxford University Press, 1973.

Fraser, Robert. "The Face beneath the Text: Sir James Frazer in his Time." In *Sir James Frazer and the Literary Imagination*, edited by Robert Fraser, 1–17. London: Macmillan Press, 1990.

Frogley, Alain. "Constructing Englishness in Music: National Character and the Reception of Ralph Vaughan Williams." In *Vaughan Williams Studies*, edited by Alain Frogley, 1–22. Cambridge: Cambridge University Press, 1996.

———— "'Getting its History Wrong': English Nationalism and the Reception of Ralph Vaughan Williams." In *Music and Nationalism in Twentieth-Century Great Britain and Finland*, edited by Tomi Makela. Hamburg, von Bockel Verlag, 1997.

———— "H.G. Wells and Vaughan Williams's *A London Symphony*: Politics and culture in Fin-de-Siècle England." In *Sundry Sorts of Music Books: Essays on The British Library Collections*, edited by Arthur Searle, Malcolm Turner and Chris Banks, 299–308. London: British Library, 1993.

———— "Re-writing the Renaissance: History, Imperialism, and British Music since 1840." *Music & Letters*, 84 (2003), 241–57.

———— "Vaughan Williams and Thomas Hardy: 'Tess' and the Slow Movement of the Ninth Symphony." *Music & Letters*, 68 (1987), 42–59.

Frogley, Alain and Aidan Thomson, eds. *Cambridge Companion to Vaughan Williams*. Cambridge: Cambridge University Press, 2013.

Fuhrmann, Christina. "'Adapted and Arranged for the English Stage': Continental Operas Transformed for the London Theater, 1814–1833." Dissertation, Washington University, 2001.

———— "Between Opera and Musical: Theatre Music in Early Nineteenth-Century London" in *The Oxford Handbook of the British Musical*, edited by Robert Gordon and Olaf Jubin. Oxford: Oxford University Press, 2016.

Gammon, Vic. "Folk Song Collecting in Sussex and Surrey, 1843–1914." *History Workshop*, 10 (1980).

Gatens, William J. "John Ruskin and Music." In *The Lost Chord: Essays on Victorian Music*, edited by Nicholas Temperley, 68–88. Bloomington, IN: Indiana University Press, 1989.

Gervais, David. *Literary Englands: Versions of 'Englishness' in Modern Writing*. Cambridge: Cambridge University Press, 1993.

Ghuman, Nalini. *Resonances of the Raj: India in the English Musical Imagination*. Oxford: Oxford University Press, 2014.

Giles, Judy and Tim Middleton, eds. *Writing Englishness 1900–1950*. London: Routledge, 1995.

Girouard, Mark. *The Return to Camelot: Chivalry and the English Gentleman.* New Haven, CT: Yale University Press, 1981.

Gould, Corissa. "Edward Elgar, *The Crown of India*, and the Image of Empire." *The Elgar Society Journal*, 13, 1 (2003), 25–35.

———— "Elgar, *The Crown of India* and the Feminine 'Other.'" In *Europe, Empire and Spectacle in Nineteenth-Century British Music*, edited by Rachel Cowgill and Julian Rushton. Aldershot: Ashgate Publishing, 2006.

———— "'An Inoffensive Thing': Edward Elgar, *The Crown of India* and Empire." In *Music and Orientalism in the British Empire, 1780s–1940s: Portrayal of the East*, edited by Martin Clayton and Bennett Zon, 147–64. Aldershot: Ashgate, 2007.

Grainger, J.H. *Patriotisms: Britain 1900–1939.* London: Routledge & Kegan Paul, 1986.

Gramit, David. "The Dilemma of the Popular: The *Volk*, the Composer, and the Culture of Art Music." In *Cultivating Music: the Aspirations, Interests, and Limits of German Musical Culture, 1770–1848*, 63–92. Berkeley, CA: University of California Press, 2002.

Grimley, Daniel. "Landscape and Distance: Vaughan Williams, Modernism and the Symphonic Pastoral." In *British Music and Modernism, 1895–1960*, edited by Matthew Riley, 147–74. Farnham: Ashgate, 2010.

Grogan, Christopher. "Elgar, Streatfeild and *The Pilgrim's Progress.*" In *Edward Elgar: Music and Literature*, edited by Raymond Monk, 140–63. Aldershot: Scolar Press, 1993.

Hardwick, Peter. "The Revival of Interest in Old English Music in Victorian England, and the Impact of this Revival on Music composed into the Twentieth Century." Dissertation, University of Washington, 1973.

Harker, Dave. *Fakesong: The Manufacture of British 'Folksong' 1700 to the Present Day.* Milton Keynes: Open University Press, 1985.

Harper, J.P.E. "Vaughan William's 'Antic' Symphony." In *British Music and Modernism, 1895–1960*, edited by Matthew Riley, 175–96. Farnham: Ashgate, 2010.

Harrington, Paul. "Holst and Vaughan Williams: Radical Pastoral." In *Music and the Politics of Culture*, edited by Christopher Norris, 106–27. New York: St. Martin's Press, 1989.

Harris, Ellen. *Henry Purcell's Dido and Aeneas.* Oxford: Clarendon Press, 1987.

———— "*King Arthur*'s Journey into the Eighteenth Century." In *Purcell Studies*, edited by Curtis Price, 257–89. Cambridge: Cambridge University Press, 1995.

Heckert, Deborah. "Composing History: National Identity and the Uses of the Past in the English Masque, 1860–1918." Dissertation, Stony Brook University, 2004.

———— "Working the Crowd: Elgar, Class, and Reformulations of Popular Culture at the Turn of the Twentieth Century." In *Elgar and his World*, edited by Byron Adams. Princeton University Press, 2007.

Hobsbawm, E.J. *The Age of Empire, 1875–1914.* New York: Pantheon, 1987.

———— "Inventing Traditions." In *The Invention of Tradition*, edited by E.J. Hobsbawm and Terence Ranger, 1–14. Cambridge: Cambridge University Press, 1983.

———— *Nations and Nationalism since 1780: Program, Myth, Reality.* 2nd edn. Cambridge: Cambridge University Press, 1990.

Holst, Imogen and Ursula Vaughan Williams, eds. *Heirs and Rebels: Letters written to each other and occasional writings on music by Ralph Vaughan Williams and Gustav Holst.* London: Oxford University Press, 1959.

Homan, Margaret. *Royal Representations: Queen Victoria and British Culture, 1837–1876.* Chicago: University of Chicago Press, 1998.

Howes, Frank. *The English Musical Renaissance.* London: Secker and Warburg, 1966.

Howkins, Alun. "The Discovery of Rural England." In *Englishness: Culture and Politics 1880–1920*, edited by Robert Colls and Philip Dodd, 62–88. Beckenham: Croom Helm, 1986.

Hughes, Meirion. "The Duc d'Elgar: Making a Composer Gentleman." In *Music and the Politics of Culture*, edited by Christopher Norris, 41–68. New York: St. Martin's Press, 1989.

Hughes, Meirion and Robert Stradling. *The English Musical Renaissance 1840–1940: Construction and Deconstruction.* 2nd edn. Manchester: Manchester University Press, 2001.

Hullah, John P. *The History of Modern Music.* 2nd edn. London: Longmans, Green, Reader, and Dyer, 1875.

Hutton, Ronald. *The Rise and Fall of Merry England.* Oxford: Oxford University Press, 2005.

———— *The Stations of the Sun: A History of the Ritual Year in Britain.* Oxford: Oxford University Press, 2007.

Hyman, Alan. *Sullivan and his Satellites: A Study of English Operettas, 1860–1914.* London: Chappell, 1978.

Jacobs, Arthur. *Arthur Sullivan, a Victorian Musician.* 2nd edn. Portland, OR: Amadeus Press, 1992.

Jaggard, Gerald. *Stratford Mosaic.* London: Christopher Johnson, 1960.

Janowitz, Anne. "The Pilgrims of Hope: William Morris and the Dialectic of Romanticism." In *Cultural Politics at the Fin de Siècle*, edited by Sally Ledger and Scot McCracken. Cambridge: Cambridge University Press, 1995.

Jonson, Ben. *Ben Jonson: The Complete Masques*, edited by Stephen Orgel. New Haven, CT: Yale University Press, 1969.

———— *The Cambridge Edition of the Works of Ben Jonson*, vol. 5, edited by Martin Butler. Cambridge: Cambridge University Press, 2012.

Judge, Roy. "May Day and Merrie England." *Folklore*, 102 (1991), 131–48.

Keith, W.J. *The Rural Tradition: a Study of the Non-Fiction Prose Writers of the English Countryside.* Toronto: University of Toronto Press, 1974.

Kemp, T.C. and J.C. Trewin, *The Stratford Festival.* Birmingham: Cornish Brothers, 1953.

Kennedy, Michael. *A Catalogue of the Works of Ralph Vaughan Williams*. 2nd edn. Oxford: Oxford University Press, 1996.

―――― "Elgar the Edwardian." In *Elgar Studies*, edited by Raymond Monk, 107–17. Aldershot: Scolar Press, 1990.

―――― *The Works of Ralph Vaughan Williams*. 2nd edn. London: Oxford University Press, 1980.

Kramer, Lawrence. "*Felix culpa*: Goethe and the image of Mendelssohn." In *Mendelssohn Studies*, edited by R. Larry Todd, 64–79. Cambridge: Cambridge University Press, 1992.

Krummacher, Friedhelm. "Composition as Accommodation? On Mendelssohn's Music in Relation to England." In *Mendelssohn Studies*, edited by R. Larry Todd, 80–105. Cambridge: Cambridge University Press, 1992.

Kumar, Krishan. *The Idea of Englishness: English Culture, National Identity and Social Thought*. London: Routledge, 2015.

―――― *The Making of English National Identity*. Cambridge: Cambridge University Press, 2003.

Kuykendall, Brooks. "Sullivan, *Victoria and Merrie England*, and the National Tableau." In *SullivanPerspektiven I*, edited by Albert Gier, Meinhard Saremba, and Benedict Taylor. Essen: Oldib-Verlag, 2012.

Lambert, Constant. *Music Ho! A Study of Music in Decline*. New York: Charles Scribner's and Sons, 1936.

Langland, Elizabeth. "Nation and Nationality: Queen Victoria in the Developing Narrative of Englishness." In *Remaking Queen Victoria*, edited by Margaret Homans and Adrienne Munich, 13–32. Cambridge: Cambridge University Press, 1997.

Lew, Nathaniel. "'Oh! By what tongue or pen can their glorious joy be expressed?': Ralph Vaughan Williams's Heavenly Choruses after John Bunyon." In *Vaughan Williams Essays*, edited by Byron Adams and Robin Wells. Aldershot: Ashgate, 2003.

Luckett, R. "'Or Rather Our Musical Shakespeare:' Charles Burney's Purcell." In *Music in Eighteenth-Century England: Essays in Memory of Charles Cudworth*, edited by C. Hogwood and R. Luckett, 59–77. Cambridge: Cambridge University Press, 1983.

Mackenzie, John M. "Introduction." In *Imperialism and Popular Culture*, edited by John M. Mackenzie, 1–16. Manchester: Manchester University Press, 1986.

―――― *Orientalism: History, Theory, and the Arts*. Manchester: Manchester University Press, 1995.

Manning, David, ed. *Vaughan Williams on Music*. Oxford: Oxford University Press, 2008.

Marker, Frederick and Lise-Lone Marker. "Actors and their Repertory." In *The Revels History of Drama in English, Volume VI: 1750–1880*, 95–143. London: Methuen & Co., 1975.

Marsh, Jan. *Back to the Land: The Pastoral Impulse in Victorian England from 1880 to 1914*. London: Quartet Books, 1982.

Marvin, Roberta. "Handel's *Acis and Galatea*: A Victorian View". in *Europe, Empire and Spectacle in Nineteenth-Century British Music*, edited by Rachel Cowgill and Julian Rushton, 249–63. Aldershot: Ashgate, 2007.

McCaw, Neil. *George Eliot and Victorian Historiography: Imagining the National Past*. New York: St. Martin's Press, 2000.

McCracken, Scott and Sally Ledger. *Cultural Politics at the Fin de Siècle*. Cambridge: Cambridge University Press, 1995.

McFarland, Alison. "A Deconstruction of William Blake's Vision: Vaughan Williams and *Job*." *International Journal of Musicology*, 3 (1994), 339–71.

McGuire, Charles Edward. *Elgar's Oratorios: The Creation of an Epic Narrative*. Aldershot: Ashgate Publishing, 2002.

————— "Functional Music: Imperialism, the Great War, and Elgar as a Popular Composer." In *The Cambridge Companion to Elgar*, edited by Daniel Grimley and Julian Rushton, 214–24. Cambridge: Cambridge University Press, 2005.

————— *Music and Victorian Philanthropy: The Tonic Sol-Fa Movement*. Cambridge: Cambridge University Press, 2007.

————— "1910, Vaughan Williams and the English Festival." In *Vaughan Williams Essays*, edited by Byron Adams and Robin Wells. Aldershot: Ashgate Publishing, 2003.

McVeagh, Diana. "Elgar and *Falstaff*." In *Elgar Studies*, edited by Raymond Monk, 134–41. Aldershot: Scolar Press, 1990.

Mellers, Wilfrid. *Vaughan Williams and the Vision of Albion*. London: Barrie and Jenkins, 1989.

Mitchell, Jerome. *More Scott Operas*. Lanham, MD: University Press of America, 1996.

Moody, Jane and Daniel O'Quinn, eds. *The Cambridge Companion to British Theatre, 1730–1830*. Cambridge: Cambridge University Press, 2007.

Moore, Jerrold Northrop. *Edward Elgar: A Creative Life*. Oxford: Oxford University Press, 1984.

Moulton, Ian Frederick. "Stratford and Bayreuth: Anti-commercialism, Nationalism, and the Religion of Art." *Litteraria Pragensia*, 6 (1996), 39–50.

Oates, Jennifer. *Hamish MacCunn (1868–1916): A Musical Life*. Aldershot: Ashgate Press, 2013.

Onderdonk, Julian. "*The English Musical Renaissance, 1860–1940: Construction and Deconstruction* (review)." *Notes*, 52 (Sep. 1995), 63–6.

————— "Vaughan Williams's Folksong Transcriptions: a Case of Idealization?" In *Vaughan Williams Studies*, edited by Alain Frogley, 118–38. Cambridge: Cambridge University Press, 1996.

Orgel, Stephen. *The Jonsonian Masque*. London: Oxford University Press, 1965.

Outka, Elizabeth. *Consuming Traditions: Modernity, Modernism, and the Commodified Authentic*. Oxford: Oxford University Press, 2009.

Parker, Anthony. *Pageants: Their Presentation and Production*. London: The Bodley Head, 1954.

Parker, Louis. *Several of my Lives*. London: Chapman and Hall, 1928.

Parry, Hubert. *The Evolution of the Art of Music*. 2nd edn. London: D. Appleton-Century Co., 1930.

———— "Inaugural Address." *Journal of the Folk Song Society*, 1 (1899), 1–3.

———— *The Music of the Seventeenth Century*. vol. 3, *Oxford History of Music*. Oxford: Oxford University Press, 1902.

Paxman, Jeremy. *The English: a Portrait of a People*. New York: Penguin, 1999.

Pearson, Charles H. *National Life and Character*. London: Macmillan and Co., 1913.

Perry, Lara and David Peters Corbett, eds. *English Art, 1860–1914: Modern Artists and Identity*. New Brunswick, NJ: Rutgers University Press, 2001.

Pierson, Stanley. *British Socialism: The Journey from Fantasy to Politics*. Cambridge, MA: Harvard University Press, 1979.

Pirie, Peter. *The English Musical Renaissance*. New York: St. Martin's Press, 1979.

Pope, Michael. "*King Olaf* and the English Choral Tradition." In *Elgar Studies*, edited by Raymond Monk, 46–80. Aldershot: Scolar Press, 1990.

Pople, Anthony. "Vaughan Williams, Tallis, and the Phantasy Principle." In *Vaughan Williams Studies*, edited by Alain Frogley, 47–80. Cambridge: Cambridge University Press, 1996.

Porter, J. "Muddying the Crystal Spring: from Idealism and Realism to Marxism in the Study of English and American Folk Song." In *Comparative Musicology and the Anthropology of Music*, edited by Bruno Nettl and Philip Bohlman, 113–30. Chicago: Chicago University Press, 1991.

Price, Curtis. "*Dido and Aeneas*: Questions of Style and Evidence." *Early Music*, 22 (1994), 115–25.

———— *Henry Purcell and the London Stage*. Cambridge: Cambridge University Press, 1984.

Rainbow, Bernarr. "The Rise of Popular Music Education in Nineteenth-Century England." In *The Lost Chord: Essays on Victorian Music*, edited by Nicholas Temperley, 17–41. Bloomington, IN: Indiana University Press, 1989.

Rich, Paul. "The Rise of English Nationalism." *History Today*, 37 (1989), 24–30.

Richards, Jeffrey. *Imperialism and Music: Britain 1876–1953*. Manchester: Manchester University Press, 2001.

Ries, Frank. "Sir Geoffrey Keynes and the Ballet *Job*." *Dance Research*, 2 (Spring 1984), 19–34.

Riley, Matthew, ed. *British Music and Modernism, 1895–1960*. Aldershot: Ashgate, 2010.

———— "Rustling Reeds and Lofty Pines: Elgar and the Music of Nature." *19th-Century Music*, 26 (2002), 155–77.

Rowell, G. *The Victorian Theatre, 1792–1914*. Cambridge: Cambridge University Press, 1978.

Roy, Donald, ed. *Plays by James Robinson Planché*. Cambridge: Cambridge University Press, 1986.

Russell, Dave. *Popular Music in England, 1840–1914*. 2nd edn. Manchester: Manchester University Press, 1997.

Savage, Roger. *Masques, Mayings and Music-Dramas: Vaughan Williams and the Early Twentieth-Century Stage*. Woodbridge: The Boydell Press, 2014.

——— "Vaughan Williams, the Romany Ryes, and the Cambridge Ritualists." *Music & Letters*, 83 (2002), 383–417.

Saylor, Eric. *English Pastoral Music: From Arcadia to Utopia*. Champaign, IL: University of Illinois Press, 2017.

Sessa, Anne Dzamba. *Richard Wagner and the English*. London: Associated University Press, 1979.

Shaw, Christopher and Malcolm Chase. "The Dimensions of Nostalgia." In *The Imagined Past: History and Nostalgia*, edited by Christopher Shaw and Malcolm Chase, 1–17. Manchester: Manchester University Press, 1989.

Southern, Richard. "Theatres and Stages." In *The Revels History of Drama in English, Volume VI: 1750–1880*, 61–94. London: Methuen & Co., 1975.

Strong, Roy. "Illusions of Absolutism: Charles I and the Stuart Court Masques." In *Art and Power: Renaissance Festivals, 1450–1650*, 153–70. Woodbridge: The Boydell Press, 1984.

Summerfield, Penny. "Patriotism and Empire: Music-Hall Entertainment, 1879–1914." In *Imperialism and Popular Culture*, edited by John MacKenzie, 17–48. Manchester: Manchester University Press, 1986.

Sykes, Richard. "The Evolution of Englishness in the English Folksong Revival, 1890–1914." *Folk Music Journal*, 6 (1993), 446–90.

Temperley, Nicholas. "Mendelssohn's Influence on English Music." *Music & Letters*, 43, 224–33.

——— "Musical Nationalism in English Romantic Opera." In *The Lost Chord: Essays on Victorian Music*, edited by Nicholas Temperley, 143–57. Bloomington, IN: Indiana University Press, 1989.

——— ed. *Musicians of Bath and Beyond: Edward Loder (1809–1865) and His Family*. Woodbridge: The Boydell Press, 2016.

——— ed. *The Romantic Age 1800–1914*, vol. 5, *The Athlone History of Music in Britain*, edited by Ian Spink. 6 vols. London: Athlone Press, 1981.

——— "Sir George (Alexander) Macfarren." In *New Grove Dictionary of Music and Musicians*, edited by S. Sadie and J. Tyrrell. London: Macmillan, 2001.

——— "Xenophilia in British Musical History." In *Nineteenth-century British Music Studies*, edited by Bennett Zon, 3–22. Aldershot: Ashgate Publishing, 1999.

Tennyson, Hallam. *Alfred, Lord Tennyson: A Memoir by his Son*. London: Macmillan, 1897.

Thompson, E.P. *William Morris: Romantic to Revolutionary*. rev. edn. New York: Pantheon, 1976.

Tillyard, S.K. *The Impact of Modernism, 1900–1920*. London: Routledge, 1988.

Torgovnik, Marianna. *Gone Primitive: Savage Intellects, Modern Lives*. Chicago: Chicago University Press, 1990.

Treitler, Leo. "The Politics of Reception: Tailoring the Present as Fulfillment of a Desired Past." *Journal of the Royal Musical Association*, 116 (1991), 280–98.

Trend, Michael. *The Music Makers: Heirs and Rebels of the English Musical Renaissance, Edward Elgar to Benjamin Britten*. London: Weidenfeld & Nicholson, 1985.

Treuherz, Julian. *Victorian Painting*. London: Thames and Hudson, 1993.

Trowell, Brian. "Elgar's Use of Literature." In *Edward Elgar: Music and Literature*, edited by Raymond Monk, 182–326. Aldershot: Scolar Press, 1993.

Twycross, Meg and Sarah Carpenter. *Masks and Masking in Medieval and Early Tudor England*. Farnham: Ashgate Publishers, 2002.

Vaillancourt, Michael. "Coming of Age: The Earliest Orchestral Music of Ralph Vaughan Williams." In *Vaughan Williams Studies*, edited by Alain Frogley, 23–7. Cambridge: Cambridge University Press, 1996.

Vaughan Williams, Ralph. "The Age of Purcell." *The Music Student*, 7, 3 (Nov. 1914), 47–8.

——— "British Music in the Eighteenth and Early Nineteenth Centuries." *The Music Student*, 7, 4 (Dec. 1914), 63–4.

——— "British Music in the Tudor Period." *The Music Student*, 7, 2 (Oct. 1914), 25–7.

——— "The Foundations of a National Art." *The Music Student*, 7, 1 (Sep. 1914), 5–7.

——— *National Music and Other Essays*. 2nd edn. Oxford: Clarendon Press, 1996.

——— "A School of English Music." *The Vocalist*, 1 (1902), 8.

Vaughan Williams, Ralph and Gustav Holst. *Heirs and Rebels: Letter written to each other and occasional writings on music*, edited by Ursula Vaughan Williams and Gustav Holst. London: Oxford University Press, 1959.

Vaughan Williams, Ursula. *R.V.W.: A Biography of Ralph Vaughan Williams*. London: Oxford University Press, 1964.

Vickery, John B. *The Literary Impact of The Golden Bough*. Princeton, NJ: Princeton University Press, 1973.

Walker, Ernest. *A History of Music in England*. London: Oxford University Press, 1907.

Walkling, Andrew. "'The Dating of Purcell's *Dido and Aeneas*'?: A Reply to Bruce Wood and Andrew Pinnock." *Early Music*, 22 (1994), 469–81.

——— *Masque and Opera in England, 1656–1688*. London: Routledge, 2017.

Walls, Peter. *Music in the English Courtly Masque, 1604–1660*. Oxford: Clarendon Press, 1996.

Weber, William. *Music and the Middle Class: The Social Structure of Concert Life in London, Paris and Vienna*. New York: Holmes & Meier Publishers, 1975.

——— *The Rise of Musical Classics in Eighteenth-Century England: a Study in Canon, Ritual, and Ideology*. Oxford: Clarendon Press, 1992.

Weinroth, Michelle. *Reclaiming William Morris: Englishness, Sublimity and the Rhetoric of Dissent*. Montreal: McGill-Queen's University Press, 1996.

Wells, Stanley, ed. *Shakespeare in the Eighteenth Century*. Cambridge: Cambridge University Press, 1998.

Welsford, Enid. *The Court Masque: a Study in the Relationship between Poetry and the Revels*. Cambridge: Cambridge University Press, 1927.

White, Eric Walter. *A History of English Opera*. London: Faber & Faber, 1983.

Wiener, Martin J. *English Culture and the Decline of the Industrial Spirit, 1850–1980*. Cambridge: Cambridge University Press, 1981.

Wiles, Patricia. "A study of 'Job, A Masque for Dancing' by Ralph Vaughan Williams." Dissertation, Texas Tech University, 1988.

Wood, Bruce and Andrew Pinnock. "'Unscarr'd by turning times'? The dating of Purcell's *Dido and Aeneas*." *Early Music*, 20 (1992), 372–90.

Young, Robert J.C. *Postcolonialism: an Historical Introduction*. Oxford: Blackwell Publishers, 2001.

Yuval-Davis, Nira. *Gender and Nation*. London: Sage Publications, 1997.

Zon, Bennett. "'Loathsome London:' Ruskin, Morris, and Henry Davey's History of English Music (1895)," *Victorian Literature and Culture*, 37 (2009), 359–75.

——— *Music and Metaphor in Nineteenth-Century British Musicology*. Aldershot: Ashgate, 2000.

——— "Plainchant in Nineteenth-Century England: a Review of some Major Publications of the Period." *Plainsong and Medieval Music*, 6 (1997), 53–75.

Index

Page numbers in *italics* are examples and figures.

New titles published under the series title
Music in Britain, 1600–2000
ISSN 2053-3217

Hamilton Harty: Musical Polymath
Jeremy Dibble

Thomas Morley: Elizabethan Music Publisher
Tessa Murray

The Advancement of Music in Enlightenment England:
Benjamin Cooke and the Academy of Ancient Music
Tim Eggington

George Smart and Nineteenth-Century London Concert Life
John Carnelley

The Lives of George Frideric Handel
David Hunter

Musicians of Bath and Beyond:
Edward Loder (1809–1865) and his Family
edited by Nicholas Temperley

Conductors in Britain, 1870–1914:
Wielding the Baton at the Height of Empire
Fiona M. Palmer

Ernest Newman: A Critical Biography
Paul Watt

The Well-Travelled Musician: John Sigismond Cousser
and Musical Exchange in Baroque Europe
Samantha Owens

Music in the West Country:
Social and Cultural History across an English Region
Stephen Banfield

British Musical Criticism and Intellectual Thought, 1850–1950
edited by Jeremy Dibble and Julian Horton